Inventing the Ties That Bind

Inventing the Ties That Bind

IMAGINED RELATIONSHIPS IN
MORAL AND POLITICAL LIFE

Francesca Polletta

THE UNIVERSITY OF CHICAGO PRESS

CHICAGO AND LONDON

The University of Chicago Press, Chicago 60637
The University of Chicago Press, Ltd., London
© 2020 by The University of Chicago
Published 2020
Printed in the United States of America

29 28 27 26 25 24 23 22 21 20   1 2 3 4 5

ISBN-13: 978-0-226-73417-0 (cloth)
ISBN-13: 978-0-226-73420-0 (paper)
ISBN-13: 978-0-226-73434-7 (e-book)
DOI: https://doi.org/10.7208/chicago/9780226734347.001.0001

Library of Congress Cataloging-in-Publication Data

Names: Polletta, Francesca, author.
Title: Inventing the ties that bind : imagined relationships in moral and political life /
Francesca Polletta.
Description: Chicago : University of Chicago Press, 2020. | Includes bibliographical
references and index.
Identifiers: LCCN 2020011825 | ISBN 9780226734170 (cloth) | ISBN 9780226734200
(paperback) | ISBN 9780226734347 (e-book)
Subjects: LCSH: Solidarity. | Collective behavior. | Social action. | Responsibility. |
Interpersonal relations.
Classification: LCC HM717.P655 2020 | DDC 302/.14—dc23
LC record available at https://lccn.loc.gov/2020011825

♾ This paper meets the requirements of ANSI/NISO Z39.48-1992
(Permanence of Paper).

Contents

Preface

In July 2019 the U.S. Immigration and Customs Enforcement Agency (ICE) began raids to arrest immigrants who had been ordered deported, many of them for missing a court hearing. The raids would include "collateral" arrests of people without documents who happened to be at the scene. The raids had been delayed because of opposition within the agency to separating children from their parents, but President Donald Trump pressed forward, and in July, 2,000 people were targeted.[1]

In a working-class section of Nashville, however, things did not go as planned. ICE agents followed a man in a van into the driveway of his home and instructed him and his twelve-year-old son to get out of the vehicle. The man knew to refuse since the agents only had an administrative warrant. If they entered his car or home without permission, a judge might rule it an illegal search. The man called immigration activists, who arrived on the scene along with curious residents. ICE agents continued to press the man to get out of the car. "They were saying, 'If you don't come out, we're going to arrest you, we're going to arrest your twelve-year-old son,'" an immigration lawyer reported. To onlookers, it seemed bullying. A local resident named Angela Glass told a news reporter, "At that point, we was like, 'Oh my God, are you serious?' And that's when everybody got mad and was like, 'They don't do nothing, they don't bother nobody, you haven't got no complaints from them. Police have never been called over there.'" Another resident, Stacey Farley, told a reporter, "The family don't bother nobody, they work every day, they come home, the kids jump on their trampoline."[2]

Residents swung into action. They brought cold drinks and snacks to the van, and as the temperature rose, someone arrived with gasoline to keep the vehicle's air conditioning running. ICE agents left after several hours, but everyone was sure they would return. Residents formed a human chain around the van and to the front door of the house, counting in Spanish to ten and then yelling to the boy to run so that he, and then his father, could get inside safely. They formed another human chain when a car arrived to pick up the family and spirit them away.

The residents who intervened did not seem to know the family. But they were neighbors. "We stuck together like neighbors are supposed to do," Felishadae Young told a reporter. Usually we think of the obligations of being a neighbor in less demanding terms: perhaps accepting a delivered package or shoveling snow off the neighbor's sidewalk when we shovel our own. Here, though, being a neighbor required more. Of course, some residents probably already had feelings about ICE or they may have reacted in a visceral way to seeing a twelve-year-old in fear. But they invoked a culturally familiar relationship to articulate moral obligations that were otherwise difficult to name. And doing so led them to act in solidarity across lines of race, ethnicity, and legal status.

In this case, the neighbors really were neighbors. In other cases that I will treat in this book, people have acted cooperatively on the basis of relationships they did not actually have. They have imagined themselves bound by the obligations of citizenship when they were not recognized fully as citizens, have imagined themselves as kin, bargaining partners, and activists when they were none of those. But invoking the obligations of culturally familiar relationships has helped people to know what they owed others, and it has led them to act cooperatively and sometimes effectively. Other times, to be sure, it has not, and studying the failures of imagined relationships reveals dynamics of cultural constraint alongside those of creativity. Either way, though, people's efforts to invent the ties that bind offer lessons, I believe, for those concerned with forging solidarities that reach across the usual lines of difference.

When I began this book, I thought that task was an important one. Now I think it is urgent. This is not because Americans are more economically stratified and politically polarized than ever before. In fact, recent polls suggest that when it comes to economic issues, Americans are coming closer to agreement. A majority of the public now supports taxing the wealthy if doing so will help to provide ordinary Americans with decent jobs, health insurance, and child care. But lest progressives celebrate too quickly, the polls also show that a not-insignificant portion of those who lean left on economic issues also favor steep restrictions on immigration. This suggests that absent a concerted effort to make the case for inclusion, a left populist agenda on its own will not produce an inclusive circle of the "we." My aim in this book is to contribute to that effort in a modest way by exploring an existing American vernacular of solidarity.[3]

•

Writing this book has reminded me of the value of relationships that are intimate and those that are not, relationships that are of long standing and brand new, relationships that are real, remembered, and imagined. Nina Eliasoph, Wendy Espeland, and Ann Mische read an earlier version of the manuscript in full. Their insights were so perceptive and delivered with such a spirit of generosity and encouragement that I've kept the three of them in my head as scholarly cheerleaders since then. Three people very dear to me died before I completed the book. Priscilla Parkhurst Ferguson, Doug Mitchell, and Marc Steinberg were consummate intellectuals. My sadness at their passing mingles with fond memories of the joy they took in discussing ideas.

Thanks to the students—many now former students and, whether or not still students, many now friends—who worked with me on the interviews for this book: Jessica Callahan, Tania DoCarmo, Kathryn Hoban, Iara Peng, Gregory Smithsimon, Zaibu Tufail, Kelly Ward, and Lesley Wood. And thank you to the activists, community organizers, debt-settlement agents, public engagement practitioners, public officials, and public forum participants we interviewed. The fact that each was willing to talk with us, often at length, was testament to their commitment to wrestling with the practical and ethical dilemmas of their work.

I was part of two remarkable communities of scholars as I wrote this book. I am grateful to the Canadian Institute for Advanced Study for sponsoring the Successful Societies program; to Peter Hall, Michèle Lamont, and Paul Pierson for so ably leading it; and to the program members who made each one of our meetings over the course of four years an intellectual feast: Gérard Bouchard, Wendy Espeland, Kate Geddie, Peter Gourevitch, David Grusky, Jane Jenson, Kristi Kenyon, Kristin Laurin, Patrick LeGalès, Hazel Markus, Rachel Parker, Paige Raibmon, Biju Rao, William Sewell, Prerna Singh, Leanne Son Hing, and Anne Wilson. Thank you, too, to the Russell Sage Foundation, where I was a visiting scholar in 2018–19, and to the scholars and staff who made my stay such a pleasure. I want to make special mention of Edwin Amenta, Peter Hall, Arnold Ho, Jane Mansbridge, and Rosemary Taylor, who joined me in series of discussions about solidarity that were truly illuminating for me.

Lynn Chancer, Paul DiMaggio, Martha Feldman, Marshall Ganz, James Jasper, Mike Miller, Thaler Pekar, Kathy Quick, and Rosemary Taylor either commented on portions of the book or helped me work out arguments for it. Participants in colloquia at the CUNY Graduate Center, New York University, Rutgers, and UCLA provided incisive feedback on material I presented there.

In addition to financial support from CIFAR and the Russell Sage Foundation, grants from the National Science Foundation (Grant #IIS 0306868), the Open Society Foundations, the UCI Center for the Study of Democracy, and the UCI Center for Organizational Research made it possible for me to do the research on which I draw in this book. Parts of chapter 3 appeared previously in "The Moral Obligations of Some Debts," *Sociological Forum* 29 (2014): 1–28 and in "Helping Without Caring: Role Definition and the Gender-Stratified Effects of Emotional Labor in Debt Settlement Firms," *Work and Occupations* 43 (2016): 401–433, both articles coauthored with Zaibu Tufail. Parts of chapter 4 appeared previously in my "Public Deliberation and Political Contention," in *Democratizing Inequalities*, edited by Caroline Lee, Michael McQuarrie, and Edward Walker (New York University Press, 2015). I thank the editors and publishers of these works for permission to reuse the material.

I am grateful to what I think of as my tribe of mom-friends: Silke Aisenbrey, Kim Blanton, Beth Cauffman, Amy DePaul, Martha Feldman, Laura Kelly, Nancy Manetta, Debra Minkoff, Kim Putnam, and Sarah Rosenfield. Raising children while holding a job has been made immeasurably easier because of their advice, support, and friendship. The University of Chicago Press executive editor Elizabeth Branch Dyson joined the tribe when she emailed me late one evening to apprise me of the manuscript's progress—while at the same time making a pie for her son's birthday the next day. Thanks to Elizabeth and to her team—Mollie McFee, Caterina MacLean, and Barbara Norton—for their combination of expert advice and good humor.

As always, I thank my family—Gabriella and Maddalena Polletta, Nagraj Gollapudi, Pedro Diez, Dante Diez, and Zohra Polletta Gollapudi, as well as the Amentas and Gareschés—for their eagerness to talk about my research when I was so inclined and to distract me from it when I was not. Edwin Amenta read every page of this book at least once, gave me suggestions that were invariably on the mark, occasionally coaxed me down from the ledge of intellectual despair, and cheered each time I announced that I just possibly might have figured something out. I am grateful for his wisdom and encouragement. Finally, Luisa and Gregory Amenta, who are sixteen, have come of political age at a time when Americans' political differences have become vitriolic. Luisa, with her deep sensitivity to the experiences of those who have been excluded, and Greg, with his willingness in every controversy always to hear the other side, give me real hope that their generation will do political solidarity better than mine has done.

CHAPTER ONE

Relationships, Real and Imagined

We [moderns] are wont to see friendship solely as a phenomenon of intimacy, in which the friends open their hearts to each other unmolested by the world and its demands.

HANNAH ARENDT,
"On Humanity in Dark Times: Thoughts about Lessing" (1968)

Worries about the ties that bind are nothing new. Generations of social critics have complained that our relationships with those outside our narrow circle of intimates have become thin, denuded of trust, care, and mutual respect, with dire implications for our society. In a recent rendering, economic processes of outsourcing and downsizing have made jobs temporary, skills portable, and attachments minimal. The counterfeit solidarity of the workplace team, in which members monitor each other's level of commitment as they jockey for position with higher-ups, has replaced ties born of stable careers. Meanwhile, the hegemony of the market has produced a new Gilded Age, in which the richest 5 percent of Americans own two-thirds of the country's wealth. Indeed, the richest three Americans (Warren Buffett, Bill Gates, and Jeff Bezos) own more in total than the bottom half of all Americans. Reflecting the fact that class often maps onto race and ethnicity, the median White family has forty-one times the wealth of the median Black family and twenty-two times the wealth of the median Latino family. We live today in enclaves of class, race, and ethnicity, chosen or unchosen. Roughly half of African Americans and more than 40 percent of Latinos live in neighborhoods where virtually no Whites live, and the average White person lives in a neighborhood that is 80 percent White.[1]

As in the workplace and personal life, so too in politics have social relationships ceded to an enervating individualism or a new kind of tribalism. The political scientist Robert Putnam's 1995 article "Bowling Alone" gave voice to concerns about Americans' declining civic participation and its costs for social solidarity. No longer involved in the associations and clubs, such as bowling leagues, that once built habits of engagement and political trust, citizens were withdrawing into private worlds and a pursuit of narrow self-interest. Meanwhile, others argued, those concerned with action for the common good were reduced to running ads featuring babies with bloated bellies and dead refugee toddlers, hoping to convince viewers to click on a link for donating money. The people clicking on the links, for their part, did so without connection to others, choosing to commit to causes that were easy, not those that were hard.[2]

Today, say critics, things have gotten even worse as political apathy has evolved into political enmity. Democrats distrust Republicans and vice versa. Not only do we oppose each other's policy preferences and politicians; we do not talk to each other, we live in different places, we watch different television shows, and we drive different cars. When it comes to our actual policy preferences, we are less different than we actually think. But our perception that people in each party hew to the extremes leads us to become more polarized. In this political landscape, the prospect that we will join the same bowling leagues becomes increasingly remote. Not knowing partisans on the other side, moreover, encourages us at election time to throw our support without question to our partisan standard-bearer. And not only has that impoverished possibilities for political compromise; it threatens the viability of our democratic system.[3]

Solidarity is a fuzzy concept, but its absence has real-world consequences. Without a sense of fellow feeling that extends beyond a narrow circle of the "we," people are unlikely to participate politically, instead free-riding on the efforts of others. They are unlikely to support policies aimed at combating inequalities or integrating newcomers. And they are unlikely to extend a modicum of trust to political ideas, politicians, even statements of fact they see as supporting the other side.[4]

What is to be done? One solution is deceptively simple. We should get to know each other as people—directly, one on one, in a setting that discourages invective and encourages trust. After all, most of us have had the experience of connecting with someone very different from us. We talk, perhaps superficially or haltingly at first, until a spark of recognition allows us to ease into the interaction, sharing personal stories and gradually revealing more of ourselves. We discover surprising commonalities: experiences we have both had, perceptions of the world we share, similar frustrations with the state of our company, our city, our nation's economy or politics. We like one another, we discover, and we begin to trust each other. Not only do we see each other in a new way. We likely begin to see the group of which the other is a member in a new way: Republicans, Latinos, our company's management, city government. The research on intergroup contact shows that when people from a dominant group interact with those from a marginalized group in a setting of equality, dominant group members' negative views of the group diminish. The original research by the psychologist Gordon Allport in the 1950s suggested that contact worked by giving people knowledge of the other group, but studies since then have shown rather that it increases their empathy and perspective taking. And it works by promoting self-disclosure. Friendship is the optimal form of intergroup contact, the psychologist Thomas Pettigrew observes, because self-disclosure is so central to it.[5]

Today, practitioners of intergroup dialogue bring people together to talk, share experiences, and, practitioners hope, develop ties across divides of race, religion, and partisanship. And that sometimes happens. But the relationships that are striven for in such dialogues—something like personal friendship arrived at by way of something like mutual self-disclosure—figure now as ideals in diverse civic initiatives. Indeed, egalitarian intimacy and its characteristic style of talk have become key terms of civic repair. Champions of public deliberation, for example, in which ordinary people talk about political issues in carefully organized forums, maintain that the relations of trust and affection participants form with each other chip away at their political disengagement even after the forum is over. Nonprofits operating in communities riddled with poverty and crime strive to forge caring relationships between community teenagers and middle-class volunteers, with both enriched by their interaction. For proponents of the "sharing economy," the friendly and cooperative relationships that form when people trade goods and services such as babysitting, carpentry, and Wikipedia entry writing represent viable alternatives to the competition of the market. Advocacy groups, for their part, now reject the politics of pity they once relied on to raise support from wealthy donors. They seek rather to create relationships of caring and mutual respect between those who bear the scars of injustice and those who, they hope, will join the struggle for justice.[6]

Just as important as the relationships these initiatives strive to create are the means they use to do so. Participants learn a distinctive kind of communication. Sometimes taught by experts with backgrounds in fields of psychotherapeutically informed communication, participants learn to share personal experiences rather than argue over ideologies or bargain over group interests, to voice their values more than their complaints, to dwell on their hopes instead of their suffering, to prize authentic connection over scoring points, and to aim for common ground. If successful, they create a kind of egalitarian intimacy. And that, in turn, say proponents, opens up possibilities for understanding and cooperative action. The relationships forged by participants should help to build the solidarity missing in contemporary society.

I am not convinced. Exercises like the ones I have described do create experiences of emotional closeness. Sometimes, though, the experiences are one-sided. One party sets the terms for the performance of equality and intimacy that the other is asked to follow. For example, victims of sex trafficking or people who were once homeless are taught to tell their stories to potential supporters in a way that emphasizes hope over pain and personal growth over suffering. This, say advocacy consultants, will empower storytellers at the same time as it raises support. But tellers' empowerment is depicted in the stories they tell more than it is exercised in their choice of how to tell their stories. Sometimes, instead, both parties experience solidarity across difference. The public forum participants I interviewed experienced a genuine sense of connection with people very different from them. But the bond felt truncated. Participants wanted relationships that continued, and they wanted relationships that allowed them to intervene in the politics that mattered. They were frustrated by organizers' insistence that public deliberation was properly removed from politics.

Writing long before the initiatives I describe, the political theorist Hannah Arendt bemoaned our modern understanding of friendship as determinedly unconcerned with "the world and its demands"; that is, as firmly restricted to the sphere of the intimate, the private, and the nonpolitical. The alternative she had in mind was an Aristotelian understanding of civic friendship as a kind of generalized regard for members of the political community. But contemporary initiatives have turned our modern understanding of friendship, not Aristotle's, into a modus operandi for civic reform.[7]

I do agree with reformers that we need new kinds of civic relationships. Those relationships should be marked by trust, care, and equality. But I do not believe that the intimacy characteristic of personal relationships is a good model for such relationships. We need relationships that are oriented to a longer time horizon than is typical of many civic initiatives and relationships that are connected to political decision making rather than kept separate from it. We need schemas of solidarity that acknowledge our membership in groups, rather than asking us to interact only as individuals. And we need relationships in which people not only talk the way that equals do but have equal power to choose the way they talk.

But here is the thing. We already have something like those relationships. People have acted cooperatively and politically by imagining themselves as religious fellows, as a team, and as nodes in a computer network. They have put their lives on the line by imagining themselves as the "first-class citizens" they were not. Where the organizers of the public forum I mentioned treated participants as something like temporary friends, participants saw themselves as members of a focus group, as a social movement, and as the United Nations. Of course, they were actually none of these, and they knew it. The relationships they drew on were metaphorical, but those metaphors helped them to work through their differences, arrive at practical compromises, and envision routes to genuine political impact.

If a particular relationship is as idiosyncratic as the people who make it up, the *idea* or schema of a relationship is cultural. We know, at least in broad outline, what is expected of members of a team compared to friends, how participants in a focus group interact, and what a bargaining relationship looks like. We do not even have to have direct experience of a relationship to know its characteristic norms. An experimental study of a prisoner's dilemma game showed that when people were told they were participating in a "Wall Street game," they were much less likely to cooperate than when they were told they were participating in a "community game." Presumably, most participants had not worked on Wall Street. So people *can* draw on the norms of relationships they do not actually have. In this book, I will show them doing so, transposing the behavioral expectations of familiar relationships to new situations.[8]

The sociologist Ann Swidler famously argued that culture operates less by defining our goals and aspirations, propelling us along paths we did not make, than by serving as a tool kit from which we pick and choose beliefs (often inconsistently) to deal with the very practical challenges we face in everyday life. People use relationship schemas in that fashion, I believe. They invoke the norms of familiar relationships to know what they owe others when those obligations are difficult to name otherwise. For example, surveys show that White Americans who consider themselves "close" to African Americans are more likely to favor affirmative action. The effect, though, is independent of respondents' perceived self-interest, their moral values regarding equality, or how much actual contact they have with African Americans. The closeness, for many, is imagined. But it captures a sense of solidarity that is difficult to articulate otherwise.[9]

To be sure, people also draw on familiar relationships metaphorically to deny their responsibility for others. When middle-class White Americans explained to the sociologist Sandra Levitsky why they wanted Medicaid to cover people like themselves but not poor people or recent immigrants, they used the language of family. One woman compared her relatives who, she said, had worked and paid taxes with "all the people that were sitting there [who] didn't speak English": "We've chosen to take care of them rather than take care of our own." But "our own" actually meant more than family. The woman clarified: "the people who live here and have contributed and our ancestors who have contributed." Taking care of our own meant taking care of native-born Americans, not immigrants.[10]

If people use imagined relationships to narrow as well as broaden the ambit of their moral concern, in the following chapters I focus more on the latter. Acting on the expectations of imagined relationships has led people to sacrifice time, money, even their physical safety for the common good. Imagined relationships have allowed groups to acknowledge real differences among their members without requiring members to subordinate those differences to some overarching sameness. They have produced solidarities with nonhostile boundaries—that is, where the strength of the "we" does not depend on its antagonism to a "them." And they have produced the kind of trust in government that is based on government's accountability rather than serving as a substitute for that accountability. These, I believe, are the kinds of solidarities we need, and they are evident in the practical imaginations of people acting in the real world.

My aims in this book are threefold. One is to identify the limitations of styling civic solidarity on a relationship of egalitarian intimacy, to be arrived at by way of mutual self-disclosure. Both the relationship and the communicative style are ill suited, I believe, to building solidarities that are egalitarian, inclusive, politically engaged, and enduring. Another is to identify alternatives, real instances of solidarity that have scaled the usual barriers of self-interest and difference, and that have scaled the cultural barrier that stands between what is often praised as civic cooperation and what is sometimes denigrated as political contention. And a third is to argue that the basis for those alternatives lies in our capacity to invent relationships we do not actually have. More than has been recognized, people turn to the obligations of imagined relationships as a way to deal with common challenges of solidarity.

SOLIDARITY AND ITS CHALLENGES

I did not intend to write this book. In fact, I thought I was done writing about relationships. I had written about them in a book that I published more than fifteen years ago about participatory democracy in movements. In *Freedom Is an Endless Meeting*, I argued that radical democrats in the pacifist, civil rights, New Left, and women's liberation movements styled their organizations on the norms of relationships that were familiar to them. For pacifists, the norms of religious fellowship provided a guide for how to make decisions, allocate tasks, and handle disagreement. In the organizing projects of the southern civil rights movement, by contrast, participatory democratic decision making was a pedagogical tool for building leadership among those who had long been deemed unqualified for it. Participatory democracy was modeled on tutelage. For activists in the New Left and women's liberation movements, friendship was the mold for radically democratic relationships. These differences helped to account for why practices of radical democracy looked so different across movements. But they also helped to account for some of the problems movement groups encountered. For example, in participatory democracies styled on tutelage, crises emerged when no one would propose new policies. Determined only to teach skills, not impose goals, organizers in the southern civil rights movement were paralyzed when the movement's previous agenda proved obsolete. In the New Left and women's liberation movements, bitter conflicts between the new and old guards reflected the limits of friendship as a model of participatory democracy.[11]

I completed that book wondering if one could create new democratic relationships, ones characterized by the trust and care typical of friendship, but without the exclusiveness and resistance to formal rules that are also typical of that relationship. I did not find an answer to the question, though. And then I moved on to other things. The 9/11 attacks happened, and wanting, like many New Yorkers, to do something to help, I became involved in an effort to solicit residents' input into what to build at the site of the destroyed World Trade Center. I ended up studying citizens' participation in that effort and in public deliberative efforts more generally. At the same time, I pursued a long-standing interest in storytelling, first in social movements and then in other forms of politics. When a foundation executive asked me several years ago whether telling personal stories was an effective tool in advocacy—or, as he put it, whether personal storytelling "worked"— I saw an opportunity to explore how people in progressive advocacy today use personal stories, and how they define what working means. So I began to interview advocates and messaging consultants about their use of personal storytelling.

Another line of investigation began with a conversation in my office with an undergraduate who had worked in a debt-settlement firm. Such firms offer people with substantial debts their services in trying to renegotiate the principal of some of their debt. In describing her experience, Zaibu Tufail mentioned that clients were usually unwilling to allow the firm to renegotiate their medical debts, even though these debts were the easiest to settle. I found that fascinating, and we began an ethnographic and interview-based study of debt settlement. When we discovered that men in debt-settlement firms held the kind of job that is typically associated with women, namely, counseling distraught clients, and that women held the kind of job typically associated with men, namely, hardball negotiating with creditors, we began to study male and female agents' different experiences of debt settlement.

I thought of these projects as completely different from one another. They were about public communication in movements, the conditions for effective civic engagement, individuals' financial decision making, and gender relations in the workplace. But I began to see that they were also about how people decided what they owed others. For the debt-settlement clients, of course, that question was central. In a situation in which they simply could not pay back all their debts, to which creditors did they have the strongest obligation? Debt-settlement agents, for their part, struggled with whether they were taking advantage of people who were already in financial trouble. To give negotiators in the company some leverage with creditors, agents instructed their clients to stop payment altogether on the debts they wanted to renegotiate. However, that rendered clients vulnerable to financial and legal penalties. Were agents helping or exploiting them?

The question of one's obligation to others was also important for the people to whom advocacy groups targeted their storytelling. Given all the worthy causes making claims on their support, why should they give money and time to one rather than another? And what, in turn, did the people who were asked to tell their stories—of poverty, homelessness, abortion—owe to the cause? The question of what people owed each other was also central to the public deliberative efforts I was studying. Participants were volunteers, with no formal obligation to the process. And policy makers were not bound to follow the recommendations that issued from the forum. How, then, did participants figure out what they could legitimately ask of each other? And how did they figure out what they could legitimately ask of policy makers?

The answer to these questions was not that people followed their self-interest. Nor did they follow a blanket moral principle—that one pay back one's debts, for instance, or not exploit people, or give money to those who need it most. Either the action entailed by the principle was unclear or it conflicted with another equally applicable principle. Instead, in each of these cases, people decided what they owed with reference to the relationship they were in—but in each case that relationship was ambiguous. Debt-settlement clients, Tufail and I discovered, thought about their creditors as people with whom they had reciprocal and continuing relationships. If the creditor had given them good service, the debt should be paid back in full; if the creditor had not, the debtor felt justified in opting to renegotiate the debt. Most of the time, though, creditors were impersonal agencies, not individual people, and they did not have any kind of relationship with the debtor other than a legal claim on their money. Debt-settlement agents, for their part, insisted that their relationship with clients was one between a financial educator and a student. They were not selling people a service that had the potential to harm them; instead, they said, they were simply informing clients of their financial options. But agents were salespeople, not financial educators. The public forum participants I interviewed had figured out how to deliberate by drawing on the norms of other kinds of organizations, some in which they had participated and others they had only heard about. They were *like* the United Nations, they told me, or *like* a jury. And they used these analogies to know what they should expect of each other and what they should expect of the policy makers they hoped to influence. The advocates I interviewed, finally, insisted that it was the bond of mutual respect and even equality that storytellers forged with their audiences that led people to contribute to the cause, this although they might never even meet.

In each of these cases, relationships served, or were expected to serve, as a kind of moral compass, indicating the kind of behavior that was right and appropriate. And in each case, relationships were less just *there*—their moral demands fixed and obvious—than they were the objects of craft and, indeed, invention. This is not to say that people were always well served by their inventiveness. Debt-settlement clients' loyalty to imagined creditors led them to try to negotiate the wrong debts and rendered them even more financially vulnerable. Debt-settlement agents who were women simply could not get away with claiming their relationship with clients was an educational one. They were expected instead to be something like therapists, and as a result their job was even more emotionally onerous. The deliberative forum participants who thought of themselves as an organized advocacy group ended up more frustrated by the forum's outcomes than those who thought of it simply as an opportunity to talk. And as much as advocates insisted that the relationship they styled between wealthy donors and the victims of injustice empowered victims at the same time as it appealed to donors, just how that empowerment took place remained unclear.

Still, the fact that people sometimes acted on the basis of relationships they did not actually have suggested to me that we might learn something about the dynamics of solidarity more broadly by paying attention to their efforts. That may seem a stretch. It is hard to see how debt-settlement clients' fantasy of being in a reciprocal personal relationship with their creditors or advocacy groups' pitches to wealthy donors would offer insight into the conditions for the kind of solidarity that is so clearly missing in American society today. And in fact, much of the recent scholarship on solidarity has been motivated by concerns like the latter. Scholars have tended, accordingly, to focus on broad solidarities and those that involve the government, asking about the conditions in which citizens espouse more or less inclusive conceptions of national membership.[12]

If we define solidarity as a sense of identity with, and responsibility for, members of a bounded group, however, it should be clear that there are multiple kinds of solidarity, which operate in different settings and come with different obligations. One form of solidarity is that which joins members of a group, community, or society and is manifest in members' adherence to the norms of the collective. This is solidarity in the Durkheimian sense; it is both the basis of morality and dependent on members' conformity to moral norms. A second kind of solidarity, by contrast, requires that members *contest* the laws and norms of the community or society. This is the solidarity of social movements (which have occasionally taken the name Solidarity). A third kind of solidarity is developed within the associations of civil society. I have in mind the voluntary organizations that Alexis de Tocqueville praised and the public forums championed by deliberative democrats. The mutuality and trust that develop in such associations, Tocquevillians maintain, lead participants to develop more generalized trust in their fellow citizens as well as in their democratic institutions. Finally, there is the solidarity that joins members of the national community and is expressed in the policies of the nation-state. Whereas the first kind of solidarity is manifest in citizens' obligations to the state, here the focus is on what the state owes its citizens, as well as residents who are not citizens.[13]

There are significant obstacles to each of these kinds of solidarity, which have been the subject of normative and empirical scholarship. I wondered, though, if the relationships people imagined helped them to deal with the challenges of solidarity in a way that had not been captured by the literature. For example, solidarity as Émile Durkheim theorized it is threatened by the possibility that members will follow their own self-interest when it conflicts with the norms of society. Scholars have treated this possibility theoretically in terms of people's inadequate socialization or, from a rational-choice perspective, in terms of the failure of social control. But the clients of the debt-settlement agencies Tufail and I studied confronted this possibility in a very practical way. They could not follow the norm that one pay back one's debts in full. One might expect, accordingly, that they would temper their moral commitments with self-interest, choosing to try to renegotiate the debts whose creditors were most likely to agree to a settlement. But this is not what they did. Instead, they rewarded creditors who had given them good service by insisting on paying them back in full. They opted to renegotiate a debt as punishment for creditors who had not given them good service, whether it was the IRS levying excessive taxes or the mother of their children demanding child support. The result, as I said, was that debt-settlement clients sometimes ended up choosing to renegotiate debts that, strategically, they would have been better off trying to pay back in full. But thinking about their obligations in terms of imagined relationships allowed them to preserve a sense of moral agency in a humiliating situation. Their imagined solidary obligations thus outweighed their self-interest and finessed the moral principle that one should repay (all) one's debts in full.[14]

If self-interest often stands in the way of solidary action, so does difference. People in any group have diverse experiences, needs, values, and priorities. How much must they share in order to cooperate? Alongside the danger that their differences make cooperation impossible is the danger that their similarities are forced. Claims of solidarity may misrecognize the experiences and priorities of more powerful members as shared when they are not. In movements, one thorny line of difference is between participants who have been directly harmed by the issue the movement is tackling and those who have not. Solidarity is different from charity insofar as the person who pledges solidarity to the cause, even if she has not been affected, nevertheless also sees herself as having a stake in the cause. But that poses a practical problem: how far should activists go to convince potential participants, and especially donors, that they have a stake in the issue? If they go too far, the movement may become more about already-privileged people's needs than about those of the people who are most harmed. Advocacy groups' efforts to craft an egalitarian relationship between people who were formerly homeless, or poor, or undocumented and people who had money, time, and political capital to dedicate to the cause seemed to be an attempt to deal with this challenge. I was not convinced that the attempt was successful, but better understanding why that was the case was potentially instructive.[15]

The relationship work that people did in public deliberation initiatives, for its part, illuminated a challenge characteristic of the solidarities that develop in civil society. As I noted, scholars have argued that the habits of cooperation nurtured in civil-society associations spiral outward, leading participants to develop trust in their fellow citizens and in their political institutions. And that trust, in turn, contributes to solidarity in the first sense in which I used it. But critics have asked what good civil-society associations are if they only legitimize government rather than also, where necessary, challenging it. This is less a practical obstacle to solidarity than a danger that may accompany it: namely, that solidarity substitute for political accountability. Consider, then, the public forum participants who, as I mentioned, drew on multiple metaphors of democratic association to understand how to deliberate. As I will show, participants, more than forum organizers, envisioned their bonds as enduring after the close of the forum, and they saw themselves as properly exercising pressure on government, not simply reaffirming their trust in it.[16]

What I was seeing in these cases pushed me in two directions. One was empirical. I turned to other cases where people found themselves reckoning with standard challenges of solidarity. I have already noted three such challenges: the competing pulls of self-interest and one's obligations to the group, differences within the group that either discourage cooperation or are unjustly ignored, and the risk that solidarity is enacted in ways that lessen the demand for political accountability. Another challenge lies in the existence of competing solidarities. We are members of multiple groups, and we are usually more loyal to intimates than to those who are less close to us emotionally. But sometimes solidary action depends on our loyalty to the latter. For example, scholars of the civil rights movement have shown that Black southerners were convinced to participate in often dangerous activism by their obligations to kin and congregation. But in some areas of the South, retaliatory violence by Whites extended to movement participants' families and churches. In that context, one's obligation to intimates would likely discourage one from participating. How did activists deal with that challenge? I returned to my earlier study of organizing in Mississippi and southwest Georgia in the early 1960s to answer that question, drawing on hundreds of field reports by organizers to better understand how they convinced people to participate. As I will show, it was imagined relationships, in this case of citizenship, community, and even kinship, that led people to sacrifice for the cause.

I also turned to research by other scholars on a variety of civil-society organizations, including churches, volunteer organizations, community organizing groups, and unions. I was interested in groups that had wrestled successfully with the challenge of difference. Had they figured out ways to recognize differences, and even inequalities, among members of the group without that recognition threatening the group's unity? If so, how? With respect to the challenge of political accountability, had groups figured out how to build ties between citizens and officials without those ties foreclosing citizens' ability to make demands on officials?

At the same time as I looked for empirical cases of solidarity, I searched for elements of a theoretical framework that would help me to explain why people sometimes claimed relationships they did not have, and what the consequences of their doing so were. I did not want to discount the importance of people's real relationships in defining their solidary obligations. In fact, after years of seeing people as making moral judgments independently, moral philosophers and psychologists had begun to take seriously the fact that people reason morally in the context of relationships. For example, when we are judging strangers, we see their failures of omission much less seriously than their failures of commission; but with friends, we judge both failures with equal seriousness. On the other hand, when a friend engages in morally questionable behavior, we judge it less harshly than when a stranger does so. People make different moral judgments about an individual depending on the relationship they are in with that person, scholars now recognized. Yet, relationships in the scholarship on moral philosophy and psychology were treated as objective and given. One was either a stranger or a friend, and that affected how one behaved morally. It seemed to me, though, that people's moral judgments are also shaped by the relationships they *want* to have as well as by the relationships that seem to be good models for moral principles that are hard to articulate.[17]

Sociologists, for their part, had demonstrated that people's position in networks of ties of varying strength, number, and centrality affected everything from their weight to their willingness to sacrifice for political causes. But exactly what those ties supplied—whether information, incentives, obligations, or something else—was often unclear. A narrow version of a relational approach missed the fact that people experience, forge, and transform relations through cultural categories. They have relation*ships*, which come with normative expectations and obligations. And there is often room for considerable interpretation in defining the relationship that two people have, as well as the normative expectations and obligations that come with that relationship. A broader version of a relational argument emphasized that all ties are discursive. All relationships are imagined, and it is through talk that we establish and alter the meaning of particular ties. I believed that was true. But I was convinced that there was also value in distinguishing between structural ties and the schemas in whose terms those ties are interpreted. For one thing, it allowed me to explore when people's obligations to an imagined community become more motivating than their perceived obligations to people they know directly. Distinguishing between structural ties and imagined ones also allowed me to capture relationships' metaphorical character. We are capable of recognizing some bonds as being *like* others. We can recognize both the similarity of the relationships and the "as if" move we are making in order to do so. Sociologists in interactionist and phenomenological traditions have long observed that people's perceptions of self and other are, as Charles Cooley put it, "the solid facts of society." My interest, though, was in how people imagine, in often creative ways, the *relationships* joining self and others, and in the cultural materials they use to do so.[18]

To make sense of the ways in which relationships, real and imagined, figure in solidary action, I turned to the literature in psychology and anthropology on relationship schemas. Combined with insights produced by sociologists, historians, and organizational scholars about the operation of institutional schemas, it gave me the tools I needed to understand how people's ideas about relationships both open up some practical possibilities and foreclose others. Let me turn to this body of work, then, before sketching the arguments I will make in the rest of the book.

CULTURE IN RELATIONSHIPS

A schema is a model for doing things. There are schemas for how to shake hands, how to experience the death of a loved one, and how to negotiate with foreign governments. Schemas are culturally and historically specific. They are modified in and through their use and may never exist in pure form but are analytically separable from their diverse enactments. You and I can agree on the key features of marriage, for instance, without describing the relationships of all the married couples we know. The same goes for our schemas of public education, political rights, and personnel management.[19]

We craft our relationships based on the idiosyncrasies of our personalities and on the contingencies of the situation. And the bonds we forge evolve over time in ways that we may not anticipate. But cultural schemas for relationships provide a kind of baseline of expectation. Imagine if, every time you went into a store, you had to negotiate your relationship with the clerk from scratch. Should you be warm or distant? Should you expect the clerk's assistance or be grateful for it? Should you tell him your name? Should you ask him his? Of course, some clerks are warmer, more helpful, and more forthcoming than others. I've found myself in clenched-teeth standoffs with some clerks and surprising intimacy with others. But having a prior set of expectations about how the two of you should interact makes it much easier to approach the interaction with minimal stress. Those expectations might be that you should expect assistance but be surprised and grateful if it goes beyond the assistance that is typically offered, that you should not talk about your personal life or ask the clerk about his, and so on. The expectations come from your having interacted with other clerks, observed people interacting with clerks, and absorbed cultural materials on how clerks interact with customers. You transform the schema as you enact it. But in new settings and new encounters, situations that are rife with uncertainty, relationship schemas provide some stability of expectation. As the psychologist G. P. Ginsburg puts it, they "facilitate the coordination of action, reduce the effort of interaction, reduce the necessity of attention to small details and allow joint action to be organized in large rather than minute chunks."[20]

Note that schemas (or models or scripts—all three terms are used) are both descriptive and normative; they tell us how we should interact. They indicate the expected level of intimacy, the degree of formality, the norms of exchange, the degree of equality, the interpersonal goals of the relationship, and the ways in which the relationship should develop over time. Note, too, that schemas exist in and through their difference from other schemas. The schema for a customer-clerk relationship is different from the schema for a patient-therapist relationship, but the schema for a bank-customer and clerk relationship is different from one for a candy-store customer and clerk, and both are different when the clerk is a woman rather than a man. In the United States, at least, an older person probably operates with a different schema of a customer-clerk relationship than a younger person does. Still, scholars have demonstrated that relationship schemas are widely shared. Their operation is evident in studies showing that people characterize typical relationships between close friends, interviewer and job applicant, teammates, and others in similar ways; that people often confuse those with whom they interact in a similar relationship; that when people's behavior departs from the schema or script they are less likely to remember it; and that people strive to behave in a manner that is in line with the salient relationship schema.[21]

I emphasize the emotional guidance that familiar relationship schemas provide. We associate relationships not only with certain norms and expectations but with distinctive feelings; parenthood with unconditional love, a bargaining relationship with an emotionally cool assessment of costs and opportunities, and so on. Indeed, feelings may be the basis for moral principles. As the sociologist James Jasper observes, many moral principles have their semantic origins in one's loyalty to the group—that is, in relationships. One reason I talk about relationships rather than roles is that relationships focus our attention on the ties between people. If the concept of role retains its theatrical connotation of performing for an audience, the concept of relationship captures the fact that both parties can be expected to know how to feel and behave.[22]

Perhaps the most expansive theory of relationship schemas is offered by the anthropologist Alan Page Fiske. Fiske argues that four relationship schemas shape action across a variety of domains, including decision making, exchange, conflict, and the organization of labor. In a *communal sharing* relationship schema, which is typical of families, communes, and, in attenuated form, ethnic and national identities, goods are shared on the basis of need, decision making is collective and consensus oriented, and values of caring, kindness, and altruism are privileged. In an *authority ranking* relationship, of which the military is the archetype, higher-ranking individuals enjoy more in the way of power, prestige, and privilege and they provide protection and care for subordinates. In an *equality matching* relationship, the emphasis is on reciprocity between equals. Characteristic of acquaintances and colleagues, equality matching relationships emphasize balancing and turn taking, tit-for-tat retaliation, and egalitarian distributive justice. Finally, in a *market pricing* relationship, relevant features of the interaction are reduced to a single metric, which is often but not always money. Decisions are made on the basis of a cost-benefit calculation of expected efficiency or utility. Fiske points out that many actual relationships involve shifting among these models. For example, I might use a market-pricing mode when I sell my student my car, but an authority-ranking one when I give him tasks to do as my research assistant. Still, Fiske and others who have tested the theory have found extraordinary consistency in people's expectations of the values, obligations, and actual behaviors associated with each relationship schema.[23]

I will draw on Fiske's theory, and in particular its insights into how people respond when the terms of a relational schema are violated. However, in the main, I find that Fiske's categorization of relationships misses the finer-grained differences between relationship types that actually matter a great deal. Fiske also tends to treat relationship schemas as matching actual relationships. He acknowledges that there may be situations where the appropriate relational schema is ambiguous or contested, but he does not really focus on them. However, these are the situations that interest me: where people treat a relationship in the terms usually reserved for another. For instance, in his study of the letters that Renaissance Florentines wrote seeking favors from powerful patrons, the sociologist Paul McLean shows that, in the aggregate, letter writers' position in preexisting networks of status determined the kind of relationship they invoked in their letters. Petitioners invoked the obligations of real relationships. Those who were closer in status to their would-be patron tended to appeal to an egalitarian relationship of honor or *amicizia*; those who were lower in status tended to perform deference, invoking the magnificence of the addressee. But this was by no means always the case. Rather, McLean's closer examination revealed petitioners writing relationships into existence. A petitioner might invoke friendship in a way that highlighted the would-be patron's self-interest in such a relationship, or combine appeals to honor (among equals) and magnificence (toward a better) so as to subtly shift the obligations of the relationship. As I will show in chapter 3, debt-settlement agents can turn a profit by supporting debtors' fantasy that they are in a continuing reciprocal relationship with their creditor.[24]

People use relationship schemas to pursue their own self-interest, but they also use them to enact the obligations of solidarity. Here I draw on the historian William Sewell's insight that institutional schemas can be transposed from one setting to another, indeed from one institutional sphere to another. The schema's familiarity makes it easy to use, since parties know its behavioral expectations, but translating those expectations to a new setting produces new effects. An example comes from the Chinese Communist Party's efforts to organize women mill workers in the 1940s. Organizers adopted a relationship schema that was familiar to the women: "sisterhoods," in which six to ten women pledged allegiance to each other in a ritual ceremony to protect themselves from abuse by employers. Mill workers had already transposed the relationship schema of sisterhood from the world of family to that of work. Now organizers sought to turn it into a force for revolutionary solidarity. In similar instances, people have used familiar forms to create novel modes of political interaction.[25]

Scholars interested in how people combine and transpose schemas have tended to focus on schemas of organization. For example, the sociologist Elisabeth Clemens shows that American women activists barred from politics in the late nineteenth and early twentieth centuries pursued political activities within formally nonpolitical organizations such as clubs, parlor meetings, and charitable societies. These organizations were seen by men as appropriately and unthreateningly feminine, and women activists used them to become a major force for reform. But organizational forms often include bundles of norms for how people within the organization should interact with each other and with people outside the organization. Just as metaphors can, by naming one thing in the terms of something different, alert us to possibilities we had not previously recognized, so too can transposing relationship schemas from one sphere to another encourage new modes of interaction. If we want to bring more conviviality and warmth into our workplace, we may treat each other as friends. If we want to promote more open sharing of information, we can treat each other as collaborators or team members, drawing relationship schemas from sports teams of which we have been members or scientific work groups we have read about. Again, these schemas provide us guidance on how to feel and act, and they provide us some confidence that the people with whom we are interacting will feel and act in the appropriate ways. They save time that would otherwise be spent constantly negotiating the terms of engagement. Although they are modified as they are enacted, their power lies in the fact that they are familiar, both to us and to those with whom we are interacting.[26]

THE CONSTRAINTS IN AND OF RELATIONSHIPS

So far I have treated people's use of relationship schemas as practical and creative. But if such schemas guide behavior rather than just describing it, they should make it harder to do some things even as they make it easier to do others. Can we anticipate the kinds of problems and conflicts that might arise when people invoke the obligations of familiar relationships in new situations?

One problem is simply that the parties to the relationship do not have equal power to define it. For example, the reproductive surrogates whom the sociologist Zsuzsa Berend interviewed characterized their relationship with the couples for whom they carried a child as a romantic one. They truly fell in love, they said. And they wanted to continue the relationship after the child was born. It was not the child they cared about; it was the child's parents. They felt betrayed when the parents pulled away from them, and even more betrayed when the parents redefined their relationship as a contractual one. But the surrogates had no way of making the parents see the relationship as something other than contractual. In similar fashion, the debt-settlement clients I will describe had no way of convincing creditors that they had the reciprocal relationship they imagined.[27]

Another limit on people's ability to use relationship schemas effectively lies in the very availability of the schema. Some schemas may not be culturally familiar. For example, the sociologist Michèle Lamont attributes White French workers' sense of commonality with Black workers to the Catholic and socialist traditions in which they were steeped. These traditions made familiar to them a schema of solidarity that was simply unavailable to the working-class White Americans Lamont interviewed. Alternatively, schemas may be culturally available but seen as inappropriate for some kinds of people. As I will show, while debt-settlement agents who were men could avoid the sense that they were taking advantage of their clients by imagining themselves to be financial educators rather than salespeople, agents who were women could not do so. Their clients insisted instead that they serve as something like therapists.[28]

Imagined relationships constrain also by levying behavioral expectations that are at odds with other behaviors necessary for the group to survive. This, I came to believe, was the problem facing activists in the New Left and the women's liberation movement who sought to run their organizations as participatory democracies. With few models for how to operate in a radically egalitarian way, activists drew on the norms that bound them as friends. Friendship is in some ways a natural model for participatory democracy. After all, friends' mutual trust and affection make it easy to make decisions quickly and fairly. Friends enjoy spending time together, so they have an interest in sustaining the relationship apart from what it provides them individually. And friends' equality is a deep one, based not on their similar strengths and competencies but on their complementary strengths and competencies, and, indeed, on their potential rather than existing ones.[29]

Many of the activists who formed the New Left had had experience of campus politics and Old Left organizations, which seemed to thrive on internecine battles waged via parliamentary maneuvers. To operate politically as friends—to allocate tasks on the basis of whoever wanted to do the job and to make decisions by consensus—was not only easy, but novel. For New Left women, whose relationships with men had always been the ones that seemed to count, the idea of friendship with women as the basis for political solidarity was even more radical. Certainly, activists transformed friendship as they relied on it. They extended friendship to more people than typical, and they incorporated political discussion and, indeed, political conflict into the norms of friendship. But the schema remained recognizable: informal, egalitarian, and based on affection.[30]

Features of friendship also undercut groups' ability to operate as participatory democracies, however. Friendship's natural exclusiveness made it difficult to expand the group without breeding mistrust between veterans and newcomers, who perceived themselves as excluded from the friendship circle. The women's liberationist Jo Freeman famously criticized what she called the "tyranny of structurelessness" in participatory democratic groups: in the absence of formal structures for equalizing power, unequal power still operated informally. But some women's liberationists *did* try to implement formal structures to equalize relations in the group. They allocated tasks by lot so that no one would have an advantage in securing more desirable tasks. Or, to prevent anyone from monopolizing the discussion, they distributed disks to participants at the beginning of meetings and had participants surrender one each time they spoke. Some groups created special occasions on which to welcome newcomers and integrate them into the group or subdivided the group when it became too large to allow real equality among members. But these efforts to create equality by way of formal mechanisms did not work. Why?[31]

A participant in one feminist collective put her finger on the problem, I believe, when she explained the failure of her group's effort to create a formal occasion for integrating new members: "One could hardly order active participants to make friends with all recruits. This was seen as a private, personal activity." In groups that were based on ties of friendship, efforts to formalize interactions seemed at odds with the informality that is a critical feature of friendship. Disk systems and lot systems seemed artificial, "mechanical," says the women's liberationist Chude Pamela Allen. They were at odds with the spontaneity and informality of friendship relations. When the feminist collective New York Radical Women experienced an influx of newcomers, straining its capacity to run as a collective, the group decided to divide into three randomly assigned groups. "Nobody had the nerve to say that they didn't want to do it by lot, that they wanted to be with their friends," recalls the group's founder, Anne Foror. Rather than question the procedure, many women simply ignored their assignments, continuing to meet with their friends. The resulting conflict led many to leave the organization altogether. As well as being exclusive, friendship is also resolutely voluntary and informal. Formalizing friendship's behavioral obligations and expectations was unappealing because it would have risked transforming the relationship into something else.[32]

Modifying relationship schemas is difficult. If you are already friends, it is difficult to ignore those bonds in favor of a more formalized relationship. Again, relationship schemas have meaning in relation to other relationship schemas. We know what friendship is because it is not acquaintanceship or a romantic relationship or a team membership. We have an emotional investment in maintaining the boundaries between different kinds of relationship. Certainly, we can and do move from one to the other. We invite an acquaintance to join our intramural soccer team, or a former romantic partner becomes a friend. But shifts like that take considerable emotional work. Fiske and his colleagues found that people strongly resisted applying the norms of one relationship type to an interaction that was seen as properly governed by another. Other researchers have shown that modifying the norms of relationships too much or modifying them in particularly stressful situations creates emotional strain. It puts the relationship in an uncertain position. People may try to avoid that emotional stress by sticking to the schema—even though doing so may come at the expense of adapting practically to the schema's limits. In sum, relationship scripts are both detachable from actual relationships and, at the same time, freighted with expectations about their use. This means that every attempt to act on the basis of an imagined relationship is both potentially effective and risky.[33]

So far, I have described individuals and small groups of people using relationship schemas creatively. But relationship schemas also become more widely available at certain moments. Today, for example, observers tout the potential of "crowds," "peer-to-peer networks," and "open-source movements" to build new forms of democratic cooperation. None of those schemas is traditional in civic action, but they are said to encourage behaviors that are egalitarian and effective. Whether or not such schemas live up to their claims, however, is an empirical question. To answer it, we need to examine what people actually do with these schemas, recognizing the constraints posed by users' relative status and by the norms that are culturally associated with the schema. This is the kind of examination I undertake with respect to a schema of egalitarian intimacy, one that I believe underpins many contemporary civic initiatives.[34]

THE DIFFUSION OF EGALITARIAN INTIMACY

If the current popularity of crowds and open-source movements as schemas for solidarity is recent, other schemas are longer in the making and produce more seismic shifts. William Sewell draws attention to one such shift, arguing that the rise of commercial capitalism in France in the eighteenth century made possible the schema of civic equality that we know today. In fact, in a society deeply permeated by relations of hierarchy and privilege, commercial capitalism led aristocrats, of all people, to turn that schema into the animating ideal of a revolution. What capitalism produced was a new appreciation for the relations of equivalence that were characteristic of the market, and for the processes of abstraction necessary to determine equivalence. Thinking of people as equals depended on viewing them abstractly. It depended on viewing them separately from how they were in the real world, where by no stretch of the imagination could they be considered equal. That schema became available with the rise of commercial capitalism.[35]

Two centuries later, in the social theorist Anthony Giddens's account, large-scale social changes produced a different understanding of equality, one based on the intimacy characteristic of adult erotic relationships. I want to rehearse Giddens's argument, since I believe that, in a perhaps surprising way, it helps to explain features of the contemporary civic initiatives on which I will focus. What Giddens calls a late-modern ideal of *confluent love* displaced the previous ideal of romantic love in the wake of movements for women's equality and sexual liberation and in the context of the diffusion of a psychotherapeutic idiom. Where romantic love is once and forever and depends on choosing the perfect person, confluent love is contingent and depends on the capacity of the particular relationship to serve each person's needs. Instead of projectively identifying with the other, confluent love involves a constant "opening oneself out to the other." Lovers enter and stay in a relationship as equals, crafting an emotional bond that satisfies their individual needs and deepening their trust in one another by way of mutual self-disclosure. Equality, joint fashioning, communication, and emotional expression: these are the values of the "pure relationship."[36]

Of course, these are ideals rather than realities. But for Giddens, intimacy as it is understood and striven for signals a profound change in personal relationships. Two features in particular are important: intimacy is based on equality and on communication. These are important not least because they are so close to the conditions for real democracy, Giddens observes. If we understand democracy as an arrangement that maximizes people's autonomy, then it should provide equality in decision making, a forum for open debate, mechanisms for the accountability of decision makers, and rights and obligations that apply to all. With its emphasis on mutual trust and on expectations arrived at and monitored through communication between equals, those things are provided by contemporary ideals of intimacy.[37]

Giddens goes one step further, however, if more suggestively. "The possibility of intimacy," he writes, "means the promise of democracy." Modern intimacy is not only itself democratic but may promote democracy outside the sphere of personal relationships: "A symmetry exists between the democratizing of personal life and democratic possibilities in the global political order at the most extensive level." Giddens cites as an example negotiation based not on bargaining, "which can be equated with a personal relationship in which intimacy is lacking," but rather on parties' attempt "to discover each other's underlying concerns and interests." In other words, a schema of egalitarian intimacy based on mutual self-disclosure might serve as a model for relationships in the public sphere.[38]

My argument is that, in a sense, it is already doing so. As psychotherapeutic ideas diffused from private life to work and politics, the notion that certain kinds of *talk* were critical to building effective relationships became widely accepted. Numerous scholars have documented the spread of what the sociologist Nikolas Rose calls the "psy discourses"—psychology, psychotherapy, and counseling—from the realm of personal life to that of school and work. I will talk about this more in chapter 5, but for now I want to make the point that, from the beginning, the psychotherapeutic project was about talking about the self. According to the historian John Durham Peters, the extraordinary interest in communication that flowered after World War II owed to the centrality of communication to two new projects: theories of information (such as cybernetics, computer science, and genetic science) and psychotherapy. For the latter, communication was at once the means of psychological healing and its goal. Thus Carl Rogers, the dean of the person-centered humanistic psychology that would come to dominate psychotherapy and counseling, insisted, "The whole task of psychotherapy is dealing with a failure in communication." Communication, moreover, would overcome conflicts not only within the individual, but also between individuals, groups, and, indeed, nations.[39]

The infusion of modes of talk with conflict-resolving, cooperation-inspiring, self-enhancing, and equality-producing purposes continues to the present. At home, at work, in volunteering with a nonprofit, in diversity workshops, in leadership seminars and organizational retreats, in career coaching, in advice columns, in relationship blogs, and in facilitated meetings, people today learn how to communicate properly. Doing so is claimed to have instrumental benefits: it will make the person more successful and the organization more effective. But the instrumental benefits of talk are touted only lightly. One does not learn how to communicate in order to dominate, manipulate, or manufacture the appearance of solidarity. Rather, talk should create authentic bonds of trust and affection. It should create genuine equality. What experts provide, then, is training in authentic communication. And just as communication characterized by mutual self-disclosure and emotional support should make for more egalitarian marriages and more cooperative workplaces, it should also make for more civically engaged and democratic polities.

This, then, is what I draw attention to in contemporary civic initiatives: an effort to build solidary relationships by way of a certain kind of talk. The particulars of the talk and the kind of relationship it is supposed to build vary across initiatives. However, common to all of them is the value placed on sharing experiences, values, and beliefs at least as a preliminary to expressing opinions, and sometimes as an alternative to doing so; striving to empathize with experiences different from one's own; and speaking as an individual rather than as a representative of a group. Interlocutors are taught to avoid talk that is narrowly instrumental, that involves bargaining rather than identifying common ground, that is abstract rather than expressive, or that seeks to elicit deference rather than reciprocity.

As I have said, I see real limits to this approach to building democratic solidarity. But I want to distinguish my critique from one alleging the so-called political triumph of the therapeutic. Complaints in that vein say that institutions today are overly concerned with meeting the narcissistic needs of individuals claiming vulnerability and pain. The initiatives I describe, by contrast, are emphatically about building relationships. They abjure the unbuttoned self-exposure, the performance of victimhood, that critics of the therapeutic decry. Nor is my main objection that such approaches improperly import into politics the kind of emotional expression that critics believe should remain within the private sphere. To the contrary, there are ways in which the *virtues* of the schema as it operates in the private sphere have been lost as it has been transposed to the public sphere. The egalitarian intimacy that is striven for in the realm of personal life exists within an ongoing relationship, a relationship that should deepen over time. By contrast, the egalitarian intimacy that is forged in public deliberation, in efforts to connect causes with distant donors, and in empowerment projects in low-income communities is often temporary. People are brought together for encounters in which the usual disparities of status are suspended. But the encounter is bounded in time. It provides at most a fleeting *experience* of a relationship rather than the basis for building one. To some extent, this is simply a practical reality. In the case of public deliberation exercises, it would be prohibitively expensive to hire professionals to structure a relationship between citizens and political decision makers that continues until the decisions are actually made and implemented. All civic initiatives operate with limited funds and on a tight timetable for demonstrating results. But the limitation is also conceptual. The relationships that professionals craft do not build in expectations about how the relationship will develop over time.[40]

The efforts to craft solidary relationships in civic life that I examine are limited not only in the temporal horizons they imagine but also in their faith that a particular communicative style can produce equality. This is what professionals provide: instruction in a mode of communication, whether storytelling, deliberation, or dialogue. Professionals maintain that this mode of talk differs from the more familiar ones that both alienate citizens from the political process and keep them stuck in old ideological positions. Teaching people how to talk, how to disclose their fears and aspirations, their pain and hope, can create mutual respect across difference. Just as important, it can empower those whose views are usually marginalized, creating relationships characterized both by solidarity and equality.

But mutually self-disclosing talk is not the same as equality. If certain topics are declared off-limits or if one party is more skilled in the privileged mode of talk than others, it is hard to imagine how talk will move the relationship toward one of equality. In fact, the supposedly mutual self-disclosure that takes place in these civic initiatives is sometimes one-sided. Certain people talk, and other people have the privilege of choosing whether to listen. Or else the talk is performed for distant audiences, with the expectations of those audiences transmitted to parties interacting in the here and now. For example, the volunteer organizations that the sociologist Nina Eliasoph studied strove to empower low-income kids: to build kids' skills and confidence by showing them they could work alongside middle-class volunteers to improve their communities. But what empowerment projects most tangibly produced, Eliasoph shows, was empowerment *talk*. Participants learned to talk as if forging bonds between middle-class White youth volunteers hoping to strengthen their college applications and poor students of color who had little chance of going to college were easy, and as if the adult volunteers who appeared for a few hours a month were like a family. They learned to talk as if there were a community bonded by trust and affection that just had to be invited to materialize and begin to solve community problems. Disadvantaged kids learned to describe themselves to funders, reporters, political officials, adult volunteers, even to each other, as problems to be solved (asked by a reporter why he was volunteering in a local event, one boy explained, "I'm involved instead of being out on the streets or taking drugs or doing something illegal"). Advantaged kids, for their part, learned to call the disadvantaged kids leaders simply for partici-pating—again, as if saying it would make it so. In the process, though (and this was not the intent), participants also learned to treat relationships of family, leadership, and community lightly, as claims that could be made and shed depending on the audience.[41]

I see in other initiatives an enactment of equality that, as in Eliasoph's case, left inequalities pretty much in place. For example, the cause advo-cates I will describe encouraged the people affected by homelessness or poverty to tell stories emphasizing their resilience and agency. Doing so avoided exploiting them, advocates said, and instead put them in a position closer to equality with their audiences. But their agency was represented—depicted—in their stories, not enacted in their own decisions about how to tell their stories. Again, a certain kind of talk was made to stand in for equality more generally, outside the moment of talk.

The same slippage between a kind of emotionally expressive talk and a relationship of equality figures in contemporary celebrations of the so-called *sharing economy*. In allowing strangers to use their apartments, power tools, and carpentry services, the argument goes, people are build-ing anti-hierarchical and community-oriented relationships. They are re-placing the instrumentalism and impersonality of capitalist relations with those of cooperation. Sharing comes naturally to millennials, the argument continues, because they are so used to sharing online: sharing photos, video clips, files, and memes. Far from attenuating social ties, then, digital media have the capacity to build them.[42]

But as the communications scholar Nicholas A. John points out, there is little reason that sending photos and video clips to people whom one al-ready knows should lead one to want to lend out one's possessions to people whom one does not know. What makes the two seem to go together is the confusion of two meanings of the term "sharing": sharing as *communication between intimates* and sharing as an *egalitarian form of distribution*. When Facebook promises its users that it will not "share" our information without our permission—meaning that it will not sell our information to advertisers—it trades on those dual meanings, representing our relationship with the company, with whom we have already "shared" our information, as one of egalitarian intimacy. Before the mid-2000s the term "sharing" was not even used in relation to social media; now it is ubiquitous. The interesting thing is not so much that sharing sometimes actually means selling or renting. It is that social media entrepreneurs' successful appropriation of the word *sharing* has endowed transactions conducted over social media with values of equality, openness, honesty, mutuality, community, and trust, whatever their actual character. Social media–enabled transactions appear to be those things because they have been cast in an idiom of intimacy.[43]

My argument is that the same slippage between a certain style of talk (one of emotional self-revealing) and a certain kind relationship (egalitarian and cooperative) also occurs outside social media. I want to be clear that equality in talk is surely necessary to an egalitarian relationship. But it is not the sum total of that relationship. To put it a different way, if a certain style of talk may be valuable as a *means* to equality, that is very different than treating a certain style of talk as an *expression* of equality, as if it has already been achieved. If our goal is to create solidarities that are based on members' equality, conflating the two may not serve us well.

ALTERNATIVES

A careful reader might interpret my arguments as contradictory. On one hand, I have said that people's creative capacity to act on relationships they do not actually have has allowed them to solve standard challenges of building solidarity. On the other hand, I have argued that a relationship of egalitarian intimacy—something like friendship to be arrived at by mutual self-disclosure—is ill equipped to provide the kind of solidarity we need. But if people can pretend so creatively, why can they not pretend to be friends? Why should that imagined relationship be less effective in building solidarity than the metaphors of a bargaining relationship and advocacy group used by the public forum participants I mentioned or that of kinship and first-class citizenship used by southern civil rights organizers? Because the norms of egalitarian intimacy, at least as those norms are understood today, are not well matched to a kind of solidarity in which people are members of groups as well as individuals and in which their equality is actively negotiated. Nor do they foster the kind of solidarity that is involved in politics rather than removed from it. In other words, my objection to the relationships that are held out, implicitly or explicitly, as ideals in many contemporary civic initiatives is not that such relationships are inauthentic, but that they are unlikely to produce the forms of solidarity we need.

So, what is the alternative? What kinds of civic relationships should we strive to create? Rather than try to outline ideal schemas for such relationships, in the following chapters I identify elements of such schemas operating today in the imaginations and practices of real people acting in civic life. As I mentioned, while the organizers of the deliberative forums I studied saw participants as a temporary and decidedly nonpolitical public, participants themselves understood the bonds that joined them differently. In doing so, they pointed to ways in which they might have had real impact on the decisions that mattered. In another context, I find government bureaucrats helping to equip the public to move from deliberation to challenge, suggesting that a more flexible conception of the public is not unrealistic. When it comes to the communicative form of self-disclosure, some among the advocates I interviewed used the form to genuinely empower people rather than only represent them as empowered. Critically, though, empowerment came from mastering the performance of a persuasive story, not from connecting emotionally with distant donors.

I also explore a variety of efforts in churches, unions, volunteer groups, and movements to build forms of solidarity across difference that are egalitarian and that are firmly oriented to institutional decision making. Paying attention to solidarity as it is crafted in these local settings leads me to yet another argument: that it is possible to create new schemas of belonging when familiar ones are inadequate. Certainly, familiar relationship schemas have the advantage that their behavioral expectations are already known. This means that people can use them with the knowledge that other parties to the interaction will recognize them too. But groups have also forged new ways of interacting. The sociologist Jeffrey Alexander argues that social movements have made moral claims that have redefined the contours of social solidarity. In a more modest way, I show that movements have produced schemas of solidary relationship that have diffused more widely.[44]

Finally, I turn to solidarities at the national level. The political scientist Benedict Anderson famously argued that the rise of nationalism depended on people seeing themselves as joined by ties of comradeship with those they did not know. Nations depended on "imagined communities." Scholars since Anderson have tended to focus on the symbolic boundaries or originating narratives that constitute national communities, however, not on the character of the bonds that are thought to join their members. But conceptualizing co-nationals as something like kin is different than conceptualizing them as something like participants in a collective enterprise or as peers or neighbors. Certain metaphors imply more permeable boundaries with outsiders than others, and tolerate more difference within the group. Indeed, certain schemas make it possible to imagine a "we" we love without a "they" we hate. In sum, paying attention to people's efforts to enact solidarity may help us to think about Aristotle's concept of civic friendship—the glue binding democratic polities—in terms of more contemporary referents. And doing so, I suggest, may have real consequence.[45]

OUTLINE OF CHAPTERS

In the following chapters I show how people have imagined and invented relationships to deal with recurrent challenges of solidarity. These include the obstacles to solidarity posed by self-interest, by members' differences, and by competing solidarities, as well as the obstacle specifically to democratic solidarity posed by the tension between political trust and political accountability. Along the way I take up elements of solidarity that have been theorized under other names, such as collective identity, ideas about fairness, and social capital. I pay special attention to the people whose job is to convince others of their solidary obligations: movement organizers, debt-settlement agents, public-engagement specialists, and the advocates who seek to build public support for their cause. Their efforts shed light on ordinary people's capacity to act on imagined relationships and on the conditions for their doing so. I detail the specifics of the data and the methods of analysis I use in the endnotes for each chapter.

Chapter 2 takes up the challenge of competing solidarities, in this case, in a movement. African Americans living in the Deep South in the early 1960s knew that attempting to register to vote would likely subject them to economic and physical reprisals. My focus in this chapter is on how civil rights organizers—most of them young, Black, and, crucially, from outside the towns in which they operated—sought to convince them to try. Drawing on field reports written at the time, I explore organizers' evolving understanding of what worked. It is no great surprise that appealing to people's self-interest or to abstract principles of freedom and justice alone did not work. More surprising, given the literature on social movements generally and this one in particular, is that appealing to people's obligations to kinfolk and congregation also did not work. To the contrary, such ties usually counseled against participation. Direct ties with particular others sometimes must be imagined away, I suggest, replaced in people's minds by imagined ties with general others in order for solidary action to take place. I show how civil rights organizers were able to help bring those ties into being.

Chapter 3 turns from the enabling dimensions of imagined relationships to their constraints: some of the things that make it difficult to successfully claim relationships that are not there. The solidarity in which I am interested here is of the first kind, enacted in a society's shared moral norms, and the challenge is that posed by self-interest. How do people's assessments of what is fair both reflect and respond to the tension between moral norms and self-interest? To decide what was fair, the clients of the debt-settlement agencies Zaibu Tufail and I studied imagined a relationship with their creditors that was characterized by reciprocity and that was personal. That fiction allowed them to retain some sense of moral autonomy in a degrading situation. And yet, it also led them to try to punish creditors who, in their view, had treated them badly, a decision that often had lasting repercussions for their financial futures. Then I turn to agency staff to identify another kind of constraint on people's practical use of imagined relationships. Agents sought to sell people who were in economic straits a service that they probably would have done better without. How were agents able to think about the work they did as fair? I show that men were better equipped to do so than women because of the schema of financial advisor they, but not women, were able to claim. The resulting moral onerousness of women agents' work points also to the likely difficulty of integrating an ethic of care into democratic solidarity more broadly.

Chapter 4 turns to the sphere of civil society. It treats the public forums that have been championed in recent years as a solution to citizens' low levels of trust and involvement in political institutions. Giving people the opportunity to talk about issues of public concern, issues ranging from downtown development to the federal deficit, in a setting characterized by civility and mutual respect should help people to learn more about the issues, arrive at areas of agreement, and provide policy makers with a census of informed opinion. Critics charge that such forums are no more than a feel-good exercise in which a carefully orchestrated show of public voice substitutes for anything like actual influence. To adjudicate between these two positions, I argue, we need to pay attention to how organizers imagine the relationships participants have before, during, and after the forum, as well as how participants themselves imagine those relationships. My observations of forums held to solicit public input into rebuilding Lower Manhattan after 9/11, along with interviews with participants, show that participants saw themselves differently than did forum organizers. Drawing on a variety of metaphors for what bound them as a group, participants imagined themselves at different points bargaining with each other, representing groups outside the forum, and advocating for the forum's recommendations with policy makers. These imagined relationships, I argue, allowed participants to envisage possibilities for impact that forum organizers did not. Then I explore the limitations of the schema of partnership favored by forum organizers for connecting policy makers and the public.

In chapter 5, I study another group of experts who use a distinctive style of communication to build solidarity—here, solidarity that is capable of transforming the status quo. Advocacy groups use personal self-disclosure to develop relationships with potential supporters: the people who will give money, time, influence, or all three, to the cause, whether the cause is fighting homelessness, human trafficking, poverty, or discrimination against transgender people. Thirty years ago, the stories advocates told, or encouraged the people with whom they worked to tell, would likely have emphasized the suffering those people experienced. Advocates today firmly reject such "victim" storytelling as exploitative. They strive to create a relationship between teller and audience that is characterized by mutual respect and something approaching equality. To this end, they coach people to tell stories emphasizing hope and resilience, stories in which the person's emotional pain is barely revealed, stories emphasizing details with which audiences can identify, and stories implying that the telling is reciprocal. Such storytelling practices depict a relationship of equality, but do little, I argue, to actually empower the teller. Contrast that understanding of the place of talk in forging solidarity with another one that I heard in my interviews. For some of the people I interviewed, intimacy was reserved for people one knew, and performing one's story was a single step in one's development as an activist.

In chapter 6, I explore some of the conditions that have made it possible for the kind of civil-society groups celebrated by Tocquevillians—churches, unions, and volunteer groups, along with workers and movement organizations—to forge solidarities marked by equality and the recognition of difference. The groups I profile have not striven to forge relations of intimacy by way of self-disclosing talk. Instead, they communicate in a variety of registers, including direct challenge, collective self-reflection, and playful humor. They use talk as a way to work out relationships of equality. And along with talk, they rely on collective rituals to reaffirm both the group's unity and its distinct way of organizing difference.

In the conclusion I suggest that efforts to invent new modes of solidarity like those I described in chapter 6 have import for broader solidarities. Indeed, they open up possibilities for enacting more inclusive national solidarities than the ones that dominate American policy and public discourse today. Then I pull together the main lines of analysis in previous chapters. The concept of relationship schemas encourages us to question oppositions that structure the way we think analytically and normatively about social life. On one side are face-to-face interactions with particular others; on the other, imagined relationships with generalized others. The former is usually privileged: the local is the source of relationships that are affectively rich and communal, while imagined others are remote emotionally as well as geographically. In contrast with that picture, I argue that people imagine relationships even with particular others; that solidary action may rely on obligations to imagined others rather than real ones; that if we want to create solidarities that are inclusive and politically effective, striving to make strangers seem like intimates may not be the best way to do that; and that, luckily, we need not be so limited.

CHAPTER TWO

Free-Riders and Freedom Riders

Two intellectuals, a scientist and a film director, were once asked to sign a protest [petition against the authoritarian regime in Poland]. One refused: "I can't. I have a son." The other one unscrewed the cap of his pen: "I have to sign, because I have a son."

KAZIMIERZ BRANDYS, *A Warsaw Diary* (1983)

The former civil rights worker Charlie Cobb remembers arriving in rural Mississippi communities to launch voter registration drives in 1962: "You were in these little towns like Ruleville, and people would say, 'Wow, that's the Freedom Riders!'" He and the other voter registration workers knew about the Freedom Rides, of course. The integrated bus trips had been planned by the Congress of Racial Equality (CORE) in 1961 to test a federal law on interstate transportation. The rides created a federal crisis when passengers were bombed in Anniston, Alabama, and attacked by chain-wielding segregationists in Birmingham. When CORE called a halt to the rides, the newly formed Student Nonviolent Coordinating Committee (SNCC) resumed them, sending hundreds of students on buses from Montgomery to Jackson, Mississippi, where they were arrested and held in the notorious Parchman prison.[1]

Few of SNCC's organizers in Mississippi, though, had participated in the Freedom Rides. It did not matter. The organizer Ivanhoe Donaldson remembers, "When you knocked on the door—and I had this I don't know how many times—people would say, "Bout time you Freedom Riders got here.' It was like they were waiting for you." Two years after the Freedom Rides, a Greenville organizer reported, "We are identified as 'Freedom Riders.' No matter where we go, we are questioned thusly; 'Where are you from . . . You one of the Freedom Riders?'" The Freedom Rides didn't even go through Arkansas, yet a West Helena organizer wrote:

People call us Freedom Riders. On a number of occasions, we have talked to someone who had heard that we were here in town. When we ask how he found out that we were here he'll say something to the effect of, 'I was talking to a man in the grocery store this morning and he said, "they're here."[2]

Being a Freedom Rider, Cobb explains, "meant that you were one of these people who were challenging the White people. And you were up here to do that too." He remarks on the irony: "The interesting thing for me was how you kind of hit town and had this identity. Not because of anything you did. It had to do with these people who came down on the bus." There was another irony: Freedom Riders' notoriety increased the level of risk for Black residents. It made it more likely they would be fired or evicted or arrested or cut off from credit on any evidence, however slim, of having associated with movement activists. When Bernice Carter's employer told her that she would be fired if she attended a meeting "with those Freedom Riders," or when a police officer told James West that he was "going to do something about you goddamn Freedom Riders" and had two prisoners beat him unconscious, it is hard to imagine that being associated with the Freedom Rides helped in organizing. And yet former SNCC activists are convinced that it did.[3]

With few resources and no guarantee of federal protection, SNCC workers could offer residents little in the way of material incentives to participate. But they did bring a sense of being part of a wider movement. Organizers broke through the isolation of rural Black residents by providing recognition for their efforts, news of other communities moving, and stories that worked their travails into broader narratives of overcoming. When they were successful, SNCC workers were able to alter the behavioral requirements of solidary ties, that is, of kinship and religiosity and community membership, and to create new ties and loyalties. The fact that people knew little about them enabled organizers to claim to have political influence that they did not. More important, insofar as they were seen as representatives of a South-wide movement, they provided the recognition of that movement for people willing to claim new, politically assertive identities. At the same time, their willingness to sacrifice their own safety—these "children" who could have left the South—levied powerful obligations on those they sought to organize.

The most obvious movement victories were not won in the rural areas of the Deep South. Organizers' efforts to register voters were mainly unsuccessful: the fear was too great and the federal government too unwilling to intervene. And yet, SNCC organizers did galvanize movements in some of the counties in which they worked. Two years after SNCC began organizing in Mississippi, eighty thousand Black residents cast ballots in a mock election for governor. SNCC projects formed the backbone of that effort as well as of the Mississippi Freedom Democratic Party (MFDP), an independent Democratic party formed the next year. Years later the counties in which SNCC organizers had worked in 1964 had higher rates than others of Black voter registration and electoral turnout.[4]

In this chapter I explore the role of relationships in people's willingness to stand up to injustice. The solidarity I am interested in here is that which opposes the status quo. Like the scholars whose work I will cite, I draw attention to the importance of long-standing relationships among members of the group in motivating people to participate in collective action. But more than previous authors, I argue for the importance of relationships between insiders and outsiders to the group, of relationships that are new rather than of long standing, and of relationships that are more imagined than real.

WHY PEOPLE PROTEST

Generations of theories about why movements emerge when they do have been based on studies of the 1960s civil rights movement. For a time, sociologists studying that movement emphasized the role of outsiders in mobilizing protest. After all, African Americans in the South lived under the yoke of economic subordination and violence. How could they be expected to mobilize, knowing that to do so jeopardized their jobs and lives, and the jobs and lives of their families? The economist Mancur Olson argued about collective action generally that it was more rational to "free-ride" on the efforts of others than to participate oneself—even when all one would give up by participating was one's time and effort. Imagine the appeal of free-riding, then, when the prospects of winning were so slim and the costs so great. Accordingly, scholars argued that northern White support was crucial to the rise of the civil rights movement. Support took the form of money, legal and political expertise, and the involvement of northern "conscience constituents," most of them White, whose resources insulated them from the free-rider dilemma.[5]

In debunking that version of history, sociologists such as Aldon Morris and Doug McAdam developed a new perspective on social movements. Oppressed people had resources other than economic and political capital. Long-standing bonds of trust and care provided people *solidary* incentives to participate, even in conditions of repression. Institutions in Black communities, especially Black colleges and churches, nurtured bonds among students and congregants, respectively, that discouraged free-riding. Ministers, for example, held one of the few jobs in Black communities that were not dependent on Whites, and they were deeply involved in the lives of their congregations. Charismatic, as well as skilled organizers and orators, they generally enjoyed their members' strong loyalty. Participation in a movement supported by ministers thus became normative.[6]

This argument has found empirical support in studies of other movements. Preexisting ties led to participation in movements ranging from the French Commune and the Russian Revolution to the Central American solidarity movement and Italian environmental activism. Yet, studies of still other movements show people mobilizing in the absence of dense ties, as was the case with animal-rights activism and movements of gays and lesbians and of the disabled. And in still other movements, dense ties, but ones characterized by competition and mutual suspicion, have discouraged participation.[7]

One can imagine, moreover, that even mutually supportive ties might militate against participation. In the Deep South in the early 1960s, joining the movement put others at risk. Retaliatory efforts by Whites could strike anyone even peripherally involved with the movement. Churches that hosted mass meetings were vulnerable to bombing, whole families who housed civil rights workers were evicted, parents who attempted to register to vote saw their children fired. If one's friend or kin or co-congregant joined a movement in circumstances like these, loyalty might demand that one try to dissuade him or her from continuing on that perilous course. And if one knew that one's own participation would likely provoke retaliation against one's family and friends, participation surely would become less appealing.[8]

Another obstacle to protest associated with dense networks also operated in the South. The relations of authority and deference that typically accompany densely networked communities gave some people a stake in accommodation rather than insurgency. Rewarded by powerful Whites for their brokerage role, some traditional Black leaders resisted challenges that could threaten that position. Even if their loyalties were firmly to those without power, they might use their authority to discourage any but moderate challenge. Together, these possibilities suggest that especially in the conditions of repression that characterized the Deep South, but probably more generally, preexisting bonds of trust and loyalty must be reinterpreted so that those bonds now require participation rather than its avoidance. Alternatively (or, more likely, additionally), preexisting solidarities must come to compete with new ones, relationships either with real people or with imagined ones that make participation an obligation of those new relationships.[9]

This work of redefining old relationships and creating new ones is what organizers do. Since the historian Charles Payne's masterly work on the Mississippi movement, we have a better sense of what organizing looked like under conditions of repression. Payne draws attention to a cadre of longtime activists who laid the groundwork for the 1960s movement in that state. Men such as Aaron Henry, E. W. Steptoe, Amzie Moore, Hartman Turnbow, and Vernon Dahmer were set on building Black electoral power. They saw strategic possibilities in the young Black students who were sitting in at lunch counters around the South, and they drafted the students into that agenda. However, Payne also shows what the young SNCC organizers brought to the table. They were smart, impulsive, and willing to confront racist brutality in daring shows of defiance. And, at their best, they were also willing to do the slow, patient work of building relationships of trust in Black communities. They worked with ministers and other "leading people" such as teachers and the owners of small businesses where those leaders were receptive, and they maneuvered around them where they were not. Organizers made it clear to residents that if they were willing to get in "that mess," the SNCC kids would be there with them.[10]

In this chapter I try to add to the picture presented by Payne and others by drawing attention to the ways in which organizers did not just build on existing relationships, but also invented them. It is the imaginative work of organizing that I explore here. Organizers appealed to residents' sense of obligation to those with whom they already had relationships, such as their own children. But they also created obligations to themselves as something *like* residents' children. They created obligations to a movement with which residents had little contact, and they created obligations to a nation whose promises lay, always, in the distant future.

OUTSIDERS

In tracing organizers' efforts to make salient and to invent relationships capable of compelling participation, I also want to explore the conditions in which those efforts took place. The head of the Mississippi project, Bob Moses, wrote a letter in late 1962 about SNCC's work in the state thus far. SNCC's Mississippi-born organizers "very seldom are free to work in their own home towns because of the pressure brought to bear on their parents and/or their relatives," Moses wrote. "And then, when this situation does not prevail, they are likely to be prophets without honor at home." Hollis

Watkins and Curtis Hayes, two of SNCC's best organizers, Moses went on, "were able to recruit some 250 people to go down and register in Hatties- burg and Forrest County, but were not successful in recruiting more than two or three in McComb, their home city." Another organizer, Lafayette Sur- ney, could not work in his hometown of Ruleville "because his parents are afraid of the pressure that would follow."[11]

Moses's report points to what theories of mobilization premised on the power of dense ties miss. The very fact that people in the community had deep ties to Watkins, Hayes, and Surney rendered them vulnerable to pres- sure *not* to participate and probably made them more determined to con- vince the young men not to recruit other participants. The fact that com- munity members knew Watkins and Hayes also probably made them more skeptical of their pitch that participating would bring them some gains along with the costs that were all too certain.

The young men were more effective, Moses observed, in communities where they were outsiders. Organizers in the tradition of Saul Alinsky have long argued that outsiders are effective because they are removed from the conflicts and rivalries that characterize most communities. Like the soci- ologist Georg Simmel's "stranger," the outsider is unconstrained by assump- tions about his allegiance. Residents are therefore more likely to assume that he is on their side rather than on that of a competitor. But the orga- nizing literature does not talk about another advantage outsiders have: the connections they are imagined to have with people and groups outside the community. SNCC organizers, I will show, claimed to have access to the Justice Department and other federal officials, as well as to Martin Luther King, Jr., and a South-wide movement. Just as important as the instrumen- tal benefits those connections might be expected to confer—for example, protection for people registering to vote—were their symbolic benefits. SNCC workers' ties to a South-wide movement and the federal government allowed them to serve as what the sociologist Alessandro Pizzorno calls a mobilizing circle of recognition.[12]

Pizzorno, like other movement scholars, maintains that people partici- pate because it is who they are. Collective identity rather than self-interest motivates participation. Pizzorno reminds us, however, that if collective identity is an awareness of one's membership in a group, it also requires that one be *recognized* as a member of the group. This suggests that when one's existing circles of recognition (friends, family, church) are counseling one not to participate, one is unlikely to do so unless another circle of rec- ognition becomes salient. Or, to put it otherwise, when participation puts at risk those to whom one has prior, identity-constituting ties, discovering a compelling interest in protest may require reconstituting the self. It may require that one see oneself as a different person. And that is only likely to happen if one is seen by a circle of relevant others as that different person.[13]

For rural Black southerners in the early 1960s, who would those relevant others be? While it is possible to feel recognized by imagined others, it is probably easier when there are real proxies for the imagined others. Organizers who are seen as connected to actors outside the community—even if that connection is more claimed than enjoyed—can play that role. Moreover, organizers' detachment from local structures of authority and responsibility makes it possible for them to recast the obligations of familiar relationships. In this case, it helped organizers to make the case that being a citizen depended on the recognition not of southern officials but on that of the movement; that being a Christian depended on a community of believers extending beyond the local minister counseling moderation; that being a parent depended on protecting the "children" who had left their own communities to lay their bodies on the line; that being a leader depended not on one's credentials but on one's ability to persuade other people to join the movement.[14]

In sum, dense ties may mobilize or inhibit action depending on the meanings that are imputed to them. Activists' structural position outside the communities in which they work may give them an advantage in reinterpreting old ties and creating new ones. But it is no guarantee. Each one of the capacities I've described—to hint at powerful resources and connections, to motivate through norms of reciprocity, to validate new identities—requires a prior relation of trust with local residents. Otherwise outsiders could be dismissed as naive about the challenges that locals faced or as motivated by personal desires for martyrdom or celebrity. They could be seen as dangerous rather than morally compelling. As I said in the last chapter, to claim relationships that are not there is potentially game-changing but also risky.

MISSISSIPPI AND SOUTHWEST GEORGIA, 1961–1963

Today we treat voter registration as part of the machinery of routine democratic politics. For African Americans in the Deep South in the early 1960s, it was a radical act. In counties with populations that were majority Black, legal voter registration would have made it more than remotely possible for Black residents ultimately to control the machinery of government. For that reason alone, it was resisted by southern Whites with fierce determination. Prospective Black voters in Mississippi were required to interpret a nearly incomprehensible section of the state constitution, and in Georgia to submit character vouchers signed by registered voters in counties where no Blacks were registered. Applicants were turned away for such trivia as having underlined rather than circled "Mr." on the registration card or would find the office mysteriously closed on registration day. Those who attempted to register knew not only that they might be harassed, beaten, fired, or evicted from their homes, but that members of their extended families might be too.[15]

The strategies were grimly effective. In Pike County, Mississippi, where SNCC began organizing in the summer of 1961, only two hundred of the eight thousand Black adults in the county were registered to vote; in Amite County, one person out of five thousand was registered; and in Walthall, none of the three thousand Black adults were. In Lee and Terrell Counties, Georgia, where SNCC began a second state project in early 1962, Black residents made up more than 60 percent of the population, but no more than fifty individuals had registered in the previous decade. "It seemed like a good afternoon," one southwest Georgia organizer wrote cautiously in a field report in 1962. "But it was like any afternoon, with the same tired phrases, the same appalling nebulous fear. What's holding you back, you ask? 'Well now, I jest ain't got up there yet. I jest ain't got up there.' You cannot come around and break a world in two. You cannot forget the force of two hundred years."[16]

To show how organizers sought "to break a world in two," I draw on several hundred field reports by SNCC organizers working in Mississippi and southwest Georgia in 1962 and 1963, in conjunction with interviews with former organizers and minutes of meetings in which organizing strategies were discussed. The level of economic and physical violence in the rural areas of the Black Belt had dissuaded the major civil rights groups from committing resources there. The radicalism of SNCC activists lay in their willingness to concentrate their work in just those areas. Bob Moses had met Amzie Moore in the summer of 1960 and returned in 1961 to pursue Moore's plan of a voter registration program. The Kennedy administration was also urging SNCC to turn to voter registration, but many within SNCC believed the administration was trying to divert them from direct action at a time when the Freedom Rides were provoking a federal crisis. The organizational dispute was eased by creating voter registration and direct-action wings of the group and then faded when it became clear that in the Black Belt, voter registration *was* direct action. By November 1962 SNCC workers were operating in fourteen counties in Mississippi and Georgia.[17]

As part of SNCC's arrangement with the Voter Education Project, which channeled funding from liberal foundations to the group intermittently between 1962 and 1966, organizers were asked to submit weekly field reports detailing registrars' treatment of Black applicants, episodes of harassment experienced by civil rights workers, and residents' reasons for opting not to join the voter registration program. At a minimum, the reports provide information on organizers' activities and incidents of White harassment. But many go much further in detailing the pitches that organizers made and the kinds of responses they encountered. Quoting extensively from mass meetings and individual conversations, they offer rich insight into the nitty-gritty of organizing. My focus on field reports from 1962 and 1963 allows me to trace the beginnings of campaigns in counties that had experienced little sustained collective action. These materials do not enable me to account for organizers' success or failure in persuading people to try to register to vote. But they do provide a sense of what young activists were learning about how to organize.[18]

The reports make clear the role of an older cadre of activists in securing SNCC workers places to stay, protection, financial support, and strategic advice. Wiley Branton, head of the Voter Education Project, wrote: "It is not clear to me precisely what role Amzy [*sic*] Moore plays in the Miss project. However, it seems certain that at the very least he serves as an advisor and coordinator for much of the activity in Bolivar, Leflore and Sunflower counties." Moore's contacts were vital. Charlie Cobb reported on a conversation he had with Moore about a town he was reconnoitering: "According to him, the police here are bad, and that I am likely to run into some trouble with them. Also, the principal of the local high school here is in the pay of the Sovereignty Commission." Another worker wrote gratefully that he "had been informed by Amzie Moore before arrival that my best bet would be to work with the cafe owners, for the professional people were brain-washed by the Whites." His most useful contact proved to be the wealthy owner of a house of prostitution who was openly bisexual and a Grand Master of the Masons: "Compliments to Mr. Moore for he warned me that this is the kind of man I will have to work with." In southwest Georgia, D. Ulysses Pullum, Agnew James, and Carolyn Daniels helped SNCC organizers find their footing.[19]

Sometimes the contacts veteran activists provided panned out; sometimes they did not. Sam Block spent the first few weeks of his stay in Greenwood, Mississippi, sleeping in the back seat of a car. Organizers were often forced to vacate their lodgings when landlords got wind of who they were. Young people were the easiest to get involved; they were most impressed by the organizers' mystique. The challenge was to move from the young people to their parents, to persuade adults to come to a mass meeting first, then to enroll in citizenship classes, and finally—most difficult—to go to the county seat and attempt to register to vote. Invariably, they lost people along the way. On one day in August 1962, a Mississippi organizer reported, a hundred people were canvassed, ten agreed to attempt to register, three actually showed up at the courthouse, and those three were frightened away by the sheriff. By the end of the year, Bob Moses estimated, they had canvassed ten thousand people in the state; eleven hundred had attempted to register, and fewer than one hundred had succeeded. In southwest Georgia three churches associated with the movement were burned to the ground, bringing national media attention and a temporary lessening of White harassment—but also making that much clearer the depth of White opposition to voting rights. The people SNCC canvassed worried about losing their jobs, their homes, and their credit. And they worried for others close to them: for example, the teacher who feared harm to her pupils and the elderly woman who worried that the men in her family would be fired from their jobs. Usually residents simply demurred when SNCC workers pressed them: they had been feeling poorly, or they didn't have time right now, or they would get up there in a little bit.[20]

Along with residents' fear of reprisals against their families, neighbors, and church, the conservatism of traditional Black leadership figured frequently in organizers' field reports. "My immediate opposition comes from the ministers of the local churches who won't consider letting me use their churches for mass meeting," a Batesville, Mississippi, organizer complained. "This is not just one preacher in Batesville—All. This means that I have to conduct my mass meetings in pool rooms, taverns and where ever else I can get an audience." "Most of the old people think the ministers can do anything for them, so they will follow them," Charles McLaurin wrote in frustration from Greenville. "I have been meeting with the ministers to try to get them to lead their members to the court house to register to vote."[21]

Getting ministers involved meant more than a space for a mass meeting. Just as important was the authority that ministers held. As Aldon Morris's account makes clear, ministers had the power to style participation as an obligation of one's membership in the church. Organizers pitching voter registration as God's will, for their part, were desperately handicapped if the local minister was saying otherwise. "If you're ever going to be effective, that's one thing you've got to do—get in the church, get with those people there, the ones in high standing—the deacons, the church officials," the Mississippi organizer John Buffington said in an interview several years later. But he went on to describe the authoritarian style of some clergy: "You're not allowed in the church to question anybody. [The minister might] say, 'Keep still, and I'll fight your battle.' Things like that. It's a hindrance, it's a help. It's . . . it's really confusing," he concluded.[22]

Whereas in cities, ministers' livelihoods came from their parishioners, in rural areas many were forced to work part-time for Whites. The small size of rural communities made clergy, heads of political and social organizations, and other members of the Black elite into easy targets of harassment. Prepared for this by veteran organizers, SNCC workers were nonetheless frustrated by the timidity of those they took to calling "leaders" with ironic quotation marks. Even when organizers found a sympathetic minister, it was no guarantee that they would gain the support of the church. Though Reverend Darby in Tate County, Mississippi, was "with us 100% . . . he has a timid board of elders," an organizer observed. Other clergymen professed personal solidarity with the struggle but explained that their insurance policies or clerical hierarchy prevented them from opening their doors to the movement. Thus an organizer reported on asking a local minister to use the church for a mass meeting: "He told me that unless all the AME churches in the district . . . opened their doors, he couldn't. 'When the Methodist church moves, it moves as a whole.'"[23]

INVENTING SOLIDARY TIES

The challenge was to convince recalcitrant ministers to get "in it": to risk the destruction of their churches, the loss of fearful congregants, and economic retaliation by Whites. Failing that, organizers sought to convince residents to ignore or defy the counsel of traditional leaders. Occasionally organizers were able to draw on direct and indirect contacts to nudge leaders into a proactive stance. The head of the Voter Education Project, Wiley Branton, arrived in Greenwood, Mississippi, following the shooting in February 1963 of a SNCC worker named Jimmy Travis. Branton's chronology of events provides a perfect illustration of how such ties of influence could operate. SNCC organizers had identified a young pastor who was sympathetic to the movement, but, without his trustees' support, he was reluctant to allow his church to be used for mass meetings. Aaron Henry, one of the core Mississippi leadership, suggested contacting the pastor's bishop in Nashville. Branton talked to Andy Young of the SCLC, who said that a key officer in SCLC was the bishop's administrative assistant, and Young offered to contact him. The bishop's administrative assistant had a conversation with the pastor, who went to his trustees to request again that he be allowed to open his church to the movement. The trustees voted against it, but within weeks the combined efforts of supporters inside and outside the community paid off. At a Greenwood mass meeting finally held in the church, SNCC workers reported, "There was also ministers from around Greenwood and other places. This is the largest n[umber] we have had to attend the mass meeting."[24]

Wiley Branton had contacts whom nineteen- and twenty-year-old SNCC workers simply did not, however, and the resources that SNCC workers brought to the communities they organized were more often claimed than enjoyed. But they took credit for whatever they could. When a Holly Springs resident pointed out to Frank Smith that the local roads had been improved without Blacks being registered to vote, Smith, thinking on his feet, said that the improvements had been made in response to movement demands. SNCC workers turned a lack of ties to their advantage. Ivanhoe Donaldson says now, "You would let people define you. I was who they wanted me to be. . . . However they saw me, I would try and build on that." Hollis Watkins remembers that several organizers had begun seminary training, and others, like Watkins himself, were skilled orators and well versed in scripture. Some ministers may have come around to supporting the movement, Watkins suspects, because they believed that the SNCC organizers were actually ministers whose popularity with the local people made them a threat to their jobs.[25]

In these cases, people imputed credentials to organizers that enabled them to compete with established leaders unwilling to take a stand. Organizers similarly sought to exploit their connections with Justice Department officials, even when those connections amounted to little more than a phone number and rarely brought about federal action. Thirty years later the Mississippi workers Charlie Cobb, Ivanhoe Donaldson, and Dion Diamond described to me in sonorous tones the speech they would make in a mass meeting:

> COBB: We said, "The government is concerned with your situation and we have here in *this* church here representatives from the Department of Justice," and you'd be pointing to—
> DIAMOND: —the one White man in the church—
> DONALDSON: John Doar. Or "I got a telegram from John Doar." Or Burke Marshall.
> COBB: I would say, "I have Burke Marshall's telephone number. Mr. Kennedy and Burke Marshall are really close and we tell Mr. Marshall what's happening to you and he's going to tell Mr. Kennedy."

Cobb continued:

> We did that kind of thing. No matter what we might have felt about the federal government. There was enough of a federal presence in these places to make what you said about the federal government believable. In Ruleville when those girls were shot, the Justice Department was there the next day. Now they didn't do anything, but the fact is that in a little

town like that, wherever you have a shooting that's directly related to civil rights activity, and then you have these White men from Washington, D.C., going around interviewing people, it does matter. I could say, well, they ain't doing anything. But for the local people, this was important. The fact that there were these people there from Washington, D.C., was probably more important than whether or not they hauled somebody off to jail for shooting these girls.[26]

SNCC workers had long been skeptical of the government's commitment to civil rights. Telephone calls to the Justice Department went unreturned, and suits that had been planned were dropped without explanation. SNCC workers were questioned by FBI agents about whether they had "staged" a bombing. Even as he recommended voter registration for its capacity to compel federal intervention, organizer Reggie Robinson in 1962 nevertheless worried that it was "a fantastic dream."[27]

But Cobb's point was that the appearance of the Justice Department after the shooting of two young girls was important not because it was likely to bring the perpetrators of racist violence to justice, but because it demonstrated to residents that they were not alone. Cobb expands: "The way that you get people to buy into oppression is to convince them that they're absolutely alone. . . . So part of organizing is showing people that that's not true." Organizers' task was to show people that they were not alone, that there were other people who were putting their lives on the line, other communities that were "moving." And that people saw the struggles and suffering of those who participated. Outside organizers' ability to claim connections to the government and to the movement gave them the capacity to serve as something like proxies for those actors. They were incapable of supplying protection or resources, but they were capable of supplying recognition for new identities.[28]

"STANDING UP"

"The most effective way to organize communities in this area is to widen the identification of 'community,'" the southwest Georgia organizer Charles Sherrod wrote to Wiley Branton in early 1963. People were convinced that things were worse in other areas, and this prevented them from rocking the boat in their own community. Showing residents that people in nearby communities were solidary in the struggle gave "people a sense of a larger movement." "All that happens in Albany is news and house gossip in the surrounding counties," Sherrod wrote. A few months later he described enthusiastically the participation of Albany residents in mass meetings in neighboring counties: "The importance of this 'outside' attendance can hardly be overstressed as a morale-builder. The sense that 'we are not alone' is important." The organizer Prathia Hall reported on a meeting "run in real SNCC fashion. We had representatives from each of the counties witness to the struggle in their county. The audience was almost transfixed in admiration and awe as Agnew James, Mama Dolly, Dec. [Deacon] Evans, and Dec. Brown gave testimony of their trials and their determination. This kind of witness increases intercounty unity and at the same time gives form and backbone to the emerging leadership in the counties." Another organizer in southwest Georgia reported on a conversation with a woman who "proclaimed that she had really better not have anything to do with us. . . . We said that people in Dawson were in this, and that people in Sasser were in this. She softened a bit and may come along." Reverend James told a Lee County mass meeting: "We got twenty from Dougherty. This means you better get twenty-five to match us."[29]

In their canvassing efforts, SNCC workers emphasized to residents the practical changes to be secured by voting: "We went from door to door telling people of their rights to vote and how with the vote they would get better schools, jobs, paved streets and all those things citizens should have." But along with those instrumental benefits, organizers and the people with whom they worked talked about the goal of "first-class citizenship." A woman planned to go to register, she said, "so she can be a first-class citizen of the United States." In Shaw, Mississippi, eighty people sang freedom songs and "discuss[ed] good Citizenship." In Prentiss, an organizer's "subject was the duties and obligations of citizens in today's world." In Greenwood, a resident committed himself to "helping the people to become better citizens." In Lee County, Georgia, a minister talked about "the Negro's responsibility to become a first-class citizen."[30]

Two things are interesting about the ways in which organizers and residents talked about citizenship. One is that first-class citizenship was treated as both an aspiration and a responsibility. It was something to be attained through struggle, but also something that demanded participation in struggle. The other was that gaining first-class citizenship did not depend on the actions of voting registrars or federal judges. The "Citizenship Honor Rolls" that recorded individuals' contributions to the movement conveyed the message that first-class citizenship depended on the recognition of the community and the movement. "Although we've suffered greatly, I feel that we have not suffered in vain. I am determined to become a first-class citizen," one resident wrote. Her suffering was vindicated by her determination—had already *been* vindicated—not by the eventual possibility that she would be able to vote without fear. Public displays of unity and determination were ends in themselves. The longtime activist Aaron Henry reported that in the wake of SNCC's work in Greenwood, "More and more Negroes . . . are eager to get [NAACP] membership cards so they will have visible evidence of the association between themselves and the organization. Apparently, in some cases, the membership card serves as a symbol of the courage of the Negro, and as a means of defying the White."[31]

Of course, Black residents had not substituted a goal of defiance for one of attaining basic civil and political rights. But many of the residents whom organizers canvassed believed that they were not entitled to vote because they were not literate or educated enough. Organizers sought to convince them that they were worthy of first-class citizenship. Mass meetings were crucial in constituting an action-compelling circle of recognition. Meetings usually began with a prayer and freedom songs: "Woke Up This Morning with My Mind Stayed on Freedom," "Which Side Are You On," "Get On Board Little Children," "This Little Light of Mine." The singing, Watkins recalls, "would help people to overcome some of the fear." "Guest speakers" were ministers from other towns and even states, national civil rights leaders, the entertainer Dick Gregory, and the baseball star Jackie Robinson. Speakers elicited curiosity but also pride. When Slater King from Albany came to a mass meeting in rural Sumter County, residents "were proud to have a 'city' man there." The Voter Education Project head Wiley Branton, urbane and sophisticated, so light-skinned he could pass for White, delighted Greenwood's Black audiences when he responded to the mayor's having described him as an "outside agitator." Although he had grown up in Arkansas, he told them, "my great grandfather was Greenwood Leflore for whom the city and county were named."[32]

Local people in a mass meeting might give testimony about their experiences trying to register, to applause and supportive amens. People "would talk about how they felt going in there, you know just going in there, filling out the form, and attempting to do it." An organizer in Greenwood thought that the meeting the night before had spurred participants to try to register the next day, not only because a minister who had run for Congress spoke at the meeting, but also because local people related "their experiences when they attempted to register." One might expect that speakers would relate the ease with which they had done so. But that was not the case. In Ruleville, Mississippi,

> the group heard Mr. Joe MacDonald urge them to stand together and fight for freedom and justice for all. Mrs. Fannie Lue Hamer [*sic*], the lady was put off a plantation because she went down to register, spoke to the group and asked them to try to get every person in Ruleville to try

to register, she also told of some of the things that had happened to her as a result of her attempt to register. Mrs. Bessie Lee Green, one of many persons who tried to get federal commodities told of the troubles she and her family is having because the county is making it hard to get the food, she also pledged herself and as many of her friends as possible to go down to register.[33]

Would not stories of suffering encountered as a result of trying to register deter those who were contemplating it? It seems instead that they made the speaker into a figure of sympathy and veneration as they united the audience in a posture of indignation.

Mass meetings, Charles Payne writes, "created a context in which individuals created a public face for themselves, which they then had to try to live up to." "That night we went out to the mass meeting in Lee County," a southwest Georgia organizer recounted. "J. C. Morer reported for Lee—and he's pretty smart. He made all the people who *hadn't* registered stand up." People were called to stand up in mass meetings, with the physical act signaling the political act: to declare themselves as part of the movement and willing to suffer the consequences. In an important sense, standing up was the goal, not merely the means to it. "I'm going to stand up alone if nobody stands beside me," said a Hattiesburg, Mississippi, resident. "I could be killed any day but I'm not going to live the life of a mouse in a hole." The southwest Georgia project head Charles Sherrod characterized the strategy: "Once in a meeting we were to make it unbelievably stimulating to the individual's need for recognition and to belong."[34]

REDEFINING SOLIDARY TIES

Mass meetings were also an opportunity to reinterpret existing ties, to transform the behavioral requirements of faith and parenthood. "Then [the SNCC organizer] John Hardy . . . gave us a talk on good citizens," a resident reported. "He said to be a good citizen you had to be a good Christian." A SNCC staffer in Lee County, Georgia, described a new pastor's "wonderful sermon on the importance of improving life on earth, of making a witness as a Christian, and of being willing to stand up and be counted"—this all "without ever mentioning the word voter registration." In Terrell County, Georgia, meeting leaders "asked the young people from Terrell to move to the front of the tent. They filled up the front half of the tent. . . . The young of Terrell are going to stay in front." In these speeches, organizers called on residents to follow the children. After Agnew James, hero of the Albany movement, spoke, Sherrod told those assembled, "'Behind this man stand thirteen people, children. He's been shot at, boycotted, harassed, and behind him have stood those thirteen. You people ought to be ashamed.'" At another meeting, Sherrod "brought eleven-year old Marion Gaines up front, stood her on a chair, and with his arm around her waist said, 'This is Albany.' It was Marion, standing on the chair so we could see her, who led the group in 'Ain't gonna let nobody turn me round.'"[35]

Invoking children was shaming: if children, in all their vulnerability, could join the struggle, then so could adults. In Leflore County, Mississippi, the SNCC organizer McArthur Cotton "introduced June Johnson, a young girl who told us how she was whipped in Winona, Mississippi because she and some others went into the White side of the Bus station. . . . She told us that she wasn't old enough to register but that she did her part by canvassing from door to door." To talk about children, however, was also to recast the obligations of parenthood. The Mississippi organizer Jean Smith describes her pitch to the residents she sought to involve: "I would say, what kind of world do you want for your children?" Invited to a Greenwood mass meeting, the SCLC's James Bevel called on the assembled not to "let the White Man do to your children as he has done to you." The organizer Faith Holsaert described Charles Sherrod: "How many [unintelligible] of unity and hope and drama is Charlie touching when he's using a child to read the [voting] registration card? He's showing that it's so simple a child can read it, natch. But what about parental pride, and competitive parental pride? We often dream more in our children's names than we dare dream in our own." To dream for one's children rather than for oneself was sadly realistic in a region that had borne the yoke of White supremacy for so many generations. But organizers were also revising the behavioral expectations of parental ties. A responsibility to one's children required that one act, even if it meant jeopardizing the livelihood on which one's children depended.[36]

Organizers also sought to foster ties to themselves, to create a sense of obligation to these "children" who were putting their bodies on the line. "Being a Freedom Rider," the Mississippi SNCC organizer Dion Diamond explained to me, "meant that you were willing to sacrifice yourself in their town." SNCC workers would later become uncomfortable with promoting the fact that they didn't need to fight the battles they were fighting in the Deep South, especially when it seemed to overvalue the participation of White workers, but its mobilizing power was undeniable. "We are slowly building loyalties to 'the kids who are working so hard'—this, of course, is SNCC," the organizer Dona Richards wrote from Jackson.[37]

Native Black Mississippians, then and now, refer to the impact of young SNCC workers' willingness to stand up to White sheriffs, police, and mobs. Amzie Moore remembered SNCC voter registration workers as they escorted Black residents to the courthouse, "tiny figures standing against a huge column," facing White "trigger-men and drivers and lookout men riding in automobiles with automatic guns." Yet, "how they stood," Moore remembered, "how gladly they got in front of that line, those leaders, and went to jail! It din't seem to bother 'em. It was an awakening to me." SNCC workers were "the little fellows with the tight blue jeans who stood in the courthouses and marched in the streets and were arrested. When they arrest a line today, another line would form tomorrow." Another resident said later, "Bob Moses was a little bitty fella. And he stood up to this sheriff and Bob said, 'I'm from SNCC.' I had never seen that happen before. From that day on, I said, 'Well I can stand for myself.'"[38]

SNCC workers' defiance—their willingness to talk back to sheriffs, to bring suit against their White assailants, to refuse to pay the deference that was the price of survival—encouraged people to participate by penetrating the supposed invincibility of White southerners, who could be made to look silly and fearful. But note in the above quotes the way residents described SNCC workers: "Bob Moses was a little bitty fella"; the SNCC workers were "tiny figures," "little fellows." The organizer Mike Miller recalls "a certain reverence for 'our children who are doing so much.'" Residents saw the SNCC organizers as brave but youthful, in need of their support and solidarity. The Greenwood resident Robert Burns later explained his decision to offer Sam Block a place to stay: "Well I thought he was a child, a young man that was trying to do a good part . . . he needed some help, he needed all our support."[39]

The Greenwood organizer Wazir Peacock remembers that after Block was arrested for the seventh time, many of the people who came to the trial had been uninvolved in the movement to that point. They were "people from these plantations, from all over, they were there, just like that. Say 'That little boy, he ain't done nothing to nobody.' This really shocked the city officials. They looked and saw all these people packed in the hallway. They were drinking out of the [White] water fountain. They really had their chests stuck out. They came to get Sam out of jail." A field report by Peacock at the time related, "The Negroes from all around the county which included farmers, clergy, and etc. crowded the corridors of the city hall to witness Samuel Block's trial. This way within itself gave us the feeling that the movement was on the way." When Block was released on bail, Payne writes, "people took it to be a personal victory. That night's mass meeting was the largest ever, and the numbers of people trying to register jumped sharply." When the Greenwood organizer Jimmy Travis was shot shortly afterward, "Many people in Albany responded as if Jimmy [Travis] were their own, and promised to leave Albany for Mississippi with us, if we called them," a southwest Georgia SNCC organizer reported. Residents' attitudes toward SNCC organizers combined a kind of parental protectiveness with respect for their bravery.[40]

Again, if one felt a sense of parental protectiveness toward the young people in one's community, it would likely mean doing everything in one's power to prevent them from endangering themselves by defying White authorities, not joining them in their defiance. But SNCC organizers' status as outsiders meant that adults could do little to dissuade them from taking action. They could help, rather, by housing and feeding the young organizers, protecting them, and in some instances agreeing to participate in the collective action they were proposing.

REIMAGINING LEADERSHIP

Finally, SNCC workers sought to persuade people to participate by reimagining the bonds of leadership. This represented an evolution in their own thinking. As I noted earlier, when they began organizing in 1962, their guidelines instructed them to identify "people who are looked up to and who are already recognized as leaders . . . [who] can bring many of their people along with them." This, the SNCC founder Ella Baker explained in a SNCC meeting in early 1963, was what made SNCC distinctive: its focus on "the development of 'leadership' rather than 'a leader.'"[41]

Sometimes ministers, teachers, or business owners were receptive, and sometimes they could be pushed into taking a leadership role. Charlie Cobb wrote of his talk with a Leland, Mississippi, man to plan a meeting of "prominent and interested people within the Negro community." "I frankly don't have too much faith in [the man], and am skeptic[al] about the other prominent people," Cobb confessed, "but I have to begin somewhere. [He] may surprise me." The Holly Springs organizer Frank Smith reported happily in 1963, "The image of students knocking on doors, the fact of their speaking at churches on Sundays, and the threat of demonstration have served to build respect for them and has challenged the local ministers no end. They see this and are beginning to work to try to build their images and redeem themselves." Smith distributed leaflets with the name of a minister prominently displayed on them "in an effort to 'make' a leader out of him, whether he wants to be or not. I believe that if we continue our campaign and the materials keep coming out with his name on them, he would wind up in an inescapable position of leadership." Sometimes, too, prominent people such as ministers and teachers supported the young organizers anonymously, in some cases so anonymously that organizers like Wazir Peacock did not realize until years later that individuals they had dismissed as "Uncle Toms" had in fact provided the food or bond money they depended on.[42]

SNCC workers relied more on people with long histories of defiance. These were families who were known for standing up to Whites, military veterans who had returned to the South having had experiences of something closer to equality, and women who were known for ignoring the counsel of traditional leaders. Organizers looked for people who were "strong," they said, which increasingly came to mean not only willing to stand up to White violence, but capable of persuading friends, neighbors, and co-workers to join the movement. Organizers began to call these people "leaders," even though their leadership was recognized neither by Whites nor by Black residents of means. The recognition was by the movement. Leadership was thus a relationship that was both imagined and real—real in the sense that leaders were simply people of whatever background who could bring others into the movement, imagined in the sense that that status remained unrecognized by people outside the movement.[43]

Fannie Lou Hamer, for example, was a poorly educated plantation worker when SNCC workers met her, but "she knew all the people on the place and they all respect her and we feel that she will play a big part in getting people from the plantation to register." Hamer would become a stalwart of the Mississippi movement and co-chair of the Mississippi Freedom Democratic Party (MFDP). "I think the kind of people we were bringing to register to vote was embarrassing to their Negro Voters' League, which we were supposed to be working with," Charlie Cobb wrote in 1963. In a discussion of the MFDP's planned challenge to the seating of an all-White Mississippi delegation at the Democratic National Convention in 1964, Bob Moses told his co-workers, "Note that Jackson Negroes are embarrassed that Mrs. Hamer is representing them—she is too much a representative of the masses."[44]

To be sure, in the reality of southern politics, championing people outside traditional leadership could go too far. If the fact that Mrs. Hamer "embarrassed" traditional leaders became the movement's purpose, then organizers would sacrifice the possibility of working with people who sometimes could be pushed to adopt an activist role. This was the razor's edge of effective organizing: both working with existing leaders and helping to develop new ones.

OUTSIDERS

The same razor's edge operated when it came to organizers' status as outsiders. SNCC's Mississippi organizers, early on at least, were almost all

Black. Bringing White organizers into Black communities drew too much attention and put too many people at risk to be effective. Even Black organizers from the state, though, found that their outsider status brought liabilities as well as resources. The belief in their extensive contacts put them at a loss when people legitimately demanded protection and financial assistance. "People asking questions. . . . What kind of aid can we give them to help clothe and feed them?" Sunflower County organizers reported in late 1962. Ruleville organizers wrote, "Some of the people have asked us for personal loans and other help because they think if we had not came with the voter registration program things would not be so bad." If organizers' outsider status led people to assume they had access to high places, it also generated questions about their motivations for being there. Greenville organizers discovered that the high school principal was telling students that they "were paid agitators, getting more money than any Negro in Greenville." Southern White authorities had long used the label of "outside agitators" as a way to discredit entirely homegrown protest. In these cases, the label was even more likely to stick. Organizers had to work hard to prove that they were not in it for the glory of rebellion, that they would not try to push people faster than they wanted to go, and that they were willing to stick it out when things got rough.[45]

Sometimes distrust yielded to admiration in a way that was equally discomfiting. When local residents told organizers that they "were Moses, come to lead them from starvation and bondage," organizers were both flattered and worried. SNCC workers' discussions returned frequently to the question of their own leadership. They didn't plan to stay for as long as it took Black southerners to win their freedom. Nor, on the other hand, did they have much admiration for the SCLC's strategy of sweeping into a town with great fanfare and winning what proved often to be only token concessions on the part of White officials before sweeping out. SNCC workers were determined to build group-centered leadership. That meant struggling against the authority that their own charisma sometimes garnered them.[46]

Southwest Georgia's project staff was racially integrated from the beginning. Organizers there worried openly about the concentration of White workers on the project, and their probing field reports (some penned by White workers) make clear the liabilities of an integrated staff. People were now asking, "'What are *you-all* going to do?' 'when are y'all going to march?'" the White southwest Georgia organizer Ralph Allen complained. "Even Slater King [one of the adult leaders of the Albany movement] often seems to be acting out of a sense of gratitude to the people who have 'given up their summers and all.'"[47]

Concerns like these grew, especially after SNCC decided to bring upward of eight hundred northern, mainly White volunteers to Mississippi in the summer of 1964. Black SNCC workers' feelings toward the White volunteers were varied and complicated. When over a hundred of the volunteers decided to stay after the summer project and were added to the staff in a move that many existing staffers perceived as hasty, those feelings became more complicated still. Some Black organizers worried about losing control of an organization that, for all its proud interracialism, nevertheless had always been a Black one. At the same time, the organization as a whole was uncertain about next steps. The failure of the government to intercede in voting-rights abuses and the failure of the Mississippi Freedom Democratic Party to unseat the regular Mississippi delegates at the Democratic National Convention left SNCC workers skeptical of the merits of voter registration and, indeed, of appealing to liberals for support. Should they continue voter registration efforts? Turn to economic organizing? Become a mass membership organization? The answer to these problems was to "let the people decide." Somehow, workers hoped, deferring to local communities would yield a radical agenda. White SNCC workers, meanwhile, reacted to the animosity they were encountering by insisting on their commitment to local Black control and attacking longtime organizers for "manipulating" the local people.[48]

The term *outsider* became one of opprobrium, a political football in organizational conflicts that were about race and about the group's purpose as much as about organizing strategy. Of course, SNCC organizers in the past had come into local communities with a program of voter registration that they had decided on in consultation with veteran Mississippi activists, not local communities. The new antipathy to outsiders' influence also ignored the fact that SNCC's best organizers had always forged complex relationships with Black community members. They were seen both as firebrands on account of their willingness to challenge authorities and, at the same time, as something like children in their need for protection and support. Those complex relationships were sacrificed as SNCC workers increasingly renounced any role that could be perceived as directive. In the process, the creative interaction between outside organizers and indigenous activists that SNCC workers had pioneered began to erode.[49]

IMAGINED COMMUNITIES

When do people stand up to injustice? When do they take the step of joining a movement, even when they know that they can free-ride on the efforts of others? Scholars have argued for the importance both of preexisting ties and a sense of collective identity. Accordingly, we should expect to see movements emerging from communities with dense ties and a mobilizing identity—a shared sense that who one is requires that one participate. But dense ties and a mobilizing identity are often at odds with each other. Participating in disruptive action requires seeing oneself as different than one was. And that is difficult to do, perhaps *most* difficult to do, in our closest relationships. Our families and friends want us to be the person we were. This is surely the case when they know that participating will jeopardize our safety, and, for the families and friends of Black people in the Deep South, their safety as well. But even in less dangerous situations, committing oneself to a movement when familiar others have not done so requires distancing oneself from them.

Social movement scholars might respond that people participate when their prior collective identity becomes coterminous with a movement identity. Sometimes, being a "Christian" or a "mother" or a "college student" comes to be seen as including protest participation among its obligations. Such a dynamic seems to be operating when movement participants say, "As a Christian, I had to protest abortion," or, "As a mother, I could not *not* fight for a nuclear-free world." But the Christian activist probably knew many Christians who were not protesting abortion and the mother probably many mothers who were not fighting for a nuclear-free world. So why would they not define their identity as Christian or mother in terms of the Christians and mothers they actually knew?[50]

To answer that question, consider the existence of two kinds of collective identity. We think about who we are as members of a group by reference to people we know, but also by reference to people we only imagine. Social psychologists distinguish, in this regard, between interpersonal identity and collective identity. My interpersonal identity as a mother develops in relation to the other mothers I know: my sisters, most of my friends, many of my colleagues. My collective identity as a mother comes from an imagined prototype of a mother, a prototype gleaned from television, movies, advertisements, politicians' speeches, friends' casual references, and all the other materials that communicate ideas about motherhood.[51]

We probably think in both ways, but social psychologists have suggested that we may shift from one to the other. For example, a study of nurses found that while new and lower-status nurses thought about who they were in terms of their interpersonal relationships with patients, more experienced and higher-status nurses thought about who they were in terms of their professional identity as a group distinct from physicians. To be sure, both interpersonal and collective identities are symbolic constructions. As the relational sociologists I cited in chapter 1 would point out, both are arrived at through language as a means of conceptualizing the self in relation to others. But the latter is more abstract, depending on imagined relationships rather than real ones.[52]

Especially when people you know are actively counseling you not to participate in disruptive protest, but probably more generally when people you know simply are not participating themselves, deciding to participate may require that you shift to this more abstract sense of collective identity: to who you are as an imagined mother or Christian. If the action required is onerous or dangerous, going to bat for your community may require that you imagine your community as more unified and likely to benefit from your activism than your actual neighbors and community leaders are indicating they are. Again, however, one's adoption of this imagined self is difficult unless it is recognized. This, I have suggested, is where outside organizers are particularly important. The fact that they are not part of existing networks makes it easier to see them as connected to actors outside the community. And outsiders who are seen as tied to national movements or to other groups can access a larger circle of recognition. That recognition can help people to begin to see themselves as activists.

As Aldon Morris and others have made clear, the southern civil rights movement was an indigenous one. I have sought to build on an indigenous perspective, however, by examining in more detail the role of organizers, many of whom were from outside the communities in which they worked. Outsiders in rural communities in Mississippi and southwest Georgia in the early 1960s were sometimes successful in recruiting people by persuading them that being a citizen depended not on the recognition of southern officials but on that of the movement; that being a Christian depended on a community of believers extending beyond the local minister counseling moderation; that being a parent depended on protecting the "children" who had left their own communities to lay their bodies on the line; and that being a leader required neither money nor status but simply the ability to mobilize others.

It is the combination of relationships forged by organizers that I find important: relationships real and imagined, relationships both in the here-and-now and ones aspired to. People who tried to register to vote because they wanted to be first-class citizens knew that the act on its own would not give them the rights that they had long been denied. But in being recognized as first-class citizens by the movement, they enjoyed that as-if relationship of citizen to nation. In a very different context, the philosopher Marshall Berman quotes a railway electrician from Leningrad who participated in a demonstration against the Soviet regime in 1968. "For ten minutes," he said, "I was a citizen, during the demonstration." The electrician was not naive. But that as-if experience of citizenship might lead him to participate again. Organizers in the South appealed to residents' aspirations but also to their obligations, specifically, to these young men and women who could be their children. Residents had no parental authority over SNCC organizers. They could not keep them out of harm's way. But they could help by housing and feeding organizers and guarding them while they slept. And they could help by making the trip to the registrar to try to register to vote.[53]

Community organizers today talk about their work as being relational. By that they mean that, in contrast to mobilizing efforts, organizing is aimed at building relationships that endure, and in which participants take on increasing leadership responsibilities. But I believe that effective organizers are relational in a more creative way. They craft diverse relationships between themselves and the people they organize. They build on some relationships and imagine others. They call people "leaders" when their leadership is potential; they appeal to people's "self-interest" but define it as including broad normative beliefs; they recruit people as members of "faith communities" in a way that downplays racial, class, and religious divides. They build leadership and community by treating relationships of leadership and community as if they were already there, but at the same time they make clear how they will get from here to there.[54]

Recently I heard a recording on the radio of an organizer talking to a woman about abortion rights. The organizer had knocked on the woman's door; the woman, who was older, born in Mexico, and Catholic, said with conviction that she was opposed to abortion under any circumstances. By the end of their conversation, she had changed her mind: women should have free access to abortion. The radio commentator attributed that striking shift to the fact that the organizer had told the story of her own abortion. But I heard the conversation differently. The organizer began by asking the woman if she had talked to anyone about abortion, and the woman said she had talked with her daughters. She had wanted to be open with them in a way that her parents had not been with her, she explained. The organizer commiserated. Her own Filipina mother had not prepared her for getting her period when she was twelve, and she had been frightened. The woman had had a similar experience, she said, and she emphasized how different she was with her own daughters. "It sounds like you are very supportive of their choices, even if you may not agree with them," the organizer commented. They continued to swap stories. Fifteen minutes into their conversation, the organizer said she had had an abortion the previous year. She did not regret it, she said, but she had been afraid to tell her mother. She worried her mother would love her less. "No, no," the woman protested. "Would you ever love your daughters less?" the organizer asked. "No. Never." It was as if the organizer had *become* the woman's daughters in that moment, and the woman wanted to be supportive of the organizer's abortion in a way that her parents would not have been had she had an abortion. It was shortly after that exchange that the organizer asked the woman again whether access to abortion should be limited. This time, she said emphatically not.[55]

Of course, the woman knew that the organizer was not her daughter. But she was able to think about the issue as if the organizer were her daughter, and, it seemed, about how she would want her relationship with her daughter to be different from the relationship she had with her own mother. I am not sure that calling organizing "relational" fully captures good organizers' skill in building relationships with potential recruits that bundle multiple relationships, real and imagined ones, linked in that "as if" fashion.

Perhaps most important, even the most local, pragmatic, and interest-driven activism may require that participants see themselves as part of imagined communities. Their ties to people already involved in activism are undoubtedly crucial: people who convince them that participating is necessary, possibly fun, and urgent. While those ties may be enough to bring people to a meeting or sign a petition, their continuing participation likely requires that they see themselves as members of groups that are abstract: that often extend beyond the local and are more unified than any real group ever is.

CHAPTER THREE

Whom One Owes

with Zaibu Tufail

Solidarity is only gesturing when it involves no sacrifice.

MARY DOUGLAS, *How Institutions Think* (1986)

Observers have long worried that the market undermines social solidarity. Karl Marx spoke famously of capitalism eroding all connections among men other than that of "cash payment," and many other theorists have described money turning intimates into arm's-length transactors, people into commodities, and an ethic of responsibility into one of naked self-interest. These developments should be especially apparent when it comes to economic debt. Today people owe money to their credit card company, not to the merchant from whom they purchased things, or to a faceless, nameless health insurance company rather than to the doctors and nurses who treated them. In this world, one would expect people to treat their debt in a purely calculative way. One would expect people to evaluate the costs and benefits of paying back a debt, and paying back a debt on time, and to prioritize paying back those debts that came with greater penalties for non-payment.[1]

If that were true, Jason's job as an agent in a debt-settlement firm would be easy. For a fee, the firm will try to work with clients' creditors to lower the principal of their debts. Jason himself doesn't negotiate with creditors; someone else in the company does that. His job is to sign clients up and help them decide which debts to try to renegotiate. Jason spends a good deal of time cold-calling potential clients, who usually reject his pitch out of hand. Once he has secured a debtor who is willing to contract with the company and has enough in the way of financial resources to pay up if the renegotiation is successful, Jason simply has to convince the debtor to choose the debts for the firm to work on that it actually has a chance of successfully renegotiating. He should be able to instruct the client which creditors

are likely to negotiate—hospitals, say, as compared to the government—
and which ones are instead likely to levy penalties for stopping payment.
The latter is important, since in order to give the firm's negotiator leverage,
Jason will advise the client to stop payment on the debts she wants the firm
to renegotiate. Jason should be able to tell the client what is in her self-
interest to do, and the client should do it.[2]

That does not work, however. Jason explains, "I wouldn't really say
things like, 'This is good for you [financially] so forget about who you owe
money to.' That, in my experience, doesn't really go over too well." In order
to convince clients to renegotiate debts, Jason has to appeal to a logic different than one of self-interest. He has to accommodate clients' feelings about
the creditors to whom they owe money. But that does not simply mean that
debtors are uncomfortable trying to renegotiate their debt to a person they
know rather than to a big, impersonal bureaucracy. Sometimes, in fact, it is
the opposite, with debtors talking about the big, impersonal bureaucracy as
if it is a person. Debtors make decisions about what is morally right based
on relationships they imagine but do not actually have. Why? As I will show,
imagining creditors as people with whom they have a reciprocal relationship—that is, as people whom they can reward or punish by paying them
or not—gives debtors a sense of moral autonomy in a demoralizing and
disempowering situation. Debtors thus use relationship scripts practically
and creatively, but they are not purely self-serving. The relationships they
invent truly serve as moral compasses. Yet, the result is that debtors end up
refusing to try to renegotiate debts that they could actually renegotiate with
minimal penalties. In other words, their creativity comes at a cost.

Selena works at the same debt-settlement company as Jason. She used
to be an agent. However, she could not bear the sense that she was taking
advantage of people who were down on their luck. When the manager of
the firm offered her the job of negotiator, she took it. The job does not pay
as well, and it is stressful: she spends most of her day yelling at and being
yelled at by creditors. But, she says, at least she can sleep at night. Jason
does not have any trouble sleeping at night, though, nor did any of the male
agents we interviewed. Women agents did—so much so that many quit.
Why? Jason gives a clue when he explains his job: "The great thing about
just being an agent is that you are educating people—they really hear what
you are trying to get across, you know? You get them to be more aware of
their options, and you let them know how things work in general."

Agents are salespeople, not financial advisors or educators. They are
trained only in how to sell debt-settlement services. Just as their clients
use relationship schemas creatively to maintain a sense of themselves as
moral people, agents' claim to relationships they do not have allows them

to avoid the morally unappealing aspects of their job. It allows them to believe they are simply instructing clients on how the system works, laying out the options rather than persuading people to buy a service they do not need.

But what about women agents? They are unable to use an educator-student relationship script with their clients. Instead, women are pushed into a quasi-therapeutic relationship with their clients. They are expected to provide emotional support and guidance, to listen empathetically to clients who are struggling to get by, and to express confidence that their financial problems will be solved. Doing those things, though, confronts women agents sharply with the fact that they are personally capitalizing on people's financial troubles. The fact that women cannot claim a relationship of financial educator to their clients makes the job of agent emotionally difficult.

In this chapter I explore the mix of creativity and constraint with which people use relationships as guides to moral behavior. The solidarity involved here is that manifest in the laws, norms, and codes of society. It is solidarity in a Durkheimian sense.[3] Just as Durkheim saw self-interest as straining against the force of social norms within each individual, the people I describe in this chapter are torn between what is in their self-interest and what is morally right. Of course, compared to the Black southerners standing up to White oppression at the risk of their own lives who featured in the last chapter, the people who feature in this one are engaged in something less than moral behavior. My subjects are debtors who are trying to figure out how to pay less than they owe, and the agents who are trying to sell them a service that may end up costing them more than they owe. Neither agents nor debtors would seem to be paragons of moral virtue. And yet, within the limits of their situation—the fact that clients simply do not have enough money to pay back their debts in full and the fact that agents need to hold on to their jobs—they do struggle to do the right thing. They use relationship schemas to enact the kinds of relationships they *want* to have, ones characterized by mutual self-respect, autonomy, and especially fairness. But they face real obstacles in doing so. As much as debtors would like to think of their relationships with their creditors as reciprocal, that is not the way creditors see it, and the latter have the power of the law on their side. As much as women agents would like to see themselves in a financially educative relationship with clients rather than a much more emotionally onerous therapeutic one, clients and employers make that impossible. Again, some people simply have more power than others to choose the relationship schema governing an interaction.

To make these arguments, I draw on interviews with the owners and employees of debt-settlement firms conducted by Zaibu Tufail, along with observations of debt-settlement work in two agencies in the Los Angeles area.

Before I describe what we found, let me briefly rehearse the ways in which previous scholars have tackled the question of how people think about fairness. I want to make the case, contrary to previous scholarship, that people decide what is fair based on the relationships they have and the relationships they want to have. Later in the chapter I will briefly take up a second literature that has to do with how people are able to do jobs that are morally tainted. There again I make the case that they do so based on the relationships they claim to have rather than those they actually do have. And again, some people have more power than others to make their claims stick. This, I argue, has implications for how we think about solidarity normatively as well as empirically.[4]

FAIRNESS IN RELATIONSHIP

How do people decide what is fair? Scholars have distinguished between people's ideas about fair *procedures* for making decisions; about the fair *allocation* of resources or costs, say, how health care should be distributed or who should bear the cost for it; and about fair *exchanges*, that is, exchanges of resources between parties, whether the resources are money, love, labor, or anything else that is valued. Focusing on fair exchanges, scholars have identified three principles. Fairness may be defined as *equity*, that is, as an equal ratio of contribution to reward. A fair exchange, in this view, is one where each party gets out of it what they put into it. Alternatively, a fair exchange may be an *equal* one, in which parties all get the same amount, regardless of how much they put in. Or an exchange may be fair if parties get as much as they *need* from the exchange. One person might contribute more and receive less, but the exchange would still be seen as fair, in this view, if she needed less.[5]

When do people rely on a principle of equity, equality, or need? Features of the exchange seem to matter. For example, if the exchange is hurried and limited to a single instance, and the value of what is exchanged is low, it is likely that parties to the exchange will rely on a principle of equality rather than one of equity, simply because the former takes less time. But assessing what is fair also depends on the relationships among the parties. Friends, for example, are less likely to use a principle of equity than one of equality or need, while business transactors are most likely to use a principle of equity.[6]

The anthropologist Alan Fiske goes further in matching the norms of fairness to different kinds of relationships. I mentioned his typology in chapter 1. In a *communal-sharing* relationship, of which family is the prototype but which also extends to communes and, in attenuated form, ethnic and national groups, fairness is based on the principle of need. Indeed, in a communal-sharing relationship, *exchange* is a misnomer, since resources belong to the collective rather than to an individual person. But even where resources do belong to individuals, there is no expectation of tit-for-tat exchange. I do not expect that my children will pay me back the money I have spent on raising them. In an *equality-matching* relationship, by contrast, fairness is based on reciprocity between equals. Think of colleagues or acquaintances. The expectation of exchanges in these relationships is that the same kind of thing should be returned, although what counts as the same kind of thing depends on partners' expectations. If I have you over to dinner, it is only fair to expect you to reciprocate, although the invitation may be instead for a lunch, and there will certainly not be the same things on the menu.[7]

In a *market-pricing* relationship, the same value of the resource, though usually not the same kind of resource, should be exchanged for the relationship to be seen as fair. Money is often transferred as part of exchange relationships, but not always. The relationship is voluntarily entered into and on the best terms that each party can self-interestedly secure. So, where a communal-sharing relationship operates on a principle of need and an equality-matching relationship operates on a principle of equality, a market-pricing relationship operates on a principle of equity insofar as there is a negotiated exchange ratio, often based on a market. Finally, Fiske describes an *authority-ranking* relationship, of which the military is the archetype. In such relationships it is considered fair for the person with the higher rank to lay claim to what she deems appropriate, as well as to accept gifts of fealty or tribute from her inferiors. There is a general expectation that the superior will protect her inferiors from harm, but the expectation does not structure each exchange.

According to Fiske, the relationships people have with each other determine the appropriate principle of fairness. He and others have demonstrated the point by examining what happens when subjects are exposed to "taboo trade-offs." These are exchanges that are inconsistent with the relationship within which they take place. For example, imagine a mother asking her son to pay her for Thanksgiving dinner, a subordinate criticizing his employer for not staying late at the office, a physician refusing to help an accident victim who cannot afford her fee, or a parent member of a baby-sitting co-op ordering another parent to take her shift. Researchers found that subjects react to such taboo trade-offs with indignation, distress, and erratic valuations of objects in the trade-off.[8]

Fiske makes one more point that is relevant to debt settlement. There may be cases where one relational scheme evolves into another. For example, when an item or service exchanged in an equality-matching relationship is so valuable as to make it impossible for the recipient to reciprocate, the relationship may become an authority-ranking one, where one party now owes the other respect, loyalty, deference, and possibly submission.[9]

One can think about the relationship between debtor and creditor as a market-pricing one in Fiske's terms. The debtor purchases a good or service from the creditor on the best terms she can. She agrees to pay for it and to pay interest for delaying her payment. At some point, however, she decides that she is unable to pay back all her debts on the terms to which she agreed. The debt-settlement agent now enters the mix. This is seemingly another market-pricing relationship. The agent advises the debtor to allow him to renegotiate the debts that the firm has the best chance of successfully settling. This makes sense for the firm and it should make sense for the client as well.

The problem, however, is that debt-settlement clients are unwilling to see their relationships with creditors as market-pricing ones. Why? Probably because clients want to see themselves as moral people. Research has shown that the experience of indebtedness is deeply dispiriting. Debtors desperately want to maintain an identity as responsible and self-sufficient. They are reluctant to ask for financial assistance when they are in need and are dismissive of people who are too quick to turn to others. They often juggle their debts—paying one bill one month and another the next—so as to avoid asking others for help. But research also suggests that people evaluate debts based on how "fair" they are and prioritize making payments on debts that they perceive as fair. Debtors personalize debts: they talk about being "duped" or taken in by particular creditors. By the same token, I argue, debt-settlement clients treat repayment in full—refusing to try to negotiate down a debt—as a reward for good service. They treat their relationship with their creditors as an equality-matching one because they want to see themselves as equals. They want their money to serve as an acknowledgment of good service rather than as something they are compelled to yield.[10]

Here we can draw on the sociologist Viviana Zelizer, who argues that people use money to create the relationships they *want* to have. They use money variously to establish, strengthen, differentiate, and transform relationships. For example, a man would likely not open a joint checking account with a casual girlfriend. But doing so with a fiancée would serve to communicate his commitment to her. There may be occasions, and not just a few, in which people do what Zelizer calls relational work by applying the "wrong" or taboo relationship model, in Fiske's terms. For example, Zelizer describes a woman who lost her job and was forced to borrow money from her great-aunt. Despite the fact that she would eventually inherit from the great-aunt, she insisted on drawing up a legal contract. "To preserve her dignity and independence," Zelizer notes, "it mattered greatly to her . . . to mark the relationship as lender-borrower, not benefactor–welfare recipient." One might say that she insisted on maintaining a market-pricing relationship so as to preserve a sense of herself as an autonomous adult rather than a needy child. The great-aunt, in turn, acceded to what Fiske might call a taboo trade-off because she had a stake in helping her niece to feel better about herself.[11]

Like the great-aunt, debt-settlement agents are willing to accept clients' view of their relationship with creditors as one it is not; here, an equality-matching one. As I will show, they can work with that view in order to secure clients' authorization to renegotiate some debts. Creditors, by contrast, do not have a stake in seeing themselves as being in an equal relationship with debtors. And they have the law and the power of financial institutions on their side. Clients' refusal to instrumentalize debt may shore up their sense of moral autonomy, but it comes at the cost of control of their financial futures.

DEBT SETTLEMENT

Debt-settlement firms emerged in the 1980s. Banks had established debt-settlement divisions to facilitate settlements with credit-card holders who defaulted on payments, and these evolved into a profitable industry of free-standing firms. In 2010 there were more than two thousand debt-settlement companies, which handled monies owed on mortgages and repossessed boats and vehicles, credit-card debt, IRS debt, and various forms of medical debt. The 465 companies in the industry's two leading trade associations had more than 425,000 customers and had enrolled $11.7 billion in credit-card debt. The industry was widely perceived to be exploitative, since relatively few clients won successful settlements, and many were subjected to financial penalties after defaulting on their debts. In 2010 federal legislation banned agencies' requirement that clients set up a separate bank account so the agency could withdraw a monthly payment (even before reaching a settlement agreement with the creditor or collection agency). After that, agencies were allowed to extract a fee only after a settlement agreement was reached with the creditor and at least one payment had been made by the client to the creditor. The industry shrank considerably as a result, with one of the industry's trade associations folding and the other representing only thirty-three companies in 2013.[12]

We know very little about the people who contract with debt-settlement agencies. In 2010, debt-settlement customers carried an average of $30,000 in credit-card debt, compared to the $15,000 carried by American house-holds generally. Debt-settlement clients typically cannot afford the pay-ments that they are asked to make. This suggests that debt settlement may be a last resort for many clients. But debt-settlement customers are not so financially distressed that agents think them unlikely to make good on their contract with the firm.[13]

As I noted, debt-settlement agents spend a lot of their time calling poten-tial clients. Sometimes people contact the firm directly, either by phone or Internet. Firms also purchase lists of phone numbers from credit agencies, and agents make cold calls. That agents' pitches often fall on deaf ears is unsurprising, given debt settlement's murky reputation. Once an agent or telemarketer has persuaded a client to contract for the agency's services, one agent works directly with the client. Agents usually have a caseload of between twenty and thirty clients. The agent reviews the client's outstand-ing debts and works with him to decide which ones to try to settle. The agent asks the client if he has any hardships, such as a disability or being unemployed, and has the client write a letter to the creditor attesting to the hardship. If the client has not already fallen behind in payments to the creditor, the agent may urge him to stop payments in order to provide the debt-settlement firm leverage in its negotiations with the creditor. At that point the file is passed to one of the firm's negotiators, who works directly with the creditor to try to obtain a settlement on the client's behalf.

In what follows I draw on agents' observations about how clients ap-proached their debts. Since we were not able to interview clients directly, I rely on this secondhand information. However, the fact that agents had a stake in persuading clients to choose to renegotiate the debts that they had the best chance of renegotiating successfully, and the fact that they described encountering similar obstacles in that task, make their observa-tions credible.

RANKING DEBTS

Agents explained that there were debts that clients were eager to try to re-negotiate, debts that they could be persuaded to renegotiate, and debts they were downright opposed to renegotiating. The last category of debts, clients insisted, had to be paid back in full. When asked which debts fell into each category, agents pieced together a fairly clear ranking of debts by clients' desire to renegotiate them. As Selena explained, "Here's the breakdown: credit cards—for sure, number one. Then mortgages and car repos. Um, hospital bills are last. What else? Oh—back taxes probably before medical bills." Other agents gave a similar ranking. Clients sometimes asked about the possibility of renegotiating student loans, although firms were only able to offer settlement services for student loans secured from private lenders rather than the government. Debt-settlement firms were also prohibited from renegotiating child support payments. But this was another debt that clients asked about, and that was perceived as more appropriately negotiated than IRS debts, student loans, or medical debts. Agents were initially surprised by this. Bradley, a former agency owner, confessed, "It was pretty shocking when I first started that there were a lot of people that tried to get their child support negotiated. We encountered that a lot." Jason, the agent I quoted at the beginning of the chapter, marveled, "It's amazing. They are more likely to try and get you to settle on child support than a dentist!"

At the bottom of the scale of debts that clients were willing to try to settle was medical debt. Logan observed, "It's just weird to me that some people call up trying to settle with the government but not a hospital. It's like 'they are the government—you would rather try to settle back taxes with the *government*? Is that really the smartest thing to do?' Not just that, but hospital bills and things like that are *insanely* expensive. One trip to the ER will cost a grand. I am pretty sure they owe more to those than on taxes." Alejandro noted, "It's known among agents that people are hesitant about medical debt the most, especially when the doctors or nurses really took good care of them." The other agents similarly attested to clients' reluctance to try to renegotiate medical debts. But they also pointed to variation within that broad category. Clients were generally more willing to renegotiate a debt for a brief hospital stay than a debt to their primary care practitioner. But they were *less* willing to renegotiate a debt for an extended hospital stay or surgery than a debt to their primary practitioner. The hospital, in both instances, was an impersonal, bureaucratic entity; what differed was the length and kind of care patients had received.

What stood behind clients' views? In line with an instrumental logic, one might imagine that debtors would be most concerned about the instrumental ramifications of settling different kinds of debts. It might make sense, practically, to settle larger debts rather than smaller ones (since the analyst Richard Briesch, for example, found that creditors are willing to settle sooner with consumers who have higher balances). Yet agents agreed that the amount of particular debts rarely figured in clients' calculations. Alternatively, it would make sense to renegotiate with creditors who were most likely to agree to renegotiate, or those who were least likely to levy financial and legal penalties for nonpayment of debt. This might explain debtors' willingness to settle credit-card debts before mortgages, since the risk of failure in the latter case was that the debtor might lose his or her home. But such a logic cannot account for debtors' greater willingness to settle IRS debt than medical debt. Nor can an instrumental logic account for the fact that even when agents told clients that they were more likely to succeed in settling hospital debts than credit card debts or mortgages, clients were reluctant to try to settle hospital debts. As Mateo, who owned a firm, pointed out, "There is a lot you can do to completely wipe out your [medical] debt. But very few will listen to this, especially when the care has been substantial and important. And this was really stunning to me in the beginning, when I realized that people are less willing to include medical debt, even when they have been made aware—and they get it—that it is the easiest, fastest, and least risky debt to settle on."[14]

An alternative explanation for clients' calculations focuses on the social distance between debtor and creditor. This is the logic of (actual) social relationship that I described in the last chapter. Here, such a logic would predict that the more socially distant the creditor, the less compunction debtors would feel about negotiating down what they owed. One doesn't try to wriggle out of paying one's full debt to a human being, but one might if the creditor is a faceless, nameless company. However, such a logic does not account for the fact that some debtors were interested in renegotiating child support payments. The debt here was to a living, breathing person who was responsible for the welfare of their child. Yet, some clients asked agents about settling those debts.

Seemingly in line with a logic of social relationship, people were more likely to want to pay back medical debt than credit-card debt. But they were more likely to want to pay a debt in full to an impersonal hospital than to their family doctor if they felt that their stay in the hospital had been important to their health. And indeed, in some of those cases, debtors had never even met the hospital physicians who treated them. As Bradley explained, "Clients that have hospital bills can sometimes hesitate to settle more than with the neighborhood doctor, especially when they were really in bad shape." Such was the case, said Robert, "even when they knew their doctor, but not the people at the hospital." This might seem hard to understand. Debts for hospital care are often substantial, and they are widely seen as inflated. The debt is not to a single doctor or even to all the doctors and nurses responsible for the patient's care, but rather to a remote entity. Yet, clients felt that if the care that they received was competent, they should repay the whole sum. Their obligation was to the doctor or doctors who had helped them; it did not matter that the doctor or doctors who helped them would probably not know one way or the other whether they were being paid fully by that particular patient. Mateo insisted, "If they feel like they owe the doctor and he did something important for them, then they still might feel like they owe the hospital that hired the doctor and the nurses and has the equipment. It sometimes isn't just about the doctor that treated them." Bradley, who described clients as more willing to renegotiate a debt to their neighborhood doctor than to a hospital, explained, "If you can't afford to pay everyone, you pay back the person who earned it most! That's being fair. And it doesn't matter that you've been with your own doctor longer and they know you."

Patterns like these are consistent with a logic of repayment based on the moral obligations of an equality-matching relationship. According to Fiske, recall, an equality-matching relationship involves the exchange of resources that are the same, but what counts as the same is determined by participants. Here, if the creditor provided a service in good faith and the service was satisfactory, the debtor felt morally obliged to repay the debt. If not, he or she was justified in trying to reduce the debt. Of course, this logic has no legal sanction: people who have purchased goods or been provided a service cannot, in most cases, decide considerably later that the good or service was unnecessary or inadequate and refuse to pay what they owe. So, to conceive of debt in terms of an equality-matching relationship was not an obvious choice. It required creative relational work in which the debtor conceptualized the creditor as an equal party to a continuing exchange and as a person rather than an impersonal agency.

In line with this logic, there was a situation in which clients were willing to try to renegotiate medical debt: when their treatment had been, to the client's mind, inadequate. For example, Logan recounted, "I had this one lady who said that the hospital gave her some really terrible virus or bacterial infection or some such thing that ended up being resistant to antibiotics when she went in for a gallbladder removal. I said 'they did what?'" Logan laughed. "You bet that lady wasn't gonna pay for that! Who in their right mind would feel like they owed the doc anything after that? Good God! I think she should sue for malpractice. But that is easier said than done." Clients like this one treated the decision to renegotiate debts as a kind of moral sanction. One was obliged to repay one's debts, but the option of not paying the full amount felt like a legitimate way to signal one's dissatisfaction with the service. This logic came up more often in clients' talk about credit-card debt, mortgages, child support, and IRS debt. Robert, the former firm owner, noted that people were more interested in renegotiating credit-card debt than other kinds of debt, not because those debts were easier to lower, but "because people realized the interest that was being charged on these credit cards—and that wasn't fair." A client at Second Chance Settlement said that he was about to stop paying his American Express card debt so that he could stay current on his IRS payments. Paying the government was more important, he said, since the government actually gave something back to people.

Agents speculated that clients who asked about renegotiating their child support payments did so as a way to retaliate against their ex-spouse. Christian ventured, "I think it's resentment at people that they are making the payments to. It may be a way to get back at them." Again, choosing to renegotiate a debt was legitimate if the creditor was morally unworthy. It is something of a stretch to see debtors assessing the quality of the "service" they received in cases of child support payments. Debtors' creativity here lay in the relationship they made the debt about. Rather than thinking about their debt in terms of their relationship with their child, they thought about it in terms of their relationship with their ex-spouse. Bargaining down the debt was appropriate given the fact that they had not gotten what they anticipated from that relationship. As Connor put it, "They are trying to punish the mom." And Christian: "They'll want to include that instead of a medical bill [laughs]. . . . If it was a really nasty break-up or divorce, why should they have to help that person out?"

An exception to the scale I described also makes sense in terms of the moral obligations of equality-matching relationships. In an interaction at Second Chance Settlement, a customer was less willing to try to renegotiate a $3,000 American Express account than a $1,000 medical bill. When the agent asked her about it, she explained that she had paid for her son's tuition with the credit card. Without it, he would not have been able to stay in school. The medical bill, by contrast, was for dental work that she described as trivial. This client felt an obligation to American Express because the company had enabled her son to complete his education. It did not matter to her that American Express was a distant, impersonal company; it was still a virtuous actor. More generally, creditors who had done right deserved to be paid back in full. Paying back in full was a sign of respect, recognition of the creditor's moral worthiness. Debt-settlement clients in effect matched the respect the creditor had shown them by repaying the debt in full.

AGENTS AND CREDITORS

Agents accommodated clients' views of debt. They did not simply appeal to clients' financial self-interest and seek to allay their concerns that renegotiating their debt would have short-term benefits but long-term costs. "No one wants to just be seen as that irresponsible," an agent at Second Chance Settlement insisted. "They need to have a reason for why not paying is okay. These are good people and they won't just do this without feeling like [the creditor] is doing something wrong. Even if [the creditor] hasn't done something wrong, I think they need to *feel* like they have been conned or had something unfair done to them." Jason confessed that he sometimes tried to make instrumental arguments: "I try to let them know that if a law firm has bought your debt, you're better off excluding that . . . because they will probably pursue litigation. But that usually doesn't work. You move on to something else." What worked better, Jason went on, was to "tell them about how bad the credit-card company or the hospital was."

If debt were a generic moral obligation, one might imagine debt-settlement agents instead seeking to reassure clients that they were moral people. Renegotiating their debt was the moral thing to do since it would allow them to make good on their obligation to their creditors by repaying the amount agreed to by creditors. But agents did not do this. Instead, they sought to convince clients that their creditors were less worthy than they seemed. As the agent at Second Chance Settlement said, clients "need to *feel* like they have been conned or had something unfair done to them." Logan recounted, "I say to clients, 'Look, it's their responsibility to treat you properly. You must be treated properly. That is their duty. You should never feel guilty about settling because they didn't do their job.'" Agents thus sought to recast the relationship between debtor and creditor as uneven. Clients were justified in trying to lower their debt—implicitly, in not holding up their end of the original bargain—because their creditors had not upheld their end of the bargain. And the bargain was a moral one. They had not been treated "properly."

Brittany drew explicitly on the contrast between an instrumental logic and one based on the moral obligations of reciprocal relationships: "You can sometimes tell them to do what's right for them [financially], but really, they are upset, hurt and betrayed by these people. . . . And you can get them to justify not paying back a debt because they are pissed off, not because it's going to improve their finances somewhere down the line." Nia, a former agent, agreed: "Some people think they have to have loyalty to their creditor. . . . But let me tell you, a lot of those people will end up enrolling [in the debt-settlement program] if they believe deep down that that lender is not looking out for them. . . . It's more important to be treated right in people's minds." Because people conceptualized debt in terms of an equality-matching relationship, being "treated right," was a legitimate expectation of that relationship.

Had clients seen their relationship with their creditors in terms of a market-pricing schema, agents probably would have sought to press the financial advantages of trying to negotiate a lower debt. Instead, they sought to capitalize on clients' view of their relationship as an equality-matching one by making the case that the relationship was, in fact, unequal. Their creditor was not a moral actor, which therefore justified not paying their debt in full. As I noted, this logic is not one that is legally sanctioned, and it is at odds with the widely shared view that one should pay all one's debts back in full. Agents played a key role, then, in legitimating clients' characterization of their debt in terms of an equality-matching relationship.

Interestingly, clients resisted viewing some debts in terms of an equality-matching relationship. These were most often medical debts. Agents said that they generally avoided trying to recast doctors as bad moral actors. "I won't push on that (medical debt)," said Darryl. "It's hard for people, especially when they had a more serious condition, to settle. I mean they are doctors after all. They are so respected and what they do may be the most important profession out there. People, especially ones that have been really sick or especially people who have had a young child that's been very sick, that kind of thing is hard for them." And Robert: "You had to reason with them but also put yourself—myself—in their shoes. They felt wrong about settling with a doctor, doctors do for you what no one else can. So I would understand. I would tell them 'you know what, if you don't want to include that debt, you don't have to. We don't want to make you do anything you're uncomfortable with. But in the meantime, we can save you some money on these credit cards or other debts.'"

Agents' comments suggest that clients typically saw doctors not in terms of an equality-matching relationship but in terms of an authority-ranking relationship. Returning to Fiske's taxonomy, although the types are mutually exclusive, Fiske argues that an equality-matching relationship can metamorphose into an authority-ranking one if a person has been provided a service so valuable or unique that, effectively, he or she can never reciprocate. In that case, the relationship becomes a more hierarchical one, with one party commanding respect and deference. "People have said to me 'if it wasn't for that doctor, I wouldn't be alive today,'" Robert, the former owner of a firm, explained. And Dustin: "People just feel guilty when they consider not repaying the doctor fully. Clients will feel like the doctor did something important for them, but now they are ungrateful because they are settling." Jenna, an agent, described a client who had been in an induced coma, during which time a variety of specialists worked on him. "By the time he left," she recounted, "he had over a quarter of a million dollars in medical bills— maybe more. But even though he wasn't awake for almost any of it, he didn't even know the doctors really, he refused to add the medical debt because he said they saved his life. Because of them, he could see and be with his family again. He said that was priceless, and that he owed them and the hospital his life."

As these agents characterized it, the debtor owed the hospital something whose value could not be assessed on a market. That made it impossible for clients to imagine applying a market-pricing scheme to their debt, but also made it difficult to recast their creditor—their doctor—as less than moral in the terms of an equality-matching relationship. Money here was not just money, and not even a reward for work well done, but rather a small token of gratitude for help that could never be repaid. To be sure, one could conceivably interpret clients' unwillingness to try to renegotiate their medical debts in terms of an instrumental logic. In this interpretation, debtors reward creditors with an eye to future transactions. They may have insisted on paying their medical bill in full because they knew that they might fall ill again and wanted to ensure the same level of treatment. Yet clients did not describe their wanting to pay back their medical debt as an investment in their future health. According to agents, clients felt "guilty" for not paying their debt in full; they saw it as "wrong," as not "fair." Agents used a language of moral obligation, not one of utility.

THE POWER AND LIMITS OF INVENTED RELATIONSHIPS

For debt-settlement clients, to repay one's debt in full was a moral obligation, even if the debt was high and even if it was owed to a creditor whom they neither knew nor likely would have any contact with, *if* the creditor provided in good faith the service that was paid for. Debt-settlement clients thought about debt in terms of an ongoing and reciprocal relationship with a creditor. They were reluctant, accordingly, to adopt a purely calculative approach in considering whether to try to settle a debt. To do so would have meant applying the standards of a market-pricing relationship to an equality-matching relationship. It would have involved a taboo trade-off. Instead, and along the lines of an equality-matching relationship, debt-settlement clients assessed whether the quality of service they had received was adequate enough to pay back the debt in full. Debt-settlement agents tried to help clients arrive at this conclusion by characterizing their creditor as operating in bad faith and therefore not entitled to full payment. They did not, however, often use this strategy when it came to medical debt. I suggested that this was because the uniqueness and importance of the service the patient had often received, in combination with the respect that doctors typically command, turned the relationship from an equality-matching one into an authority-ranking one. That is, it turned a relationship in which reciprocity was paramount to one in which deference was paramount. In that situation, settling was completely out of the question.

But why did clients not think about their debt in instrumental terms? Why did they insist on viewing their creditors as equals or superiors—even when it led them to avoid trying to renegotiate debts that they had a good chance of settling successfully and instead try to settle much riskier debts? I suspect that it has to do with the fact that the moral norm to repay one's debts in full is a powerful one. Not being able to do that is dispiriting and disempowering.[15] People may have sought to regain some sense of moral autonomy by thinking about their debt as an ongoing relationship between equals. Doing so put them in the position of assessing the creditor's virtue and using payment to reward or punish the creditor.

This account gains support from a study by the sociologists Laura Tach and Sarah Sternberg Greene of low-income Americans' views of their debt. The 194 people interviewed generally did not want to ask for assistance from family or friends, and they cared about seeing themselves as self-sufficient and responsible. So, they juggled their debts, making payments on one bill one month and another the next so as to avoid going into collections on any debt, or taking out loans. However, some debts seemed to them to be unfair, and interviewees had no compunction about stopping payment on those debts. Such debts were often on credit cards, but also on bank overdrafts and to cell phone companies. Interviewees described in moral terms being charged excessive late charges or interest. Like debt-settlement clients, they personalized the creditor. One respondent complained about his credit-card company: "They were trying to tell me six hundred and something, which I told them that they weren't gonna get, especially since my credit limit was three hundred and I never got to three hundred. So they can take the six and wish for it all they want." Another respondent described going over the credit limit without realizing it and then being charged every month. He sought to pay his balance every month, "but this guy [the card] is never finished. I said forget it; I'm not going to pay it." Debtors described being duped by immoral companies. Like debt-settlement clients, they viewed repaying or not repaying debts as a way to assess the morality of their creditors. They did not view their decision in terms of the instrumental calculation of costs and benefits or as motivated by a blanket moral imperative.[16]

Agents worked with clients' views of debt. They sought to recast a particular creditor as morally unworthy in order to persuade clients to try to renegotiate a debt to that creditor. Because they could work with clients' views, they had little reason to challenge them. However, they did so knowing that clients were choosing to renegotiate debts that came with real risks to their financial futures.

AGENTS DOING "DIRTY WORK"

Were debtors then immoral or moral? Were the relationships they imagined good or bad for social solidarity? I will return to these questions at the end of the chapter. First, though, I want to talk about agents, and their willingness to encourage people to buy a service that put them at risk of financial and legal penalty. Again, in order to give negotiators leverage with creditors, agents encouraged clients to stop payment on the debts they had chosen to try to renegotiate. Clients' credit scores were likely to suffer as a result, scores that would be available not only to future lenders but to potential employers and insurance companies. In addition, defaulting on debts rendered clients vulnerable to lawsuits by creditors. A study of one debt-settlement company found that fully one-third of its clients faced lawsuits, which some clients only became aware of when their wages were garnished. Before 2010 debt-settlement agencies often required that clients pay fees up front, despite the fact that successful settlements were uncommon— less than 42 percent, according to an estimate by debt-settlement companies' own trade association. Although up-front payments were banned after 2010, with companies now permitted to take payment only after a successful settlement agreement had been reached and clients had made at least one payment to the creditor, clients remained vulnerable to substantial penalties for defaulting on their debts, and companies' record in winning settlements remained poor.[17]

My question, then, is how agents were able to countenance doing the work they did. How did they continue to sell debt-settlement services to vulnerable clients? And why were men seemingly better able to do it than women? As I noted earlier, fewer women than men worked as agents. Many women who began as agents either quit or took the job of negotiator when it was offered to them, despite the fact that that job was, in many ways, more stressful and was no better paid. A few men opined that women were simply less effective as agents. But most interviewees, men and women, agreed that women were less comfortable with a job that involved selling vulnerable clients a service that might deepen their financial troubles. "Women quit because I think it's harder for us to accept how wrong what we're doing [as agents] really is," a woman agent at Red Heron Financial observed. The question is why that was the case.

The beginning of an answer comes from a vein of organizational scholarship focused on what the sociologist Charles Everett Hughes called "dirty work." These are jobs that are tainted either physically (because they put their holders in contact with garbage, dangerous substances, death, or bodily effluvia), socially (because they put their holders in contact with socially stigmatized groups), or morally (because they require inappropriate actions). According to the management scholars Blake E. Ashforth and Glen E. Kreiner, moral dirty work typically employs methods that are thought to be "deceptive, intrusive, confrontational, or . . . [that] otherwise defy norms of civility"—such as those used by, for example, bill collectors, tabloid reporters, telemarketers, private investigators, and police interrogators. The surprise is that dirty-job holders have no less self-esteem than clean-job holders. To account for that puzzle, scholars argue that workers have creative ways of normalizing dirty work and, indeed, of developing a powerful identification with it. They may reframe the work so as to infuse it with positive value, as public defenders do in characterizing their job as protecting citizens' rights to a fair trial, not as helping criminals to avoid conviction. Or they may neutralize the stigma of the work by, for example, asserting that victims are not victims, as tabloid reporters do in claiming that celebrities want the publicity they provide.[18]

Debt-settlement agents engaged in those strategies. In particular, they reframed their relationship with clients. Male agents described their work as educating consumers about their financial options. As an agent at Second Chance Settlement put it, "We know how to give customers information that will teach them. They need to be educated, you know?" DeShawn described his work: "What it is at the core is education." José: "To be an agent, you have to be logical, an educator." Logan: "You get them to be more aware of their options, and you let them know how things work in general. Almost like a financial advisor."

Men's self-description as financial educators and advisors helps to explain why they did not worry that they were taking advantage of financially troubled clients. "You know, they can make up their own minds when you educate them," Robert explained. "And you don't really have to sell to them. When you're sharing the different policies, rules, regulations, and laws that are available to them, when you're outlining the different options—people can make up their own mind." Robert, like others, emphasized the extent to which callers were free to make their own decisions once provided objective information by the agent. Asked what a successful call looked like, Mateo answered, "Somebody that actually understands, not just the option that we're presenting to them, which is debt negotiation, somebody that actually understands all their options. Bankruptcy, debt consolidation, credit counseling, even making the payments back to their creditors." A good client, in other words, was the opposite of an easily manipulated one; she was like a bright student. And the agent was providing the client with something she needed. As Brett put it, "I know that I am giving people information that they really need. They don't know it, and I am the expert." He reasoned, "It's up to them whether they want to take our advice or not . . . I'll lay out the information, let them know what the options are, what would work best for them, and then it's their choice." Logan similarly explained, "An agent lays it all out, and it isn't really your problem whether they choose to go with your plan or not. Your job is to alert and teach."

DeShawn was one of only three male interviewees who even referred to the fact that clients might be better off without the service his firm provided. "The firm absolutely is motivated by one thing: profits," he declared. "A lot of times that gets in the way of truly helping people." He went on, "To be quite honest, the firm's interest, always—probably 98 percent of the time or more—wins in terms of when you balance the client's interest and the firm's interest. By far the firm is in the lead." When asked if that was difficult for him as person, he said, "No." Then he went on,

> I don't want to say that it's turning a blind eye, because it's not. What it is at the core is education. And any time you're a consumer or a client, you have to be educated. The people, or the individuals, who got helped the most were the consumers and clients who were the most educated. Unfortunately, that's how it is. And the individuals who were the least educated were the individuals who got most taken advantage of. . . . So it's everyone's responsibility, no matter who you are, if you care about yourself and your financial health, to learn as much and to know as much as possible.

He went on to talk about himself as always striving to learn more about the world. He seemed to be suggesting that the advantage he had over clients was that he had sought out education about financial matters and they had not. He was willing to help educate clients, but he was not responsible for their failure to know what was in their best interest.

In line with a relationship with clients of a financial educator and student, male agents offered advice and guidance. They did listen to, and sometimes empathize with, clients' troubles, but their tone was fairly unengaged. Women agents' relationship with their clients was much different. None described their jobs as involving education. Rather, they emphasized helping and supporting clients. Being "a shoulder to cry on and to just listen to their problems" was "an important part of the job," explained Aisha, who had worked as an agent but was now a negotiator; "You needed to be there for them. To be—almost to be like a counselor." Much more than the men, women agents won clients over by being empathetic, mirroring their indignation, and reassuring them that trying to settle their debts was the right course of action. "Clients were more emotionally dependent on female agents," Jenna, a former agent, acknowledged. "We [as women] did a good amount of hand-holding because of that. It was an expectation we needed to fulfill. And that is what we did." "That's where the female agents had a lot of success," said Darryl, a current agent. "They would listen a lot and that could really resonate with clients. Some of them were really having a pretty bad time: losing their homes, upside-down on their mortgages, and just drowning in debt. Just about to lose everything. For stressed-out people, sometimes having someone who lends you an ear and who you can vent to is so comforting. Especially since sometimes they couldn't even really talk to their family or anyone else. It's therapeutic, and in that way, I think that the female agents I knew were naturals at that."

Clients' expectations of women agents were evident in an exchange at Second Chance Settlement. A client was irritated when her agent, who had another call on hold, tried to get her off the phone. The client complained that the agent was not being compassionate. She had signed with this agent rather than a male agent she named because this agent had more compassion, she said, but it seemed that the agent did not have time for her today. The agent sought to reassure her, saying that she would call right back. "I promise I'll make the time. You said it right—I always have time for you!" After hanging up, and before she returned to the call she had on hold, the agent rolled her eyes, sighed, and said, "Ugh. Just ugh."

Whether or not a therapeutic relationship was "natural" to them, women like the agent I just quoted found it emotionally exhausting. Aisha described a woman client confiding in her a series of mounting problems. "Every time we talked, she would unload all the problems she was going through and I would just listen." But "it was so hard to hear it." Nia, a former agent and now a negotiator, complained about "listening to pain and heartbreak all day." She went on, "As mothers, we already have enough to deal with in our own lives. It's depressing listening to all of that." And Selena: "I was incredibly burned out when I was an agent—and I remember that other [women] agents were too."

Clients' expectation that women agents serve as something close to therapists proved emotionally demanding. Agents were forced to engage in what the sociologist Arlie Hochschild calls "surface-acting" their emotions: feigning emotions of empathy and care and professing easy confidence that debt settlement would solve clients' problems. Men had to do emotional labor too—they had to actively listen to and sympathize with clients' financial travails. But the fact that male agents were able to style their relationship with their clients as one of financial education rather than something closer to therapy meant both that it was easier to do the emotional labor they had to do, and that they had to do less of it. The fact that emotional intimacy was not required of their job muted the conflict between a relationship schema of caring and one of selling. For women agents, that conflict was sharp.[19]

Robert, the former firm owner, acknowledged the conflict when he confessed, "To be honest, I did have more women that were agents quit than men. I'm not sure if that was because it was the environment, or if it was the fact that sometimes they needed to do more work to get the same number of sales, or if it is just harder for women to get used to the idea that they are selling a product that might not always be in the best interest of the client." Asked why other women agents often quit, Brittany said wryly, "If I was to guess, it's because maybe they care more about whether the client is better off after signing up for debt settlement than before it."

THE BARRIERS TO INVENTING RELATIONSHIPS

Why then, did women not define themselves as financial educators? Why did they not redefine the job of agent in a way that made it less emotionally taxing? Because women did not have that option. Women could not effectively style themselves as educators. Although male agents and firm owners often described men as better than women at educating clients, they also acknowledged that men had an advantage in doing so. Several male interviewees said that men tended to be agents because clients perceived them to be authoritative. Robert, the former firm owner, ventured, "If I think back on it, I just thought that men tended to be more believable as agents, and did a better job of convincing the clients. They were more forceful—" then he stopped. "Well I mean, it isn't even just that," he continued. "It's more that clients won't second-guess their expertise on debt as much if it's a male agent. A female agent has to do more work to convince a client that she is the expert. That's sad. But that's the way our society is. Even when the [female] agent knows more than a man, people just assume she knows less, and so they ask more questions, they are more suspicious. And I potentially lost more clients. It sucks—but as an entrepreneur, you need to know how people think about things—and take advantage of that to be successful." He concluded flatly, "The client doesn't see [a woman agent] as an educator. If the client can't see that, then no amount of convincing will work."

A male agent at Red Heron Financial Services observed that when calculating how much the client would pay as a portion of his or her income if the debt were to be successfully renegotiated, agents all used the same technique: "It's just a spreadsheet. We all have it." He paused. "But when you think of a lawyer or an analyst, you don't usually picture a woman. [Clients] don't have the same faith when it's a woman." A woman agent chimed in: "I've even had some [clients] who asked to see how I did their budget. I have never seen that happen with a guy." Note that the male agent was implicitly claiming a professional role: a lawyer or an analyst. Nia, a negotiator, observed: "Men can control the conversation, because they are the quote-unquote experts. They answer questions, they teach them [clients] about the laws and all that. And the clients listen."

Like Nia, but without the irony of her observation, a male agent at Second Chance Settlement connected "educating" clients with a relationship in which the agent talked and the client listened. "We know how to give customers information that will teach them. They need to be educated, you know? They lack an education sometimes, and that's why, when it's a man they are talking to then they will probably listen more. Maybe they feel like this is an authority; then they are more likely to listen and sign up and do what is right. With women agents, that's something that they have trouble with, maybe. I mean, don't get me wrong, they are good agents. But that is maybe more tough for them."

Educating was tough for women because they were expected to conform to a relationship schema of care, not education. This is clear in an exchange between a male agent and two female ones at Second Chance Settlement. The man had opined that men were more effective agents than women, and Tufail asked why. He explained:

These ladies [agents] waste a ton of time on listening to sob stories. You just need to tell them that you aren't their therapist! Bro—if I was your therapist, I'd be charging you 150 bucks an hour. [Laughs]. Unlike these [women] agents, we [men agents] just shut it down because we would let these people know—"hey, you need to listen up, or you're going to miss out on this important information." You need to approach this in a— it needs to be a logical strategy. "Crying over the phone isn't going to help you get to a better place with your finances and it's not going to make your family any more money." But the women [agents]? They just can't find a way to shut it down! They just listen and listen. Meanwhile, we [male agents] have just made two other calls and enrolled a second client.

One of the women agents cut in, protesting:

> No. No—excuse me—it's not that simple. Sure we want to shut it down! I
> get tired listening to it. It's so exhausting to just hear that all day, to hear
> people cry, complain, and vent. But when I try, [clients] won't comply. It's
> like they didn't even hear me, and keep going.

The second female agent joined in:

> Or, they say to you that, well, they accuse you, really, of being insensi-
> tive or harsh. You feel like a bitch. It's a totally different reaction [to a
> woman]! It's like they expect—it's a different standard of what they ex-
> pect from us.

The first woman agreed:

> Exactly! When I was green and just got hired, I tried to use the lines that
> the guys used, verbatim. All that got me was hang-ups and rudeness. So,
> no, trying to shut it down and tell people that [they need to listen for an
> important opportunity] won't work for us.

The two women agents were emphatic that they could not adopt the educative role that men adopted, and that it was clients who compelled them
to adopt a therapeutic role. Both women indicated that it was a role they
did not want. It was "exhausting to just hear that all day, to hear people cry,
complain, and vent," said one. Her comment suggests that she did not find
it easy to take the perspective of clients in that situation, and that the emotional work she was required to do involved a good deal of surface-acting.

The relationship expected of women agents was also evident in a call
an older client made to a woman negotiator at Second Chance Settlement.
The client called to complain about being harassed by the creditors she
had stopped paying. As I noted earlier, normally clients did not interact
with negotiators, but this client had contacted the negotiator several times.
The client described her anxiety and embarrassment about being called repeatedly by collection agents in the presence of her children. The negotiator responded sympathetically, "You know what that's called, ma'am? It's
called harassment!" The negotiator asked if the client had talked to Mike,
her agent. No, the client said, she hadn't talked to Mike because she didn't
think he really understood or cared about her situation. She praised the
negotiator for always listening to her and said that she was terrified that

the collector would call while her son was visiting. "Oh, you poor thing. That sounds just terrible," the negotiator responded. "Well, I can tell you I will do my best to get them on the phone right now and let's see if I can't work something out for you, okay? Don't worry." The client thanked her warmly and said that Mike could learn something from her.

This client clearly wanted emotional support from her male agent and felt she was not getting it. Yet she did not feel entitled to ask for it from him. She did feel entitled to ask for it from the female negotiator, despite the fact that this was not the negotiator's job. Had the negotiator been an agent, the client would likely have called even more frequently. The interaction thus highlights the different expectations of male and female agents. Women could not style themselves financial educators. This was not because they lacked knowledge or natural authority, but because clients demanded from them something else: emotional support, not education.

WOMEN AS ADVOCATES

Women, as I noted, often took the job of negotiator when they were offered it. The job was a stressful one. Negotiators were routinely stonewalled or yelled at by creditors and collection agencies. All interviewees—whether men or women, agents or negotiators—agreed that the job of negotiator was harder than that of agent. As Brett, an agent, commented, "Let's just say that I would hate to have that job [negotiator]. Like I was saying earlier, they have to work harder than agents do, and they really do put up with a lot of bull. Agents I don't think deal with as much crap from clients." What made the work tolerable, said women negotiators, was the fact that they experienced themselves as advocates for the clients on whose behalf they worked. Selena explained, "Sometimes I do get tired. I get exhausted, you know? It can be very draining switching from happy to angry to . . . to playing the sympathy card. Some days I'm like 'I can't do this today!' But then I do realize that I am fighting for these people. Helping others is always hard." Over and over again, agents and negotiators characterized the job of negotiating as "easier on the conscience," as Darryl put it. A woman agent at Red Heron Financial was emphatic: "If I could switch over [to the negotiator job] I probably would. I'd take that pay cut for a clearer conscience."[20]

Certainly, negotiators were part of the enterprise to sell clients a service they did not need. Indeed, each time negotiators were successful in securing a favorable settlement, they may have sent the message to clients and potential clients that debt settlement would work for them, even though, much of the time, it did not. But women negotiators seemed to delineate their own moral responsibility narrowly. Once a client had committed to debt settlement, something that was out of the negotiator's realm of influence, the negotiator would do whatever she could to help the client. Nia allowed, "Sometimes I have to put up with really abusive collectors. But it doesn't matter, because I know that I am doing a good thing. They are already signed up anyway, and now it's up to me to get them the best settlement offer possible." While the relationship schema of salesperson and customer felt incompatible with a schema of therapist and patient, it did not feel incompatible with one of advocate and the person in need of advocacy.

An exchange between a male and a female agent at Red Heron Financial Services reveals how women and men viewed the emotional labor of negotiating differently. The female agent averred, "Despite all the bullshit negativity, I think most [female agents] would rather have the [negotiator's] job than what we've got now. At least I'd be able to be proud of what I was doing! If [the owner] offered, I'd take it in a heartbeat." The male agent who was present cut in, incredulously, "So you wouldn't care if you made less than you do now?" The female agent: "Nope. Not even a little. I would get to make people's lives better. It's more than I can say for what I do right now."

Both men and women agents saw their jobs as helping people in debt. The difference was that men were able to conceptualize their helping role as one of educating, and women were not.[21] Men described the job of educating in ways that contrasted it to stereotypically feminine traits: education was logical and objective and depended on the educator's expertise and authority over the student. By seeing themselves as being in a relationship of financial educator and student, men avoided the conflict that women experienced between claiming to help people and at the same time taking advantage of them. This is why men were able to deep-act emotions of solicitousness and care while women were forced to surface-act them. And this is why women found the job of agent so demoralizing. Reframing strategies, in other words, are not equally available to all workers. And more generally, if people invent relationships in practical and creative ways, they do so within powerful constraints.

SOLIDARY OBLIGATIONS

If asked, most of us would say that one should repay one's debts in full. And yet, in the real world, many of us simply cannot do so. Household debt was $13 trillion at the end of 2017. A combination of financial precarity and loosening credit put growing numbers of Americans in debt with little means of repayment. The moral principle that one repay one's debts in full provides insufficient guidance on what to do in these circumstances. The moral principle that one should not exploit vulnerable people, for its part, provides insufficient guidance when it comes to the countless jobs that involve selling people a product or service they do not need: diet products, time shares, a suntan, lottery tickets, self-publishing services, cosmetic surgery—the list goes on.[22]

Given the real-world constraints under which people strive to balance moral obligation and self-interest, I have asked two questions: How do people decide which debts to try to bargain down? And how do people justify staying in a job that they know is exploitative? The answer in both cases is that they do so by imagining themselves in relationships that they do not actually have. Debtors imagined that they were in an ongoing and reciprocal relationship with real people. If the service creditors provided was personally valuable to them, then they had to reciprocate by paying back the debt in full. To treat the relationship instead as what Fiske calls a market-pricing one, in which they repaid only as much as they could get away with, would be immoral. If the service that creditors provided was lifesaving, then the relationship debtors imagined was closer to what Fiske calls an authority-ranking one. Debtors could never reciprocate fully for what the creditor had provided them, but to pay any less than the price the creditor had set was unthinkable. Agents, for their part, also reimagined their relationships. Agents—at least, agents who were men—imagined their relationship with clients as a financially educational one. Doing so allowed them to see themselves not as taking advantage of people down on their financial luck, but rather as laying out options and allowing people to make their own decisions.

Both debtors and agents thus invented relationships that they did not actually have in order to retain a view of themselves as moral actors. They were creative, but also constrained. For debtors, the constraint was straightforward. Although they may have seen creditors as equals, creditors did not see them that way, and creditors had the law on their side. For women agents, the problem was subtler. As much as they might have liked to style themselves financial educators, clients expected them to serve as quasi-therapists. Employers and co-workers described women as "naturally" good at listening to, empathizing with, and comforting people who were in financial distress. So multiple parties pushed women agents into a therapeutic relationship with clients. However, the emotional intimacy required by the relationship made sharper the conflict between what agents claimed to be doing—helping—and what they were doing: selling.

What are the implications of these findings for how we think about solidarity in a world of self-interested actors? Debtors acted against their self-interest in their bid to be seen as moral actors. This is consistent with the picture that has emerged from other recent studies of how people in poverty think about their debts. Again, the Tach and Greene study of low-income heads of households showed how important it was for people to maintain a view of themselves as financially responsible and autonomous. This led, on one hand, to their reluctance to accept help from family and friends, and on the other, to their refusing to pay back debts that they felt were unfair.[23]

Findings like these have practical ramifications. Certainly, the evidence makes clear that for most people, turning to debt-settlement companies for help is a disastrous choice. How, then, should those who are genuinely concerned about debtors' financial health advise them? Appealing to debtors' self-interest in avoiding penalties may not be the best strategy to get them to pay back their debts. An alternative would be to try to get debtors to reflect on the relationship schema they are operating on—and then try to debunk that schema. Make clear that creditors are usually not people and not entities with whom the debtor has a reciprocal relationship. Perhaps that information would help debtors to assess their situation more instrumentally. Alternatively, debt counselors might take a cue from debt-settlement agents' willingness to serve as something like the circles of moral recognition that I described in the last chapter. Tach and Greene found that interviewees were motivated to work energetically to pay off all their debts, even ones they perceived as unfair, when doing so seemed to be a route to upward mobility. Debt counselors—again, ones who are not seeking to make a profit off vulnerable clients—might recognize debtors as moral people, and perhaps as the kinds of people who are striving for upward mobility. That kind of moral recognition, in turn, might help debtors to act in line with such an identity.

Agents, like debtors, strove to see themselves as moral people. However, women agents were unable to draw on relationship schemas that might have allowed them to do so. They were, as a result, disadvantaged relative to men. This has implications for how we think about work, but also how we think about solidarity. Scholars have argued that since women's caregiving roles are socially valued, jobs that build on caregiving roles, including sales and service jobs, tend to be emotionally satisfying for their holders. But I argue that such jobs may instead confront their holders with the gap between the expectation that they provide care and the expectation that that they turn a profit. Far from proving emotionally satisfying, such jobs may be even more onerous, requiring that women feign feelings of care and connection and actively suppress their guilt about taking advantage of their clients. The fact that women were willing to trade the job of agent for the more obviously stressful and sometimes lower-paying one of negotiator suggests that, however familiar caregiving is to women, it was not something they wanted to do. This in turn points to one of the ways in which the limited number of relationship schemas that are culturally available to women translates into real inequality.[24]

The pressure on women agents to serve as emotional caregivers also points to a problem that lies well outside the world of work. It has to do with the call by some feminist philosophers to style political solidarity on an ethic of care. The argument is that, contrary to liberalism's view of people as unencumbered selves, women have always known that people exist in relations of dependency. And our interdependence is not a bad thing. To the contrary, recognizing the value of the care that women routinely provide opens the way to forging solidarities in which care is ranged alongside such liberal virtues as equality, autonomy, and justice.[25] The experience of women agents, however, points to the difficulty of getting from here to there. If care were made an expectation of liberal politics, one danger is that more care and more emotionally intense care would be expected of women. But another danger is that women in politics, like the women debt-settlement agents, would experience conflicts between providing care and the other kinds of activities that are valued in politics, such as competing and strategizing. The moral obligations and emotional performances required of competing and strategizing typically are defined in opposition to those associated with care. The danger, again, is that women would bear the emotional costs of striving to do both.

CHAPTER FOUR

Publics, Partners, and the Promise of Dialogue

The people is a master at once imperious and impossible to find. "We the people" can take only debatable form.

PIERRE ROSENVALLON, *Democracy Past and Future* (2006)

On a warm July day in 2002, 4,500 New Yorkers gathered in a midtown convention center. Their charge was to make recommendations about what should be built on the site of the former World Trade Center, destroyed in the 9/11 terrorist attack the year before. Seated at tables of a dozen, with a facilitator at each one, forum participants reviewed preliminary plans for the site and discussed priorities for the surrounding neighborhood. They traded ideas for a memorial to the victims of the attack and deliberated over the scale of the buildings that would replace those destroyed. Participants' conclusions were transmitted via linked laptops to a Theme Team, who identified areas of consensus and projected them onto giant video screens. Occasionally participants were asked to register their individual preferences using personal digital voting pads, and these results too were projected onto the screens, sometimes to enthusiastic applause. In a city known for rancorous battles around development, many observers hailed the forum—"Listening to the City," it was called—as something genuinely new. "At each table, they debated in a sober, thoughtful, civil way," the *New York Daily News* columnist Pete Hamill marveled. "We have a word for what they were doing. The word is democracy."[1]

Hamill was not alone in his enthusiasm for public deliberation. In the last twenty-five years, efforts to bring ordinary people together to make recommendations on issues of public concern have proliferated. Hundreds of thousands of citizens in this country, and many more worldwide, have participated in forums to discuss issues ranging from local urban development to the federal deficit. Participatory budgeting, once synonymous with the city of Porto Alegre, Brazil, has spread to thousands of municipalities around the world. Canada empowered a citizens' body to define a constitutional agenda. Finland crowdsourced its constitution. As its champions see it, public deliberation can give policy makers the benefit of public opinion that is genuinely informed and free of the polarizing effects of political manipulation. Even if sponsored by civil society organizations rather than the government, deliberation encourages people to become more trusting of their political institutions and more politically engaged. In the view of its champions, deliberation makes for better policies, more active citizens, and more solidary societies.[2]

Others are less persuaded. Michael Sorkin was a progressive architect who participated in the Listening to the City forum of which Pete Hamill was so enamored. As the day wore on, he said afterward, he increasingly felt like a delegate in a "1950s Soviet Party Congress." The options for how to develop the site had been determined in advance and were basically identical. When the master of ceremonies for the event gave a "brief pep talk on how the meeting was democratic as all get out because 'in democracy, the people have a chance to speak!'" Sorkin had had enough. He stood up and yelled "Buuuuuulllllllshiiiiiiit! Democracy means the people have the power to choose!" His "tiny act of insurrection went completely unnoticed," he commented ruefully.[3]

Sorkin's experience may have been unique, but his indignation is not. Critics of today's deliberative initiatives charge that the people speak but have no control over the decisions that are made. Indeed, critics argue, grand spectacles of public participation may make it that much easier for backroom decision making to carry on as usual, without scrutiny or challenge. Such spectacles provide participants a satisfying experience of democracy in the moment, but they are no substitute for mechanisms of democratic accountability.[4]

Who is right? Scholars have sought to adjudicate between champions and critics by probing the operation and impacts of particular deliberative initiatives and identifying the conditions in which policy makers take seriously the recommendations that citizens arrive at. But to grasp the democratic possibilities of public deliberation, I argue, we also need to understand how the people who organize such initiatives think about the power and limits of deliberation. In particular, we need to understand how forum organizers construct the participating public. In the terms that I use in this book, what relationships do forum organizers imagine members of the public having before they join the forum? What kinds of relationships do they strive to create among participants during the forum? And what kinds of relationships do they envision forum participants having with the decision makers whom the forum is intended to influence? Deliberation organizers' views of the public are important, I argue. They influence who is invited to participate and whose participation is discouraged. They determine how participants are instructed to talk and listen to each other during the forum, and what they are encouraged to do or not do after the forum is over.[5]

Yet, forum participants themselves also have ideas about what binds them as a group. They have ideas about the appropriate character of their relationships within the forum, whether and how those relationships should continue after they leave the forum, and what their relationship with policymakers is and should be. These views matter too. Not least, they point to potential sources of frustration if they are different from the views of forum organizers. But they also point to possibilities, I believe, for making deliberation more effective. In the forums I studied, which included Listening to the City, participants saw themselves as representatives of groups outside the forum. They also saw themselves, along with the forums' organizers, as advocates for the recommendations they arrived at. Whereas deliberation's champions laud its capacity to transcend contentious politics as usual, the participants I interviewed believed that democratic outcomes required contention. In ways unrecognized by theories of democratic deliberation, they may have been right.

As I noted in chapter 1, one of the challenges of solidarity centers on its role vis-à-vis the institutions of government. Deliberation's champions argue, along with Tocquevillians, that the generalized trust produced by people's civic participation makes for more effective government. Critics maintain that if public trust in government becomes the overarching goal, it may release government from needing to be responsive to the public. In this chapter I explore how deliberation practitioners and participants draw on familiar relationships to deal with this dilemma.

DELIBERATION TODAY

Public deliberation has an impressive intellectual pedigree, but it has been embraced by politicians and civil society groups for eminently practical reasons. The claim is a simple one: giving people the opportunity to talk about matters of public concern, in a setting characterized by civility and mutual respect, and in which participants exchange reasoned arguments for their opinions, offers the best hope for arriving at public agreement on political issues. Even if deliberators do not reach consensus, the thinking goes, they are more likely to agree with the decision that is eventually taken if they have recognized the reasons behind it.[6]

For the philosopher Jürgen Habermas, the free, public, and reasoned exchange of opinions is what defines democracy. According to Habermas, something like this kind of democratic discussion took place in the eighteenth-century coffeehouses, salons, debating societies, and journals of opinion in which private citizens debated issues that had previously been the exclusive purview of the state. Such debates were conducted without regard for an individual speaker's status, and they formed the basis for criticizing the state in the name not of private interests, but of public ones. Habermas by no means advocated resuscitating the public sphere of the eighteenth-century, which he acknowledged was exclusive in terms of class and gender. But he did see democratic power in the notion of public debate governed by reason rather than status. In his later work, he sought to ground that potential in the norms of ordinary speech rather than in a historical precedent.[7]

Habermas's theory was pitched at the macro level: he thought about whole societies as being more or less deliberative. However, beginning in the late 1980s, scholars, foundation executives, planners, and public officials began to see public deliberation more practically. Giving people opportunities to deliberate in organized public forums might combat the public's disengagement from politics. The specific problems to which deliberation was the answer varied across regions. In the European Union, public deliberation was a response to concerns that shifting decision making beyond nation-states was hollowing out democratic accountability, while in England, it followed controversies over how the government had communicated about scientific risk. In Brazil, new programs for participatory budgeting were led by a left-wing party. In India, they were supported by the World Bank.[8]

In the United States, deliberation's proponents enthused about the specifically educative function of citizen talk. For foundations such as the Kettering Institute and academics such as James Fishkin, public deliberation was capable of producing the informed public opinion that was lacking in an era of media manipulation and spin. Sponsors of the intergroup dialogues that took place as part of President Bill Clinton's national Initiative on Race in 1992 also believed in public talk. However, their goal was less to develop informed and competent citizens than to promote racial reconciliation. Increasingly, however, a coterie of experts began to share approaches. In urban development, planners had long sought alternatives to the traditional municipal hearing, in which a line of cranky citizens came to the microphone to speak their piece, with little interest in other speakers' points of view. Sometimes with guidance from new national outfits sponsoring deliberation, sometimes on their own, local agencies and coalitions began to experiment with more deliberative forms of public input. Yet another push to deliberation came from cities that were promoting private investment in response to budgetary crises. As part of those efforts, urban visioning involved citizens in imagining creative futures for their cities.[9]

These were very different agendas: educating voters, promoting racial reconciliation, and creating municipal plans capable of attracting private investors. Deliberation's forms also varied. Some deliberative forums were one-off events, while others extended over weeks and even months; some included "stakeholders," while others aimed for broad representation of the public; some were convened by a governmental agency with a specific set of questions, while the vast majority were sponsored by coalitions that included foundations, universities, civic groups, and others. But these diverse exercises were increasingly organized and run by specialists in what is typically referred to as "dialogue and deliberation." Dialogue is more oriented to mutual understanding than to making a recommendation and is sometimes treated as a first step to deliberation. More commonly, deliberation is organized and facilitated using tools from dialogue. A 2009 survey found that the people who organized and facilitated public forums had backgrounds in organizational development, human resources, management training, facilitation, conflict resolution, and communication, but most had been trained in at least one group communication technique such as Appreciative Inquiry, Future Search, Open Space, Nonviolent Communication, Dynamic Facilitation, or Technique of Participation. As I will discuss in the next chapter, deliberation practitioners' skill sets reflect the diffusion of psychotherapeutically informed communicative techniques into schools, workplaces, and, increasingly, public administration. Handbooks and guidelines on deliberation emphasize empathetic listening more than persuasion, telling stories more than making arguments, and focusing on the personal dimensions of issues. In this sense, deliberation today is organized to foster the egalitarian intimacy I described in chapter 1.[10]

THE PUBLIC IN PUBLIC DELIBERATION

The case for public deliberation has not gone unchallenged. Feminist critics of Habermas early on took issue with the notion that deliberation could be both rational, at least in Habermas's terms, and egalitarian. They argued that men, the middle class, and native English-speakers were both more comfortable with an abstract language of reason-giving and more likely to be seen as rational, no matter how they actually spoke. As deliberative democracy was turned from a normative standard into an institutional blueprint for citizen forums, critics pointed to dynamics in group conversation that might well compromise the rationality as well as the equality of deliberative talk. For example, those with minority opinions in conversations are often pressured to agree with the majority opinion, no matter how ill-informed; high-status participants tend to be perceived as more accurate in their judgments even when they are not; and people tend to credit information they already know over information they do not, even when indications are that the latter may be more accurate. Finally, critics point out that decision makers are rarely bound by the recommendations that emerge from a deliberative forum. Deliberators might be disappointed and angry when they see policies adopted that contravene the recommendations made in the forum. They might, as a result, become more skeptical of the political process and less likely to participate in politics. Alternatively, they might accept a disconnect between what happens in the forum and the decisions that are made after it, and more generally, see themselves as having "voice" only in a therapeutic rather than political sense.[11]

Defenders of public deliberation have countered that these criticisms ignore how deliberative forums are actually organized. Practitioners never promote a Habermassian exchange of abstract reasons, they say. Instead, as I noted, they use the tools of dialogue to encourage participants to get to know each other, recognize common experiences, and appreciate one another's perspectives. Only after that are participants asked to jointly assess practical options. Skilled facilitators encourage participants to share their opinions by means of personal stories as much as rational arguments, and they work to ensure that no one feels silenced or marginalized. With respect to the charge that deliberation gives people only the illusion of influence, practitioners emphasize the importance of bringing policy makers into the deliberative process early on so that they can be engaged as genuine partners.[12]

I will come back to these claims, but I want to draw attention to yet another set of criticisms, which have focused on deliberation as it is practiced rather than theorized. The argument which has been made mainly by European scholars, is that as much as deliberation's organizers want forums to influence policy, the ways in which they conceptualize the public may undermine such influence. Policy makers and forum organizers invent the public, these scholars argue. They project some skills and interests and not others onto people they call "ordinary," and they define ordinary people in contrast to other groups that are also invented: experts, special interests, stakeholders, and so on.[13]

The public that is sought for deliberative forums typically is viewed as properly lacking expertise, involvement in advocacy, and even strong opinions. Aside from the irony that the people who "abstain from participation in political life . . . become the most highly valued constituency," the public is sometimes constructed in ways that conflict with what members of the real public want and are capable of. In forums on genetics in the United Kingdom and Germany, for example, people with a genetic disorder were listened to attentively by policy makers, but they had to be careful not to speak as members of advocacy groups, since advocates were seen as outside the public. A Canadian network of scientists and policy makers sought to include "ordinary citizens" in their discussions about genetics policy, but their view of citizen participants as valuable only by virtue of their "disinterestedness" made it impossible for them to take advantage of the knowledge that the citizen participants actually brought to the table. Sometimes, instead, policy makers construct the public in ways that levy competing demands on them. Citizen representatives on a health-care management committee in the United Kingdom were supposed to be "ordinary" and therefore typical of other community members. At the same time, however, they were expected to conform to the expectations of the professionals on the committee: to devote extensive time to the task, to be knowledgeable about the health-care system, and to work effectively with other professionals. In each case, deliberation's organizers limited citizens' capacities to influence policy—not intentionally, but rather because of their ideas about who the deliberating public was.[14]

Again, studies in this vein have focused almost exclusively on deliberation in Europe and Canada, which differs from that in the United States. Most of the forums I just described, for example, were convened by governmental agencies, whereas in the United States, forums typically are sponsored by coalitions of civic organizations and foundations, and sometimes local public agencies—rarely national ones. The question of impact accordingly becomes a more complicated one. As I noted earlier, American experiments in public deliberation have a different history than those in Europe and were developed to address different kinds of public deficits. Accordingly, it makes sense to examine how American deliberation practitioners conceptualize the public with whom they work.

To do so, I draw on books, articles, white papers, online forums, and guidelines produced by deliberation practitioners in conjunction with the results of a national survey I conducted with the sociologist Caroline Lee. I also draw on my interviews with, and observation of, practitioners who designed and ran a series of forums in New York City in 2002. Listening to the City, which I described at the beginning of the chapter, was one of these forums. It was initiated by a coalition of planning, environmental, and community groups that had been formed in the wake of the 9/11 tragedy and co-sponsored by the main agencies involved in rebuilding Lower Manhattan. The day-long forum was organized and facilitated by AmericaSpeaks, a national deliberation organization. Participants discussed preliminary plans for the site as well as transportation, housing, and economic-development options, and their recommendations were compiled and presented to rebuilding authorities. The in-person forum was followed by a two-week online forum involving another 570 people.

Another series of forums, Imagine New York, was spearheaded by the Municipal Art Society (MAS), a longtime civic actor in New York, and was organized by a planning firm famous for its urban visioning exercises. The project brought 3,500 people from the metropolitan area to 230 facilitated workshops in the spring of 2002 in venues ranging from private homes to museums and universities. Participants were asked to identify priorities in rebuilding and then worked together to identify themes and practical ideas in the answers that were generated. These were recorded by group facilitators, and the resulting nineteen thousand ideas were synthesized into forty-nine draft vision statements. The draft vision statements were reviewed, amended, and ratified by three hundred returning participants at a Citizen Summit. The final visions were released to the press and submitted to rebuilding authorities.[15]

In the following, I also draw on participant observation of the forums themselves and interviews with their participants in order to explore how participants conceptualized the public. Scholars who study the construction of publics often argue that deliberation would be improved by admitting real publics into deliberation. They call for "engaging actual rather than imagined citizens": people who are members of civil society and activist groups as well as those who are less socially connected, and people with diverse kinds of competence. This makes sense. But valorizing "real" publics risks obscuring the extent to which participants also construct themselves as publics. Participants have ideas about who they collectively are and what their role in decision making should be. These ideas are just as much imagined as are those of policy makers and forum organizers. If those ideas conflict, we can see the potential for disappointment on both sides. But we may also be able to see possibilities for alternative constructions of the public than those that dominate the current practice of deliberation.[16]

THE PUBLIC VERSUS SPECIAL INTERESTS

Most briefs for public deliberation in the United States begin with citizens' desires for "voice" in a politics that has been captured by "special interests." "People are confused by spin on every side as special interests succeed in blocking significant reform," write the Public Agenda founder Daniel Yankelovich and his coauthors. A "Primer" for public engagement opens, "In our society, public decision-making is typically the domain of powerful interest groups or highly specialized experts." Caroline Lukensmeyer, who founded AmericaSpeaks in 1995 to help decision makers "connect quickly and authentically with citizens," observes, "Over the past few decades, politics has become far more partisan, elections far more expensive, and policy making far more beholden to special interests. In the process, one key voice continually gets squeezed out: the citizen's." While citizens are increasingly "alienat[ed] from the political process" (according to a memo for potential funders), policy makers, for their part, are denied the benefit of public opinion, save for superficial opinion polls and public hearings that are "free-for-alls, where only the loudest voices prevail" (in a description of the deliberative method Citizen Choicework). The solution, according to briefs like these, is to provide decision makers with citizens' informed and deliberative opinion. Giving citizens the time and space to talk with their fellows in a setting of civility and mutual respect, with information available to help them understand the larger issues, should yield recommendations that are sensitive to the challenges faced by decision makers and oriented to the common good.[17]

As in Europe, there is an emphasis on finding "ordinary citizens" and going beyond "the usual suspects," who routinely dominate public hearings. Deliberation organizers seek "to reach out to voices that are not heard, people who normally don't turn out to community board meetings and planning hearings." In addition, practitioners emphasize the value of diversity in participants' experiences and opinions. James Fishkin's Deliberative Polls attempt to secure a stratified random sample of the public, but most deliberation organizers recognize that they cannot claim true representativeness. Instead, they aim for "a broad cross-section of the community," "diverse" participants, "diverse representation," to have "all voices at the table," and to tap "hard to reach" populations. As Everyday Democracy advises, "One of the biggest challenges is to recruit people who don't often get involved in community events. This will take extra work, but without it, you will be missing many important voices in your program."[18]

The public that deliberation seeks, then, is made up of people who have opinions but have not organized to press them. Groups that *are* organized are special interests, which should not be included in a deliberative forum. On the other hand, deliberation practitioners do see people as members of community institutions such as churches, schools, clubs, and ethnic community groups, and they rely on those organizations to help them recruit. Guidelines emphasize the importance of creating relationships with "community leaders" as a way to recruit participants. Indeed, recruiters should use tools familiar to community organizers. In sum, practitioners do not see the public as an atomized mass. Members of the public have solidary bonds of community, but they are alienated from politics.[19]

Although participants in the forum are recruited to it by way of preexisting ties, once in the forum they should speak as "I's" and not as "we's." A common ground rule introduced at the beginning of discussions is, "You speak only for yourself and from your personal experience." A guide for study circles instructs facilitators to "encourage participants to use 'I' messages, and to preface strong opinions with 'I feel. . . .'" Facilitators should "remind people to speak for themselves, not for others or a group." The Public Conversations Project encourages "speaking that is personal rather than positional or constituency-oriented." A facilitator who was asked by researchers to identify instances of successful and unsuccessful deliberation zeroed in on a participant speaking "as a Muslim—using the pronoun 'we.'" The facilitator had just praised the forum for its demographic representativeness, but, she explained, "I would argue that deliberation works best when participants are speaking as individuals and not viewing themselves as representatives of particular groups."[20]

Speaking as an "I" makes it more likely that the participant will be open to the ideas and perspectives that are voiced in the group rather than remaining tied to the perspectives with which she came. Deliberation practitioners agree with theorists that a central virtue of deliberation is that it encourages people to move away from their original preferences. Deliberation is thus different from voting, in which people simply register their preferences, and bargaining, in which they seek to maximize their preferences. Deliberation practitioners frequently contrast deliberation with "narrowly defined negotiation," "bargaining among . . . pre-established preferences and individual interests," "bargaining," and "voting, negotiating a consensus, bargaining."[21]

On the other hand, a Habermassian notion of reason-giving is much too narrow a conception of deliberation, practitioners argue. They encourage participants to trade jokes, tell stories, and be passionate about issues they care about. This is in part to free people to communicate ideas in a way that is comfortable to them. But it is also to build a sense of cohesion among participants, which facilitators see as crucial to their ability to work together effectively. Participants' openness to diverse perspectives depends on the existence of emotional bonds among them. In that sense, facilitators work hard to turn the "I's" into a group "we." Doing so creates the mutual trust that does not come naturally to strangers asked to discuss a potentially controversial issue. It may not lead to consensus, nor should it; rather, deliberation's value for policy makers as well as participants is in identifying areas of common ground along with areas of disagreement.[22]

If practitioners seek to turn "I's" into a "we" in the course of the deliberative process, the "we" is not a political "we." It does not extend beyond the end of the forum. Participants should go back to their daily lives with, ideally, a greater sense of trust in the political process. They should also retain a commitment to remaining engaged, but as individuals. Some dialogue and deliberation approaches encourage participants to plan how they will stay engaged. Everyday Democracy, for example, has participants come up with an action plan for how they will work to implement the ideas they have arrived at, which may include establishing a task force or some other continuing entity. More typically, dialogue and deliberation initiatives end with exhortations for participants to remain involved as individuals. No manuals for running a deliberative forum encourage sponsors or organizers to lobby decision makers on behalf of the recommendations produced in the forum. Instead, practitioners emphasize the value of bringing decision makers into the deliberative process as "collaborators" or "partners." According to the website of the National Coalition for Dialogue and Deliberation, "Dialogue and deliberation emphasize 'power-with' principles instead of the typical 'power-over' norms in practice today." If sponsors want to influence policy, "Running a D and D Program" instructs, "Get the power-holders on board as planners, participants, sponsors, or supporters." In 21st Century Town Meetings, the "involvement of decision-makers and key leaders throughout the project is central to the success of these initiatives." The head of Everyday Democracy similarly argues for involving "public officials from the outset, as full partners in the organizing process and in the dialogue, with a commitment to sharing decision making"; "policymakers [should be involved] as participants on an equal basis in the dialogue."[23]

In sum, deliberation experts view the public in ways that are simultaneously practical and radical. They are clear-eyed about ordinary people's low levels of interest in the issues that policy makers confront every day. But they believe that ordinary people have not been given the chance to reflect on those issues with the information they need alongside people who have different points of view. To bring these conversations about, practitioners argue for capitalizing on the bonds that people have with friends, fellow church members, co-ethnics, and so on. Once in the forum, participants should speak for themselves. As they share experiences and values, practitioners explain, they may come to see issues in a new way and identify actions they can take after the forum is over. Again, deliberation practitioners join the practical and the radical: they do not expect that decision makers will unquestioningly take their marching orders from forum participants. But they envision the possibility of a relationship between citizens and their government of partnership and collaboration rather than advocacy and conflict.

THE PUBLIC CONSTRUCTS THE PUBLIC

In some respects, this picture is tremendously appealing. The New Yorkers who participated in the Listening to the City and Imagine forums were enthusiastic about their experience. "I broadcast this to everyone I knew," said a participant in Listening to the City. "I said, 'The most amazing thing happened: I was in this town hall and no one argued, and I was listened to and it was a great day.'"[24]

Few of the people my team and I interviewed had participated in a deliberative forum before. But they likened their experience to groups they had participated in—and ones they had only heard about. They cited, variously, think tanks, juries, teams, the United Nations, focus groups, branding workshops, educational seminars, and activist coalitions. All the analogies are interesting, but some are especially so, I argue, since they depart from the models of deliberation on which the forum organizers operated. Interviewees, I show, described themselves as representatives of a public outside the forum. They described themselves as something like bargaining partners within the forum. And they described themselves as advocates for the recommendations reached in the forum. Each of these conceptions of the deliberating public is at odds with deliberation conventionally understood. But each one points to possibilities for impact that organizers may have missed.

In line with what deliberation practitioners hope to accomplish, interviewees saw themselves as "I's" joined into a "we" in the forum. To their relief, the "we" was a nonpolitical one. They referred frequently and admiringly to the fact that the forums were not, as they put it, "political," by which they meant contentious and partisan. "It was as nonpolitical as it could have been," said a Listening to the City participant; "people weren't campaigning." Our interviewees appreciated that their tablemates had been "respectful," that discussion had been "calm," that people didn't "rant," that "there was no shouting and everyone heard us." They referred frequently to the fact that they liked their tablemates, that their group had, as one put it, "clicked."

Facilitators' emphasis on forging bonds of respect and openness clearly seemed to work. Participants also appreciated the diversity of their groups. Indeed, for many participants, it was what they liked most about the forums. Why? Some interviewees drew attention to the impact on their own opinions of talking with people who were different from them. One said, "Families and evacuees say the whole thing should be a memorial site. And yeah, I understand what they're saying. And then you hear businesspeople saying, we need business . . . I became more open to a tall building. . . ." I asked the interviewee to clarify. "So, you were exposed to ideas that you hadn't been exposed to?" "I became so *through the people*," she emphasized. Another explained, "Much of my thinking prior to the event had been solo thinking. The experience made me aware of other people's experiences."

More than simply exposing them to different views, however, interviewees talked about participants' diversity as carrying the force of representativeness. They were a "microcosm of New York," a "tiny little miniature New York at each table," a good "cross-section" of the city, with "people from all different socioeconomic groups" who were "representative" of the "population at large," "a good demographic representation," and "not a bad sample." One participant appreciated the fact that "those representing the interests of the very rich and the very poor were in the same space." Articulating the distrust of opinion polls that is common among Americans,[25] another participant compared Listening to the City favorably to a poll: "Usually when they do polling they use a much smaller sample size, about a couple hundred people or so. Here they had a sample of five thousand people."

Interviewees, especially those who participated in Listening to the City, also suggested that they were representative of the public in a more political sense. "I felt I was a representing a voice of the city," one said. Another explained her participation by remarking that "I think the voice of the residents [of Lower Manhattan specifically] needs to be heard." One interviewee was disappointed "that there wasn't more Hispanic representation." She went on, "The Hispanic community is abdicating responsibility here." Another observed that "the majority of people were in the demographic age thirty-five to fifty-four, so I would have liked to see more African Americans and other nationalities in that age group." An interviewee who found himself at a table with mainly Cantonese-speaking Chinatown residents wished that there had been "demographically a better cross-section . . . so although in my table the Chinatown view was overrepresented, it means that on other tables that view wasn't even being expressed."

Two interviewees likened Listening to the City to the United Nations, again alluding to a body made up of representatives. It is also a body whose members are charged with finding compromises in the interests of the greater good, and this too seemed to have been important to participants. Many interviewees talked about the group's ability to reach compromises and, indeed, about their own willingness to compromise as something they had appreciated. As a Listening to the City participant recounted: "I guess I come from a higher income family than some of the people at the table, and other people have different priorities. You can't ignore them when there is someone in front of you rather than just a statistic. You have to say, 'I guess they're right, we should compromise on this fact, on affordable housing, and things like that.'" Another noted, "Some of my opinions were changed but nothing drastic, more compromises that I could see." A woman said she was pleased to discover that "people are much more willing to compromise" than she had thought.

Together these comments suggest that participants saw themselves as something like negotiating partners who were representing larger constituencies. Both parts of this image, though, are at odds with deliberation as it is understood by practitioners. Participants were not representative. They were not authorized, either by decision makers or by the public, to speak on behalf of the public. Nor were they descriptively representative of New York City or some larger region in the sense either that they were a random sample of residents or that they reflected accurately the demographic makeup of the region or the range of interests at stake in the decisions to be made about Ground Zero. This is typical of deliberative forums, and the reason that deliberation practitioners emphasize diversity rather than representativeness. Practitioners worry that if participants imagined that they were truly representative, they might expect that their recommendations should carry the force of public will.

For deliberation practitioners, the other part of the image that emerged from our interviews, of participants as negotiating partners, is similarly both wrong and risky. Deliberation, practitioners make clear, is different from bargaining. Seeing deliberation as something like bargaining might lead participants to hold on to their preexisting opinions in order to cut the best deal they could. It might lead them to see successful deliberation as more about gaining concessions than about arriving at areas of agreement. But I am not convinced that participants thought about themselves and the deliberative process in these ways. Compromise, as the people we interviewed saw it, was a way to deal with disagreements that they believed were inevitable. Of course, practitioners do not deny that disagreements exist, nor do they try to gloss them over. Rather, they aim to help participants identify common ground, acknowledging that common ground exists alongside disagreement. But participants seemed to want to go further than identifying what they agreed on. They saw compromise as a way to take up what they disagreed about and possibly move beyond disagreement.

Even more than that, compromise was a way for participants to acknowledge changes in their preferences or in the importance they attached to their preferences. Let me explain. People generally are reluctant to change their minds, scholars have found, and are reluctant to acknowledge doing so. The focus group members studied by the political scientists Pamela Conover, Donald Searing, and Ivor Crewe viewed changing one's mind as being weak-willed, ignorant, or naive. Compared to changing one's mind, however, being willing to compromise is usually seen as a virtuous act. Compromising involves giving up some of what one desires, not giving up who one is. While the person who has changed her opinion is seen as irresolute, the person who has compromised may well be seen as cooperative and forward-looking. Participants in the New York City forums may have shared these views. They frequently said that they had not changed their minds but instead had learned about the issues, clarified their views, or arrived at compromises. I wonder if it was easier for them to think of themselves as compromising than as changing their opinions. For example, when one interviewee said that though she had not changed her mind, she was now able to "see compromises," I read her as acknowledging that she had reevaluated the importance of one of her previous preferences. To be sure, the potential downside of a language of compromise is that people might define success as winning acceptance for a version of their preferred solution and as a result fail to consider other options. However, the fact that our interviewees often talked about the value of the "brainstorming" they did in the group suggests that they were able to shift from generating possible solutions to scrutinizing those already on the table.[26]

Participants' view of themselves as representative of people outside the forum, as members of groups rather than as "I's," also referred to a different kind of relationship than that usually featured in briefs for deliberation. Seeing themselves as representatives invested their deliberations with a seriousness of purpose. Participants saw themselves as representatives of people with distinct experiences: of living downtown, for example, or of being the owner of a small business. They did not treat those experiences necessarily as producing a set of fixed interests, but rather, as the political theorist Mark Brown suggests, as producing common questions and concerns.[27] Participants wanted to get as many perspectives on the table as possible. And if all perspectives were not represented in person, participants were comfortable imagining them. Rather than simply registering their own personal views, they wanted to do the work of hashing out areas of agreement and potential compromise by articulating the arguments they imagined people with different experiences might make.

However, this effort to imagine other people's experiences sat uncomfortably with forum organizers' injunction to speak only from one's own experience. During my table's discussion at Listening to the City, I commented that the family members of people who had died in the attack understandably did not want new buildings on the footprints of the towers (families had voiced this view publicly). The facilitator interjected that family members were at the forum and could represent themselves; our job was not to speculate about what the families wanted. A short time later another member of my group commented that his view of the appropriate size for a memorial would probably be different if he had lost a wife or child in the attack. Again, the facilitator instructed us not to consider views other than our own. My notes record my own discomfort and my sense that the other participant felt uncomfortable too. One can see the facilitator's point. Perhaps not all family members felt the same way, and perhaps their views might change in deliberation with others. Still, there is another way to interpret what the other participant and I meant. Perhaps we were trying to say, "My preference is to build on the footprints or to have a small memorial, but I am willing to yield on that preference given the claim that I believe family members have in this regard." We were separating a preference we recognized as narrow from one we believed properly considered the greater claim of family members.

DELIBERATION THAT IS RESPONSIVE TO PARTICIPANTS' UNDERSTANDINGS

I have suggested that participants' view of themselves as in a bargaining relationship with people in the forum, and in a representative relationship with people outside it, was at odds with the way forum organizers, and deliberation experts more generally, conceptualized them. But occasionally, and in somewhat ambiguous ways, deliberation experts do recognize as legitimate something like those relationship schemas. Thus, although briefs for deliberation often contrast it with bargaining, they sometimes qualify what they mean by bargaining. David Matthews of the Kettering Institute, for example, contrasts deliberation with "negotiation narrowly understood," leaving open the possibility that a broader understanding of negotiation would be consonant with deliberation. What that broader understanding of negotiation would entail is not spelled out, however. I noted earlier that facilitators tend to talk about seeking common ground rather than consensus. As the deliberation scholars Jane Mansbridge, Janette Hartz-Karp, Matthew Amengual, and John Gastil describe it, however, common ground "is a kind of compromise, but far more than a crude aggregation or averaging of participants' private interests." Again, that "far more" is not spelled out. In the terms I use, compromise is something arrived at through a process of figuring out what is truly important and what one can yield.[28]

Somewhat at odds with the overall emphasis on speaking only from one's experience, deliberation experts also sometimes, and again ambiguously, do recognize participants' capacity to represent experiences outside their own. For example, a moderator's guide for National Issues Forums instructs moderators to ensure that "participants talk about their personal stake — why this issue matters to them, their personal experiences with it." This is the familiar injunction to speak only from one's personal experience. But then the guide includes as a sample question, "How has this issue affected you, your family, or your community?" One's personal experience is treated here as encompassing that of one's community. AmericaSpeaks, both in the Lower Manhattan forums and in the others it organized, sought to include "stakeholders" — that is, those directly affected by the issue — among participants. The notion of a stakeholder implies that people have preexisting group interests and that individuals can represent the group. It reflects the idea that the representation of certain social experiences is important.[29]

So the gap between participants' ideas about who they were as a group and those of deliberation experts was perhaps not as great as much of the literature suggests. Deliberation need not be opposed to bargaining and representation. Accommodating forum participants' imagined relationships may not be terribly difficult, and doing so may have a productive effect. However, a third way in which deliberative forum participants conceptualized themselves may not be so easily accommodated by existing theories of deliberation.

A COLLECTIVE ACTOR

As I noted, interviewees were pleased and surprised at the sense of solidarity they felt in their groups, even across differences of opinion. My table at Listening to the City engaged in spirited arguments for most of the day and then spontaneously posed for a group photo at the close. When one member offered to create a website for our table, we eagerly exchanged email addresses. Another member later sent us plans for the site that his architectural office had produced. Perhaps my table was somewhat unusual in its effort to sustain ties, but it was not unusual in its belief that we had become a *group* and one that should continue.

This was not just sentimental. Participants in both Imagine and Listening to the City believed that the forums' impact depended on forum organizers' capacity to keep them mobilized for impact. Our interviewees recognized that the process of rebuilding Lower Manhattan was a complex and contentious one. There were numerous interests involved, including those of victims' family members, residents of Lower Manhattan, small and large businesses, the lessor of the site, and other developers. There were also multiple agencies with claims to rebuilding authority. Given that situation, interviewees were clear-eyed about their prospects for influence. What impact the forums would have, they said, would likely be due to the fact that the scale of the tragedy had forced government to be more responsive to residents. In addition, the fact that rebuilding authorities had endorsed Listening to the City and that it had received so much media attention would create pressure on authorities to respond. "It took away some of their wiggle room," an interviewee explained. "It didn't eliminate it, but it took away some of it."

Interviewees also emphasized that the organizers of, and indeed participants in, the forums would have to press their case in order to have real influence. Asked whether he thought Listening to the City would influence decision makers, one man answered, "It depends on the people who put Listening to the City together, how vigilant [they are]. . . . If they back off and let [rebuilding authorities] maneuver and manipulate this situation, it will be null and void what we did." Another Listening participant said that had he been running the event, he would have pushed the rebuilding authorities to make a firmer commitment, to "strip them bare," as he put it. "They were still wearing their skivvies when they walked out."

Participants hoped, and sometimes expected, that they would be involved in advocating for the recommendations they had arrived at. Several people who had been in Imagine workshops offered suggestions when my team and I interviewed them for how to maximize the forum's impact. The organizers should get a story in a high-profile local magazine, they suggested, or get a powerful person in politics to take on the rebuilding agenda or mobilize participants for a letter-writing campaign. Listening to the City participants, too, imagined a continuing effort. "I hope that we will have some kind of influence, being that we were a collective, what you would say an alliance," said one. "Because there's power in numbers." This interviewee went on: "We need to protest, shut things down if we have to, to make sure they commit to really taking our—the stuff we did with the selection process and voting and the whole democracy thing—taking it seriously." Another participant became less confident of the possible impact of the forum, she said, when she saw that "they weren't talking about expanding the process." Indeed, when interviewed a year after Listening to the City, participants complained that organizers had not capitalized on their enthusiasm. "We were never invited to participate again. I think there should have been a second or a third follow-up with the rest of the plans," said one. Said another, "There's nothing that I really see that continues to involve this group of people." As these comments suggest, participants in both forums saw the exercises as something more than a one-time effort to solicit public opinion about rebuilding options. They saw themselves as a *group*, a group that should be mobilized to press for the recommendations they had reached. They operated with a model of political influence that combined pressure with persuasion.

However, these views were in tension with those of the civic coalitions that sponsored the forums as well as of the practitioners who organized them. Imagine New York participants were told throughout the process that the project's goal was to ensure that the voices and ideas of "the broad public" were "heard by decision-makers." When it became clear that rebuilding authorities were unlikely to publicly acknowledge the project's forty-nine visions, the project's organizers had little in the way of an alternate plan. By the time of the Citizen Summit, where participants ratified the visions, organizers had shifted gears, encouraging participants to write their own letters to rebuilding authorities rather than proposing any collective strategy for political influence. Again, with the forum over, participants were treated as properly I's, with their impact to be determined exclusively by their individual actions.[30]

Listening to the City did have an immediate impact when participants vocally rejected all six plans that were being considered. Following huge media coverage of the event, rebuilding authorities withdrew the original plans and invited architects to submit new designs. This was a significant win. But Listening to the City participants had also called for building less office space and for more affordable housing on the site, and rebuilding authorities made no mention of these demands. AmericaSpeaks worked behind the scenes to try to persuade rebuilding authorities to hold another forum, but it was unsuccessful. Publicly, the organization maintained its self-described role as a "neutral, honest broker" and made no public criticisms of the rebuilding process.[31]

The civic coalitions that had sponsored the two forums, for their part, struggled with how hard to press for the recommendations that had come out of the forums. Both coalitions had styled themselves expert consultants in the rebuilding process, and they worried that criticizing rebuilding authorities too publicly would take them out of the consultative loop. One Imagine coalition staffer described her organization's modus operandi as "having a quiet relationship—influential board members talking to people in [the main rebuilding agency]." An activist in the coalition that sponsored Listening to the City explained that there was also reluctance to be perceived as "obstructionist," given New York City's long history of community advocacy derailing development projects—and given the tragedy that had prompted this development project.[32]

Eventually both coalitions became more publicly critical of the rebuilding process and its failure to take up issues outside the narrow purview of the design of office buildings and a memorial. By that time, however, opportunities for public input had diminished. At the time the forums were taking place, New York's governor was up for election. He was sensitive to being perceived as ignoring the needs of the family members of people killed in the Twin Towers, and more generally of being seen as allied with wealthy developers rather than with New York City residents. With his election, some of the ambiguity of authority that had allowed the civic coalitions to press for public input receded. When the governor overruled the choice for the architectural design that rebuilding authorities had arrived at and then the lessor of the site overruled the governor's choice and hired his own architect, it became clear that in the end the public had had little impact even on the design of the buildings, let alone any other uses for the site.

It is worth asking, then, whether the civic groups involved in Listening to the City and Imagine might have been able to win more earlier on. Right after Listening to the City, the public was cast as having virtuously forced narrow-minded rebuilding authorities to change course. This might have been the moment for Listening to the City's sponsors to press hard for more of the recommendations that came out of the forum. Sponsors might have reminded authorities that "the people" wanted not only an iconic tower but also affordable housing at the site. They wanted not only the restoration of the street grid but also a reduction of the amount of planned office space. We do not know, of course, whether sponsors would have succeeded had they adopted a more contentious role. But this is the scenario that the forums' participants, if not the forums' organizers, seemed to have envisioned.[33]

PARTNERS AND PUBLICS

Why were forum organizers so unwilling to consider a more adversarial effort to press for the public's recommendations? Deliberation professionals here, as is usually the case, emphasized their neutrality, and for good reason: it is easier for decision makers to ignore a forum's recommendations if they can say that the process was tainted by special interests seeking to manipulate the public's opinion. Reporters, for their part, may find allegations that a forum has been rigged more newsworthy than the results of the forum. AmericaSpeaks encountered just this problem when it ran a nationwide series of forums on the budget deficit in 2010. The effort was widely criticized when it was reported that a conservative foundation was funding the forums and had set the agenda. Organizers protested futilely that liberal foundations had also funded the forums, that left-of-center groups had participated in setting the agenda, and that forum participants ended up taking a strong liberal position on the deficit. But those facts proved less newsworthy than the whiff of partisan bias. Indisputably, it is critical that sponsors and organizers be seen as committed to a process rather than to a particular set of outcomes. But what about after the forum has been completed? Why should deliberation organizers not press to have the forum's results taken seriously?[34]

Deliberation professionals are not unconcerned about the prospects for citizen discussion to have an impact on policy. As I noted, though, their solution tends to be to involve policy makers early in the deliberative process. Certainly there is nothing wrong with that. In the Lower Manhattan case, as participants themselves recognized, that rebuilding authorities had endorsed the Listening to the City forum—and, indeed, that they appeared at the forum—surely made it more likely that they would take seriously the recommendations it produced. But what if policy makers end up acceding very selectively to the forum's recommendations, as they did in this case, or ignoring those recommendations altogether? In a rare willingness to consider this possibility, the deliberation specialists Allison Kadlec and Will Friedman suggest that deliberation organizers might try to bring forum recommendations into an election debate or use petitions, television ads, demonstrations, or media strategies to press policy makers to respond to the recommendations produced by the forum.[35] I would add that forum organizers might take advantage of the fact that electoral contests offer opportunities for securing allies as well as putting policy makers on the spot, and that the policy-making process invariably involves multiple actors, one of whom may see a benefit in promoting "what the people want."

Why are these strategies so rarely used or even contemplated? I believe there are a couple of reasons. One is that practitioners are specialists in deliberative *process* rather than in deliberative *results*. As the sociologist Caroline Lee observes in her ethnography of the field, practitioners market their services to corporations as often as they do to municipalities, foundations, and civic actors. They are emphatic that the same deliberative methods transfer across these settings. But surely the points of leverage differ in government and corporations. The fact that practitioners are generalists may lead them to ignore outcomes altogether in favor of a focus on process or lead them to consider outcomes at the level of the individual—did people feel that they learned something? did they feel heard?—rather than at the level of the organization or institution.[36]

Another obstacle to pressing for influence, I believe, lies in the "power with" rather than "power over" relationships that deliberation's champi-

ons imagine between the public and policy makers. Remember that deliberation is touted as an alternative to political contention. As the public-
policy scholars Carmen Sirianni and Louis Friedland describe the larger
movement for "civic renewal," of which deliberative forums are a part, "The
master frame of the civic renewal movement stresses the potential role of
government as a 'catalyst' for citizen problem-solving and a 'partner' in
multi-sided collaborative efforts." The movement is opposed to "advocate"
identities and instead "attempts to constitute not an adversarial but a collaborative 'we.'"[37] The problem with this notion of government as a partner
in a collaborative "we" is that it forecloses the option of citizens' exercising pressure on government. In principle, of course, deliberation organizers could aim for a collaborative relationship with policy makers and then,
if the collaboration did not materialize, move to a more challenging stance.
However, if deliberation's sponsors truly do imagine their relationship with
policy makers as one of partnership, that schema may discourage them
from considering actions inconsistent with a relationship of partnership.

In an ethnographic account of municipal decision making in two cities
in America's Rust Belt in the late 2000s, the sociologist Joshua Pacewicz describes just this happening.[38] What he calls "partner politics" emerged in the
1980s in cities that were devastated both by the loss of manufacturing and
by the cuts to federally funded urban development that followed the aban-
donment of Keynesian policy. In that context, community leaders based in
long-standing party networks were replaced by a new kind of leader. These
new leaders were energetically oriented to securing competitive grants
from state, federal, foundation, and business funding sources. They were
willing to make their cities seem all things to all potential sources of outside
investment and were convinced that success lay in erasing any taint of partisan division. They promoted a view of government as about collaboration,
big tents, and win-win solutions. In this new practice of leadership, efforts
to involve residents were aimed at drumming up the civic enthusiasm that
could be used in pitches to outside investors.

Pacewicz describes a series of "Envisioning forums" held in one city to
identify community priorities. The forums took a form virtually identical
to that of Imagine New York, with residents invited to brainstorm ideas for
their city and the resulting ideas turned into a list of vague priorities such as
"support livable neighborhoods." The "partner" who organized the forums
was enthusiastic, describing them as "the heart of the democratic process,
it gives you goosebumps." He and Pacewicz could probably sit down and
come up with a comprehensive plan for the city that was better than what
the forum had produced, he explained. "The difference would be that only

[we] would have ownership of it." By contrast, for citizens participating in the forum, "even if their idea does not make it to the plan, they have been part of the process and you can say, 'This is ours!' [and] *justify whatever plan you can link to it*" (my emphasis).[39] That is, if the partner could identify a funding opportunity, say, for a new arts center, and he could link that to the community's expressed desire for "livable neighborhoods," then he had a win-win solution. He could ignore other, potentially conflicting interpretations of what community members meant by a livable neighborhood — whether it was one without immigrants or one with more public parks. The partner did not see this as manipulative or undemocratic because it was consistent with the way in which partners did politics. Partners did not represent community members by serving as a conduit for their priorities, Pacewicz observes. Rather, partners represented community members in the aesthetic sense of depicting their desires to outsiders in a way that would win outside support.

There is nothing wrong with the idea that the recommendations produced by a deliberative forum should serve as resources in policy makers' entrepreneurial efforts to secure outside funding. The danger, though, is that that is *all* they are: resources, rather than also obligations. The danger is that decision makers feel free to ignore those recommendations that get in the way of their entrepreneurial plans. In the case of the New York City forums, participants wanted architecturally exciting buildings rather than what seemed to be the bland buildings planned (in fact, the initial plans were site plans, not architectural ones, so they were not intended to be architecturally exciting; but no one cleared up the confusion). A staffer within one of the rebuilding agencies told me that he was able to leverage the public's expressed desire to press for the architectural competition his group within the agency wanted. But in the model of partner politics, the other recommendations that came out of the forum — notably, for less office space on the site and more affordable housing — could be ignored. Insofar as the sponsors and organizers of the forums signed on to that model of partner politics rather than the more adversarial model that our interviewees articulated, they were ill-equipped to do much when those other recommendations fell by the wayside.[40]

Public deliberation need not be mere democratic window dressing for decisions that are made elsewhere. The solidarity that emerges from civic engagement need not foreclose efforts to secure responsive government. But striving for a relationship of partnership between citizens and policy makers, at least as that relationship is currently understood, may not be a recipe for such responsiveness.

ALTERNATIVES

Practitioners of dialogue and deliberation are right that the style of abstract reason-giving privileged in classic briefs for deliberation is both unfamiliar and unproductive. They have responded by encouraging participants to speak as "I's," to share personal stories and values and listen respectfully to those of others, and to strive more to understand than to persuade. Those recommendations are certainly worthwhile. But consider too what participants want. Those we interviewed wanted to bring into their discussions the views of people other than themselves. They wanted to bargain and strike compromises rather than only share experiences and priorities. And they wanted their conclusions to be advocated for. I have suggested that those desires are worth paying attention to.

In her study of six dialogue groups that met repeatedly over the course of six weeks to discuss race relations, the political scientist Katherine Cramer Walsh similarly found that participants strained against the norms promoted by dialogue organizers. Participants were repeatedly told by their facilitator that the goal was "dialogue, not debate." In line with that injunction, participants often recounted poignant stories to make others understand what it was like to be discriminated against, or why they had never thought about their Black friends differently than their White ones. They listened to one another respectfully. But the moments in the dialogue when people seemed to genuinely shift perspective occurred when participants defied the ban on debate. Direct challenges and people's effort to rebut those challenges forced participants to think hard about their positions. They prevented White people in particular from sliding by with bromides about everyone being the same and led them to think instead about what a real appreciation for difference would mean. "It was the most intense exchanges that resulted in expressions of 'I didn't realize' and other indicators of newfound awareness," Walsh observed. Talking about their commonalities was the easy part. The hard part was truly recognizing their differences while still envisioning some kind of relationship. The more confrontational exchanges, and the fact that participants strove to make sense of those confrontations and continue talking, allowed them to begin, however tentatively, to build relationships.[41]

In short, productive public talk may admit of more forms than often recognized. What about the New York City participants' desire to represent groups outside the forum? And their desire to stay involved in advocating for the recommendations they arrived at jointly? With respect to the second, it should be possible for policy makers to have a more communicative back-and-forth with their constituents. On a model of what the political scientist Jane Mansbridge calls *recursive representation*, policy makers listen to what their constituents want, account for what they end up deciding, and do so repeatedly.[42] Something like that kind of recursive representation characterized city planning in Grand Rapids, Michigan, as studied by the public policy scholars Kathryn Quick and Martha Feldman.[43] Over the course of twelve years, Quick and Feldman found, some public engagement efforts mounted by city managers were perceived as highly democratic and produced plans that sailed through the city council with little controversy. Other efforts were perceived by residents as democratic in name only and often ended in stalemate. In the latter category, curiously, was an initiative that combined a citywide survey with community meetings intended to solicit residents' priorities for city services to be preserved in the face of budget cuts, priorities that were then entered directly into the budget. And in the former category, perceived by residents as truly democratic, was a citizens' advisory panel of just twenty-one members who provided only nonbinding recommendations to the city in the face of the same budget cuts.

Why was the less representative and nonbinding initiative perceived as more democratic? One key difference was the kind of communication that went on between city managers and participating residents. In an earlier effort to update the city's master plan, which involved thousands of participants and hundreds of meetings, planning staff not only provided participants the information they asked for in the course of their discussions, but, noting that discussants kept talking about finer-grained development decisions, launched a set of parallel discussions about those issues. Planners encouraged participants to work with local businesses to draft land-use plans for several neighborhoods, all of which were incorporated into the updated master plan. When participants expressed interest in how the plan would be implemented, planners initiated a new public process for creating zoning ordinances, and then another public process for creating environmental standards. In subsequent updates to the plan, managers used what they called a "50/50 rule," in which 50 percent of participants would have had prior involvement in the process and were thus familiar with the issues and the process, and 50 percent were new, in order to bring in hitherto-unrepresented perspectives. City managers did not incorporate everything residents wanted into the plan, but they kept coming back to explain why they decided what they did.

The effort to make necessary budget cuts by surveying residents on their preferences for cuts—the seemingly democratic and binding initiative—came after this process, and it met with widespread condemnation for simply presenting residents with either-or choices that they had had no say in framing. In response, city managers scrapped the plan and invited the most vocally critical residents to serve on a new advisory panel. The intention was to convene a new set of public meetings, but the panel members argued that the wide range of opinions among them made additional meetings unnecessary. City managers agreed and provided the targeted information that advisory panel members requested in the course of intense and extended discussions. In their discussions, panel members reported also on concurrent conversations they were having with friends, neighbors, and co-workers. The result was a set of budgetary priorities for this and future budgeting cycles. City managers ended up making cuts in line with those recommended by the panel, including laying off members of their own management team. The process also made clear, however, the difficulty of saving the city's pools and parks in the face of future budgetary pressures. In response, city managers formed a mayor's blue-ribbon panel, on which several panel members served, and then a nonprofit organization dedicated to securing outside funding for the city's parks.

Over and over again, then, city managers asked residents to weigh in on issues, assisted them by providing tailored information in response to their questions, and then responded to their recommendations. Residents represented the groups of which they were members by seeking out their views and bringing them into the discussion. City managers, for their part, responded to residents' recommendations by, variously, altering the decision-making process, altering substantive policies, and creating a new organizational mechanism for protecting a community resource that residents cared about. One could call the relationship between residents and city managers collaborative or, indeed, a partnership, but I want to emphasize the extent to which the partnership was actively negotiated. City managers accepted conflict. Indeed, the managers' goal, said one, was to "arm [residents] for a better fight" by providing them information.[44] Managers felt bound to respond to residents' demands and concerns, though not simply by acceding to them, and they treated public engagement exercises as a way to build an ongoing relationship rather than as evidence that such a relationship was already in place. These features of the relationship that government and citizens created—its acceptance of conflict and its orientation to the longer term—seem to me to be important to democratic relationships more broadly.

CONCLUSION

Democracy is based on rules, but also on relationships. I do not mean that in the sense that legislatures accomplish little without relations of trust, and often friendship, among members; nor do I mean it in the sense that the bonds people form in their volunteer groups and bowling leagues contribute to a larger sense of civic trust. Rather, I mean it in the sense that people's ideas about how to *do* democracy, and what to expect from it, come from familiar relationship schemas.

The case for public deliberation begins with the claim that the schemas available to us today are impoverished. After all, we vote and then become passive observers while our representatives do the bidding of shadowy actors whose clout depends on money and connections. We arrive at our opinions on political issues within a small circle of intimates and encounter the views of people outside those circles only in caricatured form. Meanwhile, our representatives are exposed to our opinions as data points in one of a never-ending series of opinion polls. The deliberative exercises I have described in this chapter seek to create new schemas for relationships among citizens and between citizens and their representatives: ones that are more trusting, more open to diverse perspectives, and more thoughtful than those we typically have. Deliberative exercises try to create these relationships by gathering ordinary people and asking them to share something about themselves; giving them topics to discuss and asking them to do so in a respectful way; providing them materials to inform their discussions; and then asking them to come up a set of recommendations for policy makers. Forum organizers strive to create a relationship of egalitarian intimacy among participants and a relationship of partnership between participants and policy makers.

I have argued, though, that forum participants drew on a more extensive repertoire of relationship schemas. Although few had participated in public deliberation before, they were familiar with relationships that can be characterized, in different ways, as democratic: juries, school boards, focus groups, town meetings, Congress, the United Nations. Forum participants drew on these and other relationship schemas to characterize what they were doing and, I argue, to do it. The schemas gave them a sense of how to deliberate: how to talk and listen, how to disagree without antagonizing each other, and how to define success.

The schemas that forum participants drew on suggest that they understood deliberation differently than did organizers. Forum organizers envisioned participants sharing their personal stories and values and coming to recognize areas of agreement. They imagined participants discovering bonds of affection and respect that would last until the end of the forum. Forum participants, by contrast, were comfortable with the idea not only of recognizing areas of agreement, but also of hashing out compromises where there was not agreement. They thought about compromise not as a way to avoid changing their minds, as organizers tended to conceptualize it, but rather as a way to change their minds without seeming fickle. Participants also felt that their diversity gave them the mandate and, importantly, the responsibility to act for the wider public. They wanted to speak as representatives for their own group as well as for groups not present. Finally, participants saw less tension than did organizers between deliberation and advocacy.

These differences are important, I have suggested, because they point to an alternative to deliberation conventionally understood. In this alternative, participants speak both as "I's" and as "we's." They seek out and bring into the discussion the views of family, friends, and community members outside the forum, they work out compromises between themselves and imagined others, and they move from deliberation within the group to advocacy on behalf of it. My point is not to celebrate the wisdom of ordinary people against the narrow-minded expertise of professionals. Indeed, nonexperts' vision of the political process is blinkered in all kinds of ways. My point, rather, is that ordinary people are less committed to a single model of what democratic deliberation should look like. Instead, they draw on and combine diverse familiar ways of working together for the common good—some that they have directly experienced, others that they have observed. They capitalize on the convenience and mutuality of expectations associated with those models while adapting them to the situation at hand.

For deliberation practitioners, the lesson is not necessarily to remake deliberation along the lines of what participants want, but rather to consider what it would mean to reconceptualize the relationships that make up deliberation. Would deliberative outcomes be truly compromised by relaxing the ban on participants' reporting on the opinions of people in their circles rather than speaking only as individuals? Would allowing participants to aim for compromises really make deliberation too much like bargaining? And would treating policy makers as partners when they behave like partners and targets when they do not threaten deliberation's status as an alternative to special interest–dominated politics? Identifying the relationship schemas that underpin contemporary approaches to deliberation may open up possibilities for modifying those schemas.

Clearly, we need new ways of conceptualizing the relationship between the public and policy makers. In this regard, although briefs for public deliberation begin with the impoverished bond between citizens and their representatives, their solution focuses mainly on citizens' relationships with each other. They do not talk about citizens' relationships with their representatives. But as the political scientist David Plotke points out, more public participation is not necessarily the best solution to insufficiently representative democracies. "The opposite of representation is not participation," Plotke observes. "The opposite of representation is exclusion. And the opposite of participation is abstention."[45] In Plotke's view, the challenge is to make democratic representation more truly democratic, not to compensate for its failures by way of more citizen participation.

The metaphor of partnership is appealing insofar as it highlights cooperative norms that we think of as democratic. What would happen, the metaphor encourages us to ask, if citizens, advocates, and political representatives saw themselves as equally responsible for, and necessary to, achieving reform for the common good? What if those actors approached their interaction with the assumption that their interests were congruent rather than conflicting? Again, the schema's cultural familiarity is important. Even if we have not had the experience of business partnership, we have some basic sense of what it entails and what it requires in order to work effectively. The schema can encourage people to approach their interactions in a new way, with at least some expectation that other parties to the interaction will respond in kind.

My concern, though, is that although metaphors of relationship have the power to encourage new modes of interaction, they also have the power to describe modes of interaction as something other than they actually are. In particular, I argue, such metaphors can evoke equality and solidarity in a way that makes it seem as if inequalities and conflicts have been overcome. Consider in this regard another relationship that recently has been vested with democratic possibility: the crowd. Crowds used to be seen as irrational and dangerous. People were swept up in crowds, surrendering their capacity to make independent decisions and becoming prone to violence and destruction. In recent years, however, crowds have been reinterpreted. In books such as the journalist James Surowiecki's *The Wisdom of Crowds*, the Internet guru Howard Rheingold's *Smart Mobs*, and the media scholar Clay Shirky's *Here Comes Everybody*, crowds are portrayed as producing informed decisions, not irrational ones, and as engaging in surprisingly generous rather than destructive action. Crowds have the ability to accomplish things fast, with a minimum of negotiation. In a crowd, status and power differences fall away as people appreciate each other for their contributions to the task at hand. These and other virtues are claimed by those who promote crowdfunding, crowdsourcing, and other crowd-based, often digitally enabled collective action.[46]

However, as critics have noted, crowdsourcing initiatives not uncommonly capitalize on crowds' association with casual, informal fun to obscure the fact that they are asking people to contribute their labor for very little in return. And in fact, many participants in crowdsourced projects are not the much-vaunted amateurs described by crowdsourcing enthusiasts, but underemployed professionals who are hoping that this job might help them latch on to something more permanent. "Collaboration" and "co-creation" similarly have become business buzzwords but, critics say, are just new names for getting people to do more for less.[47] Relationships termed "flat," "participatory," or "democratic" can likewise serve as slippery metaphors, endowing practices that are not those things with democratic bona fides. And the metaphor of "partnership," I have suggested, can operate to discourage challenge, even when it has become clear that the putative partners are not fully on the same side. The caution I want to lodge, then, is that while a new metaphor for a political relationship can highlight values that deserve enactment, this should not substitute for striving to enact those values.

CHAPTER FIVE

The Art of Authentic Connection

Relationships, after all, are the one thing you can't commoditize.

DON TAPSCOTT AND ANTHONY D. WILLIAMS,
Wikinomics: How Mass Collaboration Changes Everything (2006)

Imagine that you are walking by a shallow pond and you see a small child in it, struggling to hold her head above the water. There seems to be no parent or adult nearby. The child will drown if you do not wade into the water and grab her. But you are reluctant to do so. You have on expensive shoes and they would be ruined.[1]

This would not be you, of course. The idea of standing by instead of helping anyone, let alone a small child, and, worse yet, standing by because you fear sullying good shoes surely seems offensive. And yet standing by is what you do when you fail to send money to the victims of a hurricane in Houston or ethnic cleansing in Myanmar—and perhaps buy yet another pair of shoes instead. You would object to this characterization, of course. The people in Myanmar are far away. You do not know them or know their situation. You cannot be responsible for the pain of everyone in the world. But how far should your sense of responsibility extend?

The challenge of distance is one that humanitarian groups wrestle with. But it is also one that regularly confronts groups seeking to combat homelessness or poverty, or fighting for the rights of undocumented immigrants. How do you convince people to care about people in need whom they do not know? How do you convince them to care enough that they will support the cause represented by those people—that they will give money, lobby their political representatives, participate in demonstrations, or vote for candidates who are aligned with the cause? The very words we use to denote feelings of caring depend on relationships. We would not say that parents felt compassion or pity for their injured baby. We feel compassion and pity for strangers, not intimates. To say that we feel love, worry, or pain for strangers would sound odd.[2]

Yet, this is not always true. When a baby named Jessica McClure fell into a well in Midland, Texas, in 1987, the nation was riveted to its televisions as emergency workers labored for fifty-eight hours to rescue her. Hundreds of thousands of dollars' worth of donations poured in. President Ronald Reagan observed that "everybody in America became godmothers and god-fathers of Jessica." Reagan captured the "as if" relationship presumably felt by donors: Jessica wasn't kin, but she was something close to it. At the same time, scores of children were suffering from the aftereffects of the recent famine in Darfur, Sudan. And countless American children, some of whom were located in the same towns as donors, were suffering from poverty, homelessness, and abuse. That "as if" relationship did not extend to them. The distance was too great.[3]

In this chapter I consider the people whose job is to try to build rela-tionships between Americans and those who are distant from them. The distance is sometimes geographic, as is true for the advocates who work with sex-trafficked young women in Cambodia; but it is also social, eco-nomic, and/or political, as is true for the advocates who work with homeless Americans or transgender young people or women who have had abortions. The connection advocates try to create may be aimed simply at getting the person targeted to give money to the cause or to click on an Internet peti-tion, but in most cases advocates hope that the relationship will endure. The British fundraisers for humanitarian causes whom the communication scholars Shani Orgad and Bruna Seu interviewed often talked about want-ing donors to "go on a journey" with them, with the implication that in the course of that journey, they would forge a lasting relationship. Similarly, the advocates I interviewed often talked about wanting the people they tar-geted to themselves become advocates for the cause.[4]

If the deliberation specialists I described in the last chapter also sought to create solidarity among strangers, the advocates I treat in this chapter in some ways have a more difficult job. Most of the time the strangers they must bring into relationship never even meet. The bonds are completely in-vented, and they require more than simply talking with one another. They require giving something up: money and/or significant amounts of energy and time. Certainly, advocates today have resources for relationship build-ing that their counterparts fifty years ago did not. They have the technologi-cal means to make strangers visible and audible and to do so with music, narrative plotting, and high production values. But they also labor under new constraints. Advocates know how to produce messages that will tug at audiences' heartstrings and elicit their pity. But they are deeply wary of manipulating their audiences and, worse, of exploiting the people who appear in the videos or on the fundraising dais to tell their story. Advocates are unwilling to ask victims to perform their suffering. They reject relationships that are, as they put it, transactional. They want potential supporters to come to know those affected by the issue, but to know them as being just as agentic and self-aware as they are. They want to create relationships characterized by both intimacy and something approaching equality.

To handle that challenge, advocates can draw on a veritable industry of experts in eliciting and producing people's personal accounts of social injustice. They can hire coaches to train people to recount their personal stories, and media producers to craft the kind of video that, with any luck, will go viral. They can participate in one of the many workshops and webinars that offer guidance on how to recount people's experience. They can seek funding from one of a dozen foundations that offer financial support for new storytelling initiatives. And they can consult one of the hundreds of books, articles, blog posts, and websites that offer the three features, five ingredients, or four secrets of effective personal storytelling.[5]

The result, I argue, is a set of norms for how to describe one's experience in ways that "connect"—this is the term my interviewees often used—victims with potential supporters. Advocates learn how to appropriately recount their experiences or those of the people with whom they work. And what do their accounts look like? They feature a performance of what I call *modulated suffering*. Victims do not wallow in their pain. They subtly betray their emotions rather than performing them. They show "scars, not wounds," as one advocate put it. They express hope more than hurt; display resilience rather than pain. They focus on the detail of their abuse that audiences can easily understand and perhaps have experienced. They share their experiences with the implication, if not the reality, that their audiences will reciprocate with their experiences in turn.

Advocates maintain that they have figured out how to empower victims at the same time as they raise funding and build public support. Yet, I am not convinced that the result is a win-win for everyone involved. Aside from the fact that the people affected by an issue may sometimes *want* to talk about their suffering, there may be experiences that should not be neatly packaged as inspirational. In addition, new modes of sharing personal experiences take a great deal of skill. Conveying just the right amount of wry self-consciousness, capturing the detail of an experience that seems telling rather than trivial, knowing, as one interviewee put it, when tears are appropriate; those things demand fairly specialized know-how. Professionals help, but a reliance on professionals is in some conflict with the notion that people gain power from telling their own stories in their own way. Moreover, because storytelling consultants often market their services to diverse organizations, including for-profit companies as well as nonprofits and advocacy groups, they are not especially expert in the distinctive institutional requirements of telling stories in a congressional hearing, say, rather than in a fundraising luncheon. In these ways, contemporary norms for sharing experiences in advocacy may disserve those whom they are supposed to help.

In chapter 2, I criticized scholarship that overemphasized the role of White liberals in launching the southern civil rights movement. Still, it is almost always the case that movements of and by oppressed groups also depend on support from the privileged. If that support is to be based on solidarity rather than charity, says the philosopher Klaus Peter Rippe, the privileged should also have a stake in the movement: "The concerns of the assisted are therefore always related to the assistant's own interests, values or goals, or become so in the course of the solidarity process." The question, though, is how far advocates should go to persuade potential supporters that the movement is, in a sense, about them. Surely, there are significant differences between the experiences of members of the oppressed group (the assisted) and members of the privileged group (the assistants). Yet, the advocates my team interviewed were confident that a certain kind of communication, namely, personal storytelling, could create solidarity across those gaps. The deliberation specialists I described in the last chapter were similarly confident that dialogue could bridge the interests of diverse citizens and those of citizens and policy makers. Professionals in both cases acknowledged that communication could be used to disguise unequal relationships rather than build equal ones. But they insisted that *authentic* communication could avoid those things. And they maintained that they could train people to communicate authentically. My question is whether that was true. And even more broadly, it is whether a relationship of egalitarian intimacy, crafted through professionally facilitated forms of communication, is a good model for democratic solidarity.[6]

TALKING RELATIONSHIPS

The idea that communication is important to creating relationships is so widely accepted today as to go largely unnoticed. Yet, as the sociologist Eva Illouz has shown, it was only with the ascendance of a therapeutic cultural repertoire in the early to mid-twentieth century that communication came to be seen as central to good relationships. Beginning in the 1920s, psychologists offered guidance to the American military, advertisers, and corporate management. In the workplace, for example, the psychologist Elton

Mayo's substitution of a "human relations" model of management for that of scientific rationality led corporations to pay increasing attention to affective relations among workers and to cooperation arrived at through skilled communication. The communication required of managers involved empathetic listening as much as forceful talking, as well as putting oneself in the place of the other in order to craft an effective self-presentation. Communicative competence became the sine qua non of good management and the standard of corporate success.[7]

As the psychological profession grew and diversified after World War II, it reached larger swaths of the public and deeper into Americans' lives. The emphasis on communication remained strong. It was central to the rise of the humanistic psychological approaches that came to dominate therapy and counseling. Thus the psychologist Carl Rogers wrote in 1951 that "the whole task of psychotherapy is the task of dealing with a failure in communication. . . . We may say then that psychotherapy is good communication, between and within men. We may also turn that statement around and it will still be true. Good communication, free communication, within or between men, is always therapeutic." Improving communication had benefits extending beyond individuals, moreover, to groups, organizations, and nations. The psychiatrist Harry Stack Sullivan, for example, who coined the term *interpersonal*, brought to the newly founded United Nations Educational, Scientific and Cultural Organization (UNESCO) the idea that better communication could resolve conflicts among nations.[8]

Inflected with a feminist ethos in the wake of the women's movement in the late 1960s, communication came to be seen as essential to intimate relationships between men and women. "Equality, fairness, neutral procedures, emotional communication, sexuality, overcoming and expressing hidden emotions, and centrality of linguistic self-expression are all at the heart of the modern ideal of intimacy," Illouz writes—all goals to be arrived at through communication. As the women's magazine *Redbook* put it, "Communication is the lifeblood of any relationship." And as the sociologist Anthony Giddens reports, "Any and every therapeutic text on the subject of relationships will demonstrate why revelation to the other—as a means of communication rather than emotional dumping—is a binding aspiration of democratically ordered interaction."[9]

The key to building successful relationships was talk. But it was talk that was prescribed by professionals—psychologists, counselors, therapists, and human-relations experts—and relationships that were rationalized in a Weberian sense. And it was talk infused with a distinctively American belief in self-improvement—Freud democratized. Thus, the therapeutic injunction to recount one's own suffering that gained force in the 1970s was accompanied by an optimistic faith that doing so would free one from the grips of an original trauma. From the talk show host Oprah Winfrey on down, Illouz argues, Americans confessed their experiences of abuse, addiction, and self-loathing as a way to free themselves from the demons that had prevented them from achieving psychological, and often worldly, success.[10]

Illouz's account does not capture the widespread discomfort with stories of suffering and, more broadly, with therapeutic discourse that became common in the 1990s. The discomfort extended to those who used stories of suffering for humanitarian causes, and it was voiced by the advocates my team and I interviewed. Asking people to disclose their suffering on demand came to be seen as a fake intimacy, profoundly at odds with a commitment to respecting people's dignity and agency. But I want to make note of another tension that accompanied the growth of expertise in relationship building. On one hand, the goal of interpersonal communication was self-realization, becoming the self that one truly was through mutual recognition by an empathetic other. And at the same time, communication was a strategic tool, a way to pursue instrumental goals by treating the other not as a source of recognition, but as the object of one's persuasive efforts. The belief in communication as a way to forge relationships has always borne with it the nagging anxiety that the same communicative tools could be used also to manipulate. The relationships created by communication might be exploitative ones.

The anxiety persisted as whole professions emerged to manage relationships at work, at home, and in civil society by means of specialized forms of talk: not only public relations specialists, marketing experts, management consultants, psychotherapists, and coaches, but also public engagement specialists, organizing trainers, development specialists, and facilitators. Such professions have always had to defend themselves against the charge of manipulation. Anxieties of influence, moreover, have been articulated not only by people outside the professions, but also by those within them. Public relations textbooks, for example, consistently represent the history of the field in terms of its historical evolution from manipulation to two-way dialogue. To neophytes, textbooks thus articulate the worry and present it as solved.[11]

We can see the same anxiety among the specialists in public dialogue and deliberation that I profiled in the last chapter. As the sociologist Caroline Lee shows in her ethnography of the field, specialists often locate their own origins in the movements of the 1960s and proudly echo those movements' belief in popular empowerment. They see themselves as missionaries for a process that can truly transform the way people interact. At the same time, however, they enthusiastically promote their services to corporations wanting to secure employees' acquiescence to downsizing initiatives and to municipalities charged with reducing services. Simultaneously marketing their deliberation services and bemoaning the marketization of the public sphere does not feel inconsistent, however. What matters, as deliberation specialists see it, is that deliberation be authentic. Trained in therapeutically informed fields of life and workplace coaching and facilitation, specialists insist that participants spend time getting to know each other's motivating values and to dig deep into their own experiences. They discourage conflict and work tirelessly to ensure that no one feels marginalized or demeaned.[12]

If deliberation is authentic, specialists maintain, then it can be used in any venue without jeopardizing its integrity. What specialists do not consider, however, is the possibility that, no matter how authentically the forum itself is structured, the reasons for having a forum or the purposes to which a forum's recommendations are put may undercut its democratic character. As I argued in the last chapter, if decision makers are free to pick and choose among the recommendations that emerge from a forum without having to justify their choices, then it is hard to imagine that the forum could still be structured in a democratic way. But the premium on authenticity turns the political problem into a technical one. Authenticity becomes something that can be broken down into its component parts, taught, and evaluated. Authentic deliberation is made into deliberation that is managed expertly, with participants encouraged to speak from the heart, domineering speakers gently curbed, and the group adroitly moved to common ground rather a premature or coercive consensus. In the process, deliberation specialists—and, I argue, other professionals charged with building relationships by way of talk—simultaneously pose the risk that talk can be used for manipulative purposes and locate the solution in the kind of talk that is used. The authentic feel of the talk becomes synonymous with the authenticity of the enterprise itself.[13]

In similar fashion, the storytelling specialists I will describe in this chapter pose the danger of exploiting people by packaging their stories for consumption by well-to-do audiences and then avert the danger by packaging their stories in the right way. They use stories to craft a relationship. Their artfulness lies not only in the sense that they are strategic, but also in the sense that what they create is an aesthetic representation of a relationship. It depicts the parties as equal and autonomous, depicts their disclosure of intimacies as reciprocal, and depicts their bond as based on shared experiences. Specialists sometimes produce those representations themselves, but they also coach people affected by the issue on how to represent themselves. And they do so with the conviction that they are helping storytellers to be true to themselves in the process.

CHANGING ACCOUNTS OF THE SUFFERING SELF

I had not realized that progressive advocates had become so enthusiastic about personal storytelling until I was contacted by a foundation executive who had read my earlier work on the topic. His foundation was providing training in personal storytelling to all its grantees who worked in advocacy, and he wanted to know whether telling stories worked. I said I had no idea but that the first question, probably, was figuring out what "working" meant. Accordingly, with my students Tania DoCarmo and Kelly Ward, I began interviewing advocates who used storytelling. We ended up interviewing sixty-eight people who recruited people to tell their stories, coached them on how to do so, coordinated the performance of their stories for different audiences, and/or produced their stories for use online or in other media. Interviewees were staff members of advocacy groups or of nonprofits serving the groups from which storytellers were drawn, communication and strategy consultants who contracted with advocacy groups, and organizers who worked with advocacy groups on training and leadership development. As opposed to participants in more grassroots organizations, the people we interviewed worked as paid staff. They used stories variously to raise funds, advocate for policies, and raise public consciousness. The stories they helped to produce were often delivered in person (in speeches to potential donors, congressional testimony, and interviews with journalists), but they were also written up in brochures, ads, articles, and blog posts and turned into online videos. The issues with which they were involved included homelessness, immigration, the rights of sex workers, issues facing drug users, the rights of transgender people, reproductive choice and justice, human trafficking, and police brutality. These were predominantly progressive causes, and with the exception of some participants involved in anti-trafficking, most of our interviewees identified as progressive.[14]

Why has storytelling become so popular now? Probably for several reasons. Losses around reproductive rights and welfare and wins around marriage equality and the undocumented student Dreamers convinced many advocates that telling personal stories was the best bet for winning the hearts and minds of the public. At the same time, and from a very different perspective, messaging professionals who were expert in digital communication maintained that evocative personal stories had the capacity to cut through the barrage of information to which people were subjected daily. A new field of public-interest communication emerged in the 2000s, distinguishing itself from public relations in its orientation to nonprofits. Firms in the field promoted storytelling as a way to raise funding, secure media coverage, and build public support. Meanwhile, public health researchers had turned to personal storytelling to encourage positive health behaviors such as mammogram screening and safe sex. Finally, foundations embraced storytelling, first as a way to communicate about the work they were doing, and then as a political strategy in its own right. "Another day, another storytelling initiative," led a 2016 article in *Inside Philanthropy*.[15]

STORIES IN RELATIONSHIP

The advocates we interviewed were convinced that having people recount their personal experiences with the issue in question, whether abortion or sex trafficking, homelessness or immigration, would powerfully advance their cause. And they believed that stories worked by forging a bond with the audience. Told well, personal stories enabled audiences to connect emotionally with the advocate: "allows somebody to really connect with an individual" (an anti-trafficking advocate); "connect with a person" (a human-rights advocate); "connect emotionally" (an anti-homelessness advocate); "gets to emotional connectedness" (an antipoverty advocate); "connect . . . with people" (a women's-rights advocate). That connection, our interviewees argued, should last past the moment of hearing or seeing the story. Stories should help to forge a relationship. As an antipoverty organizer explained, stories provided "an opening for a relationship." "Storytelling [is a] medium of relationship," an anti-trafficking advocate explained. "That's the whole point of telling a story: just to deepen a relationship." The relationship forged through storytelling would lead donors, legislators, and ordinary people to act on behalf of the cause. In telling stories, "you're trying to engage a community of people around your work, to become your advocates," as an anti-trafficking advocate put it.

Note the goal that audiences would become advocates, not benefactors or donors. Parties to the relationship that advocates sought to create were not equal in terms of wealth or influence, but their joint commitment to the cause would equalize them. Interviewees took pains to distinguish their approach from one associated with marketing and public relations. In that approach, our interviewees explained, storytelling was an instrumental rhetorical tool. Public relations experts encouraged organizations, including nonprofits, to create a "story bank" of organizational stories that could be trotted out to demonstrate progress and impress funders. These experts talked about "demand-side" and "supply-side" issues in the provision of digital stories.[16] The economistic language was striking, and our interview-ees emphatically rejected it. They were sharply critical of what they called "transactional" or "extractive" storytelling, in which tellers were treated simply as the producers of valuable objects that were then taken from them and circulated in remote networks. An immigrant-rights activist and an antipoverty activist both criticized stories becoming a kind of "currency."

Instead, stories should build a relationship, and a relationship based on empathy, not pity. "The best stories are when the audience will have some level of personal connection to it," an anti-trafficking advocate explained, but then emphasized, "It doesn't just have to be someone sharing all of the gory details of their abuse . . . [it should not be] a relationship of pity be-tween the audience and the person who was abused." People should tell their stories in a way that led audiences to have the same "respect [for them] that they hold for themselves and they hold for decision makers," as an immigrant-rights advocate put it. The relationship should benefit the teller as much as the audience and the cause. It should be "empowering."

For this reason, interviewees were adamant that storytellers should not have to perform their suffering. "[I hate it] when the value gets placed on emotion and it's great when someone cries," an organizing consultant averred. Telling one's story of pain on command could be "retraumatiz-ing," since such stories could force survivors to relive their suffering. "What are the ethics of bringing people in over and over again to tell a traumatic story?" a progressive filmmaker asked rhetorically. An economic-justice or-ganizer said flatly, "If it's still traumatic for somebody, then the campaign doesn't mean that much to [make it worth it to] traumatize, retraumatize people." "Almost having to relive this experience can also have the potential to be traumatizing," an anti-homelessness advocate observed.

Advocates' wariness of personal storytelling in this respect reflects a widespread reaction to the performances of suffering that became common in the 1990s. The more familiar part of the reaction was the wave of conser-vative attacks on victims as self-pitying crybabies, who appealed for help rather than taking responsibility for their own condition. But a very differ-ent line of criticism asked whether telling stories of suffering was beneficial for the tellers themselves. Criticisms of South Africa's Truth and Reconcilia-tion Commission and other transitional-justice initiatives were in this vein. The goal of such initiatives was that victims gain therapeutic closure from having their experiences of abuse witnessed and validated. Critics pointed out, however, that storytellers were being forced to relive experiences of torture and violence not in therapy, where storyteller and therapist could process the experience over a period of time, but rather before an anonymous audience and with little follow-up. The result could be psychologically damaging. These concerns spread to storytelling in other settings. Requiring that women tell their stories of sexual assault in court only forced them to relive traumatic experiences. Pushing people who had experienced disasters such as 9/11 to tell their stories to counselors risked immersing them in situations that they would be better off processing in their own way and in their own time. Our interviewees' frequent reference to the possibility that telling one's story could be retraumatizing suggests their familiarity with these criticisms. They were committed, they said, to protecting storytellers, to preventing their being exploited or turned into an object of compassion. "An object of compassion is still an object," as one put it. Again, telling one's story should be empowering, not demeaning. Accordingly, advocates' job was to create a relationship between tellers and audiences both of intimacy and of something close to equality.[17]

That was a tall order. How does one create intimacy between people separated by distance and experience? And how does one create anything like equality when one party has money and sometimes political influence and the other does not? How does one get audiences to care about another person's suffering without encouraging that person to seem to be a victim, lacking agency and power? The answer, interviewees explained, was to tell authentic stories. An organizing consultant declared, "People need to tell their stories in ways that are authentic to who they are." An economic-justice organizer explained that stories should be told "in an authentic way that's real and true to their experience"; and an advocate for transgender youth wanted "young people to be able to speak out in a way that felt authentic to them." Stories should be expressions of tellers' experience, identity, and perceptions; they should not confront their tellers as something alien and apart.

One can imagine, though, that stories told the way the teller wanted might not be especially persuasive to audiences. The teller might come off as pathetic or self-aggrandizing, mired in self-pity or angry and off-putting. His story probably would be meandering, at times confusing, at others boring. Interestingly, in this respect, interviewees also talked about stories' authenticity in another, quite different way from the one I just described. Authentic stories were true to the audience rather than to the teller. They revealed something to the audience that was fundamental and important about the teller's experience. An abortion advocate described an authentic story: "Look into my eyes. I have a heartbeat and I'm a real person." And a progressive filmmaker: "We want to really reveal . . . the authenticity of all these families." How-to guides similarly defined authenticity in terms of the story's relationship with the audience, not with the teller. "Authenticity is what sustains the connection between your audience and your character," as one put it.[18]

To be sure, the two meanings of authenticity could be made consistent—stories could be made true both to teller and audience—if the teller focused on reliving the experiences she described. In fact, this is what popular guidelines on personal storytelling outside the world of advocacy sometimes advise. For example, a piece in the *Huffington Post* on writing authentically counseled, "If you can recall that specific moment of your life and channel it while you're writing your piece, hopefully the tears from your eyes or the wave of nausea that passes over you is a sure indicator that what's getting typed will connect with those who are reading your work." But using this standard in the field of advocacy would require storytellers to relive their experiences of suffering, something to which advocates strenuously object.[19]

Interviewees did not wrestle with this tension, I believe, because they were confident that stories could be crafted so as to be simultaneously empowering for the teller (authentic in the first sense) and effective for the cause (authentic in the second sense). This was why expertise in storytelling was essential. Authentic storytelling was not spontaneous storytelling, our interviewees agreed. As an advocate for Serbian women's rights observed, "If it is an authentic story, no matter how much time you invest in rehearsing that, it will still be an authentic story." An anti-homelessness activist agreed: "You have to coach. I mean, that's all there is to it. . . . With any storytelling endeavor, there has to be a sense of rehearsal, of timing, of intentionality." These views were consistent with how-to guides produced by messaging and fundraising consultants, which similarly insisted that effective storytelling required specific tools.[20]

Interviewees also described strategies to protect the storyteller even before she told her story. They took care to make storytellers understand they might have a permanently public role, and that they might not now be able to anticipate how they would feel later about their story circulating in public without their permission. When storytellers had had traumatic experiences, interviewees strove to determine whether they were ready to tell their stories. Interviewees described stopping journalists' questioning when it became intrusive and pushing back against people in their own organization who were asking them to supply what they perceived to be voyeuristic accounts.[21]

More surprising, however, was the suggestion by many of our interviewees that the same things that protected the storyteller also gave the audience access to her. This was true in two senses. First, interviewees suggested that storytelling by its very nature made for both equality and intimacy. And second, they suggested that stories communicating the teller's autonomy, agency, and dignity, which were the stories people wanted to communicate, were also the stories that audiences wanted to hear. I will outline these views and then identify the potential problems they created.

STORYTELLING AS ESSENTIALLY EGALITARIAN

Our interviewees, like the countless briefs for storytelling available now, emphasized the fundamentally human quality of storytelling. Interviewees asserted that people "are hardwired for storytelling," that people have been telling stories for thousands of years, and that we are "storytelling animals." In either a physiological or anthropological sense, then, storytelling is who we as humans fundamentally are. How-to guidelines for advocates similarly cited research on readers' altered brain patterns to argue that people are "wired" to remember stories, that "narrative is basic to what it means to be human" and that people are "narrative animals." The literary critic Barbara Hardy was quoted in how-to materials: "We dream in narrative, daydream in narrative, remember, anticipate, hope, despair, believe, doubt, plan, revise, criticize, construct, gossip, learn, hate and love by narrative. In order really to live, we make up stories about ourselves and others, about the personal as well as the social past and future." Storytelling was thus characterized as universal and natural.[22]

There was rarely any distinction made in these briefs between telling stories and hearing them. The needs of speakers and those of the audience meshed: as much as audiences naturally wanted to hear the stories of those affected by the issue, those affected wanted to tell their stories. Storytellers were not being forced to do something that was foreign or unappealing to them. Moreover, if everyone lived in and through the stories they told and heard, then storytelling required no natural talents; it was inherently egalitarian. Stories could be more or less effective, but with a little coaching, anyone could tell a persuasive story.

Our interviewees framed storytelling as egalitarian not only in the sense that it was a form available to all, but also in the sense that it was inherently reciprocal. When an interviewee said that humans are "kind of campfire people," the image was one of stories traded among a group rather than that of a performer speaking to a passive audience. Often the imagery invoked was one of an intimate encounter. Thus, a blurb on a handbook for storytelling as an advocacy tool observed that "when two people sit down to tell stories from their lives and to listen, something happens"—this, although the book was about telling stories to much larger and often distant audiences. In the same vein, advocates often described people "sharing" their story rather than telling it. Recall the communication scholar Nicholas John's argument that the contemporary language of sharing conflates communicative and distributive meanings of the term: sharing means communicating in a self-expressive and therapeutic way *and* allocating things in an egalitarian manner. Sharing stories was thus assimilated to the equality-matching relationship that anthropologist Alan Fiske describes. Sharing stories implied reciprocity. Rather than a "transactional" or "extractive" relationship, in which tellers were treated simply as the producers of valuable objects that were then taken from them and circulated as a form of political currency, the relationship between teller and audience was made reciprocal and therefore egalitarian.[23]

In most advocacy contexts, though, storytelling was not reciprocated in the sense that audiences told their own stories. Some groups, especially those involved in grassroots organizing, did insist that trainers, leaders, and those new to the organization share their stories as a form of leadership development. But in most cases, the storytelling went in one direction. The audiences were either large ones, in the case of public presentations, or were not likely to tell their stories in return, in the case of journalists or policy makers.

THE AESTHETIC REPRESENTATION OF AGENCY

The relationship between victim and supporter was made simultaneously intimate and egalitarian also in how the subject was represented in the story. Our interviewees, as I noted, emphasized that stories could be crafted and rehearsed and still be authentic to the teller's experience. An authentic story was not necessarily told spontaneously. Rather, the goal was that the subject would not be "embarrassed by it and they would still own their story and say yes, this is mine," an anti-trafficking advocate said. A fundraiser for a Cambodian anti-trafficking group used the language of kinship: she hoped that audiences would say, "If this was my sister . . . this is actually how I would want that story told."

Interviewees were also agreed on how people would want their story told. They would want to be represented as agentic, dignified, and as hopeful rather than despairing. It was a misconception to think that authentic stories were "very difficult scenarios," said an organizer who worked with low-income people. "That, for me, is a very important piece to really work on. That it's not actually about trauma, it's about agency." An anti-trafficking advocate noted: "I think particularly the picture of the girl being rescued and being completely helpless, it's a very negative picture in trafficking because it kind of gives the impression of they're just needing complete and utter help and there's nothing we can really do, nothing they can do to help themselves. Which of course is really unhelpful for them."

Another anti-trafficking advocate recounted that his group had "really shifted gears to not telling the individual rape stories . . . [but instead a] story about an individual girl's move towards the future, what her hopes and dreams were, what she was becoming, what she's learned about herself, and moving further away from salacious details that quite frankly are personal and belong to that particular survivor." Anti-trafficking advocates in particular, but others too, insisted that painful stories were disrespectful to the subject of the story. "[I want to find] storytellers, the clients, who are able to speak from a position of power instead of a position of victimization and vulnerability," said one. The strategy was ethically motivated: the point was to avoid exploiting the storyteller. However, interviewees also dismissed "sob stories," "victim stories," or "despair porn" as ineffective. An anti-trafficking advocate explained, "Part of the healing process is not to carry guilt and shame because of what's happened to you. And when a girl is able to do that freely, then that's a win-win. It helps the organization, it helps not just the organization, it helps the cause." A child-rights advocate insisted, "You don't have to rely on the sad pathetic pictures of starving children to generate people's interest and concern. When you see people being empowered, then they feel happy to be able to give money." A human-rights activist observed, "If the stories are developed with more emphasis or focus on the challenge, it comes out like a pity story or a victim story. And I don't think it works much for—people wouldn't want to share it anyway."

Note how the last interviewee shifted from saying that victim stories were unappealing to the audience to saying that they were unappealing to the teller (who "wouldn't want to share it anyway"). An anti-trafficking advocate made the same shift when describing the importance of conveying "hope" and "how important it is to not just smack people over the head, punch them in the face with this awful message. That's not enough, and it also doesn't serve a client very well either. It reinforces all these ideas about pity that we can have toward people in a different culture." Donors admired organizations that portrayed survivors with dignity, one advocate observed. Interviewees often used aesthetic terms. One wanted to tell "beautiful stories of redemption," and another worried that negative images "strip people of their agency"—as if positive images would give them agency.

The point of telling stories of resilience and hope was to honor the teller's dignity and agency. But it was also to appeal to audiences who were turned off by despair porn and inspired by stories of overcoming. In this vein, a writer in the *Nonprofit Quarterly* complained about storytelling becoming "abuse" when nonprofits featured children in their efforts to raise funds. Such storytelling was "re-traumatiz[ing]" for the children, she wrote. But it also did not work in a practical sense. In the case she featured, it led funders to fund the wrong things.[24] Again, the argument remade the ethical problem as a practical one. More generally, advocates alluded to a possible tension between an instrumental commitment to using the story and an ethical one to not "using" the storyteller, and then solved that tension: telling stories ethically also happened to be what made them effective.

Advocates thus equalized the relationship between the victim and supporter by representing the victim as agentic, dignified, and hopeful. Representing victims as hopeful gave audiences hope, and when one represented victims as empowered, as a drug-legalization advocate promised, "then you"—meaning the audience—"also get empowered."

MODULATED SUFFERING

To be sure, one should not omit the suffering altogether. In her study of contemporary humanitarian appeals, the communications scholar Lilie Chouliariaki argues that communication specialists have traded a politics of pity for what she calls a politics of ironic spectatorship. There is little effort to forge a bond of solidarity between the sufferer and the donor. Instead, the emphasis is on the donor's experience rather than that of the sufferer. Helping is represented as easy and fun. By contrast, I find that victims still appear in advocacy groups' stories. They appeal not to the audience's pity, though, but to something more intimate and egalitarian; they seduce the audience without discomfiting it.[25]

In analyzing a collection of videos that our interviewees rated as effective, my collaborators (Jessica Callahan, along with DoCarmo and Ward) and I were struck by the fact that the people featured in the stories tended not to display strong emotions. For example, in a video commissioned by anti-homelessness organizations, a young man described his homeless childhood as a series of adventures. His account of living in cars and under bridges was interspersed with original rap lyrics and images of dragons. In a matter-of-fact tone, and betraying no sadness or resentment, he recounted being turned down for jobs and finding it difficult to fall asleep in indoor spaces as a result of his chaotic upbringing. A video produced by the Center for Reproductive Rights and picked up by multiple media sites featured the actress Jemima Kirke, famous from the television series *Girls*, recounting the story of her abortion. In an affectless tone, she described discovering she was pregnant and deciding to have an abortion. The only point at which she showed some emotion was when she wryly laughed before saying that she did not have enough money for the abortion and had to borrow it from her boyfriend. We found this pattern in other online videos. Sometimes the subjects were simply happy, determined, or hopeful. But often the subject was shown either struggling to restrain his or her emotions or speaking in an intriguingly flat tone.[26]

Advocates occasionally encountered well-meaning fundraisers or other advocates who urged them to push storytellers to cry, they said. But they retorted not only that doing so was unethical, but that it was unnecessary. A filmmaker recounted, "I definitely have worked with some organizations who are all about making their subjects cry on camera because they feel like that's what's going to get the best total response. I push back and say no, it's if your audience cries at the story, not necessarily if your subject cries." Indeed, too much emotion on the part of storytellers could backfire, alienating audiences rather than affecting them emotionally. An advocate for women's rights told of hearing a young woman tell a deeply moving story to a small group about abuse she had suffered and inviting her to tell her story to a larger group. When she became emotional, "it just didn't work," the interviewee observed. "It felt like she was just—everybody was: what's the point of this? And it felt awkward. It felt awkward for her, it felt awkward for the audience." Similarly, an anti-trafficking advocate described a situation in which a survivor broke down in tears during a fundraising event in a private home. "We walked out of there with zero dollars, the entire event," he commented. "And it was because it was emotionally moving but it was really awkward." Another anti-trafficking advocate observed, "It's not that tears are always a bad thing but . . . you have to be intuitive in those moments to know if it's okay or not." The goal was that survivors are "able to own that past and they present it like it's a scar, not like it's a gaping open bleeding oozing wound . . . the best storytelling is scars."

The point of modulating tellers' emotional performances was to treat them with respect, to avoid a voyeuristic presentation of victims overcome by pain. But the resulting performance also avoided discomfiting audiences and possibly made the performance even more engaging, because audiences knew that at any moment the teller might dissolve in tears. Adopting an affectless tone may have indicated to the audience that the story was so traumatizing that the storyteller could only disclose the unemotional parts of it. The audience was invited in to elicit the meaning of the tight grin or the shaky voice. Again, the same thing that, according to advocates, made storytelling ethical—that tellers were discouraged from performing their suffering—was also what made it effective.

JUST LIKE YOU

Storytelling consultants instructed storytellers to focus on the particulars of the events they recounted. They should precisely describe what they saw, heard, and touched. Doing so would give the audience a sense of witnessing the events being recounted. Coaches encouraged storytellers not to explain or interpret events or even to describe their emotions. Rather, they should capture the details: whether a car was blue or green, whether the doctor was wearing glasses, and so on. However, storytellers should not provide indiscriminate detail. A storytelling coach recounted, "A woman told a story about a coal mining town where the coal mining company . . . was so cheap and so controlled the light for the town, she said they didn't even put up streetlights in the town. They told the people that, in their houses, . . . at a certain time every night, they had to turn their porch lights on. That's how they lit the streets. . . . I said those are the details where the *authenticity* of a story really starts to ring true" (my emphasis). What made the story authentic was that the woman provided the *telling* detail. She captured the coal company's tightfistedness in a single, mundane experience of having to turn on one's porch lights every evening to light the street. The task of authentic storytelling, in this rendering, was to capture the detail of one's experience of injustice that would best illuminate the injustice to the audience.[27]

The illuminating detail tended to be the one that was familiar to the audience. An article in the *Nonprofit Quarterly* advised storytellers to "ensure others can see themselves in the story" as one of the "Five Ways for Nonprofits to Tell an Ethical Story," elaborating: "We can all be inspired to give money or time because we see our own moments of need reflected in our neighbors' stories." Note the author's argument that *ethical* storytelling required that the audience see itself in the story. Similarly, a how-to guide on storytelling quoted the executive director of a center serving religious minorities: "We never want to 'other' our clients," in their storytelling, the director said. "We want people to relate." Casting clients as similar to audiences was a way of treating them respectfully. "Asking people to tell their stories is ultimately not about you; it's about the storyteller, since this is a very personal process for most," a storytelling guide counseled, emphasizing, like our interviewees, the importance of being true to the storyteller. "If, however, *you take the time to listen fully and authentically, you are likely to hear stories that reflect both your key messages and messages that will resonate with your audiences*" (my emphasis). Again, expert-guided authenticity was what connected the needs of the teller and those of the audience. A communication consultant criticized a union's messaging campaign during a strike of rapid-transit workers. The union erred in showing the transit workers in their trains, she explained, "rather than showing them with their families or coaching Little League or whatever it is they *authentically do*" (my emphasis). One might ask why operating a train was not what train workers authentically did. In the contemporary discourse of storytelling, the answer was that what was authentic to the teller just happened to be that which made the teller similar to her audience.[28]

Sometimes advocates argued that the person who might connect with the audience was either not the most typical victim or not the victim at all. Storytellers who did not fit the stereotype might effectively challenge the stereotype. "The more surprising or unlikely a storyteller is, the better," explained an anti-homelessness advocate. He went on: "To illustrate my point, if [the formerly homeless person] looks like an executive, nice pressed suit, and they've been working at their job that pays a living wage for X number of years and then they come in and then they share their story about how addiction had led them on the street and they were spiraling into substance abuse for five plus years and now they've been clean and sober for the past five because of a program that allowed them to get off the streets, that's pretty powerful. . . . Oh wow, I never would've expected that person to have that story." A story like this would make clear to audiences that they too could fall victim to the issue in question. Their middle-class status would not necessarily have protected them from homelessness, abortion, or unemployment. This in turn could build the empathy that would lead audiences to act on behalf of the issue.

Alternatively, stories might feature not the victim himself but the person who helped the victim. A video created to spur American intervention in Syria combined footage of an infant being rescued from a collapsed building in Aleppo with an interview with the rescue worker. Because the infant was saved, the focus was on heroism and triumph rather than on suffering. The film also relied on the same modulation of emotion that we saw in victims. After the rescue worker recounted the rescue, the interviewer asked him if had visited the family of the infant since then. No, he said, with a knowing laugh; there was no time. The camera lingered on his face as he seemed to be processing emotionally the fact that there were so many lives to be saved, and so many lives lost. The effect was to give the audience the sense of being present in the moment when the rescue worker realized the enormity of his task. The rescuer contained his emotions, but the viewer had the sense that doing so was difficult.

In another example of focusing on the heroes rather than the victims, advocates for the homeless in an American city proudly described a video they had produced featuring a landlord who had decided to rent to formerly

homeless people and another one about a community that helped a homeless family. Advocates in this approach told the story not of stigmatized
groups, but of their supportive allies, who tended to be more like audience
members. The effort to empower the victim by challenging stereotypes of
typical victims thus dovetailed neatly with the instruction to ensure that
audiences be able see themselves in the story. Advocates recognized, however, the danger of presenting the supportive ally as a hero rescuing a piti-
able victim. This would be at odds with a view of storytellers as agentic.
Accordingly, stories of heroic allies tended to include passing testimonials
to the agency or courage of the victim. For example, in the video in Syria,
the rescuer noted the courage of the two-week-old infant he helped rescue,
although courage is not something we commonly associate with infants. In
an anti-trafficking video that was told from the point of view of a man who
liberated a trafficked young woman, the man said, "she inspired me with
her determination and courage," although the film up till then had given no
indication that the man even knew the young woman.[29]

RISKS OF THE CONTEMPORARY
DISCOURSE OF STORYTELLING

Interviewees were contemptuous of a style of storytelling they characterized as victim storytelling. Asking victims to retell their stories was voyeuristic and exploitative. It asked people to define themselves in terms of their
pain and represented them as without agency, there to be helped only by
way of the intervention of the audience. In the alternative that interviewees
favored, one did not wallow in one's emotions; one subtly betrayed them.
One emphasized hope as much as pain, resilience as much as suffering.
One used irony to demonstrate one's distance from the trauma. Stories told
in this mode, interviewees argued, were true both to the teller and to the
audience.

But were there also risks associated with storytelling in this new register? Yes. For one thing, victims sometimes wanted to tell stories of their
suffering. An interviewee worried, he said, that people "default to trauma"
in their stories. But framing the problem in psychological terms implied
that telling a story of suffering was necessarily bad for the teller, which it
may not have been. Certainly, the stories curated by advocates never depicted subjects as angry or indignant. One interviewee wrestled with the
liabilities of that decision. She had done a participatory filmmaking project
with Latina teenagers who were mothers. The young women told a variety
of stories, she said; some happy, some not: "[They were] difficult stories that
maybe they hadn't told before like grief around their mother's death or stuff

about sexual violence. . . . Still the executive director, when she saw them, she was very critical. And she said, you know, these are not the kinds of narratives that we want to put out there. These are victim narratives. We want to show the positive aspects of what our girls do . . . [she wanted] to stay away from stereotypes or negative portrayals of all the trauma and drama that these girls have gone through. But that's kind of ignoring the reality of their experiences." A development consultant I quoted earlier, who argued for telling stories of empowerment, remarked: "But I suppose the other side of that, though, is a lot of the work we do isn't always about success stories. Sometimes we do a lot and at the end of the day, things are still really difficult." The two options of victimization or resilience—or, as the participatory filmmaker put it, "narratives that are either problem-saturated and oppressive or relentlessly upbeat"—did not encompass storytellers' experiences.

Choosing as storyteller the person who defied the stereotype, for its part, risked compromising advocates' commitment to empowering the people most affected by the issue. The danger was that only the most acceptable representatives of the group would tell their stories: the undocumented students who were high school valedictorians, the women who aborted only because fetal anomalies had been detected, the elderly people who lost their home when their landlord raised their rent, the people who had contracted hepatitis C through a blood transfusion rather than drug use. An interviewee described with dismay a training session for advocacy around transgender issues she had attended in which the trainer explained that they wanted the "right-looking" transgender people to be spokespeople.[30]

There may have been more narrowly instrumental costs to relying on personal storytelling and on professional consultants in personal storytelling. Some experimental research suggests that while personal storytelling is effective in persuading people to change their own behavior—to wear sunscreen, for example—it is not effective in persuading people to support the kind of social change that requires government action. Audiences tend to focus on what the person featured in the story might have done to change her situation rather than on what policies are needed to help people like her. In the same vein, an interviewee complained that poignant personal stories of homelessness sometimes led audiences to want to contribute money to the person or family featured—not to the organization combatting homelessness.[31]

I noted that advocates' frequent references to story sharing implied that storytelling was reciprocal, which it rarely was. But had stories been truly shared, would the exchange have been empowering to those affected by the issue? Proponents of intergroup contact initiatives, in which members of groups with histories of conflict are brought together to talk, cite compelling evidence that the mutual self-disclosure involved in such talk leads to reductions in prejudice. However, some researchers have found that members of subordinate groups typically want to talk about different things than members of dominant groups: subordinate-group members want to talk about disparities in group-based power, while dominant-group members want to talk about commonalities in experience. One can imagine, then, that intergroup contact perceived as successful insofar as the group shared stories and recognized commonalities might be deeply unsatisfying to members of the subordinate group.[32]

Another series of studies found that something like story sharing could combat ill-feeling on the part of both dominant and subordinate groups, but it would have to be a form of story sharing that was quite different from that championed by storytelling experts. The research showed that while dominant-group members benefited from taking the perspective of subordinate-group members, say, by hearing or reading their stories, that was not true for subordinate-group members. They benefited instead from having dominant-group members hear their stories and communicate back that they understood them *as they, the subordinate group members, intended.* I emphasize the latter part of the sentence because it runs directly counter to the instruction that those affected by an issue tell their stories in a way that their audiences can identify with, and indeed, that they focus on experiences that their audiences have had. This, advocates say, is necessary to storytelling that empowers members of subordinate groups. But the research on intergroup contact initiatives challenges that claim. It suggests once again that the storytelling that benefits the audiences for advocacy storytelling may not benefit the storytellers themselves.[33]

The professionals who taught people how to tell their stories, for their part, marketed their services to for-profit groups as well as to nonprofit and advocacy groups. This made sense, they argued, since the essentials of telling an effective story were the same whether the audience was a corporate board, congressional representatives, or social media users. In fact, however, the requirements of effective storytelling probably differ across institutional settings. For example, research suggests that public audiences tend to be turned off by a clear "ask" at the end of a story, but policy makers expect the ask. Narrative consultants may not have been well equipped to counsel advocates on which kinds of stories were institutionally required.[34]

One could certainly have assessed these possibilities. Were there ways to tell personal stories that connected to the larger social problem? Could one balance the needs of storytellers and the needs of the audience? Were there distinctive requirements of stories told in particular institutional settings? But there was little effort on the part of consultants or advocates to engage in those kinds of assessment. Nor were there efforts to assess the relative costs and benefits of personal storytelling that was upbeat and emotionally modulated, with familiar characters and dilemmas. Surprisingly, given foundations' usual insistence on measuring initiatives' impact, storytelling seemed to have been insulated from that requirement. Instead, proponents' reference to stories' natural qualities of intimacy and equality seemed to be enough to warrant their use.[35]

ALTERNATIVES

It may make sense strategically to represent those who suffer from injustice as agentic and hopeful, if that is what is needed to compel people to support them. And there may be real benefit to the victims of injustice in encouraging them to recognize their own agency and develop a sense of hope about the future. The problem to which I have drawn attention, though, was in the conflation of the effort to empower and a representation of people as already empowered. That conflation obscured trade-offs that advocates might have wanted to consider before making. Had they instead distinguished tasks of empowering victims from persuading audiences, advocates might still have asked victims to tell their stories in ways that emphasized their hope, resilience, and similarity to their audiences. But advocates might also have acknowledged the sacrifice storytellers made in doing so. Alternatively, recognizing that a storyteller's empowerment did not depend on forging emotional intimacy with the audience might have made it easier for that person to gain a sense of power from her ability to communicate persuasively to an audience. Emotional support, meanwhile, would come from a circle of real intimates.[36]

Two of our interviewees who had been trained in community organizing described something like that. There was often a division of labor in community organizing, they said, where one person affected by the issue would tell their personal story to policy makers, and another person affected by the issue would articulate the group's demands or describe the importance of the policy reform they sought. In the next encounter with policy makers, the person who had told her story would move up the ladder of leadership to articulating the group's demands. The sociologist Ruth Braunstein similarly describes an interfaith organizing group training a woman to recount her struggles with health care in a public meeting with a health official. When she told her story, her satisfaction came from the audience's applause and the praise she received from her fellow organizers, not from any feeling of intimate connection with the official. An interviewee who worked with people with hepatitis C said that people in his group who told their stories of illness publicly were also asked to master a great deal of technical information so that they could "engage in debate with any kind of scientist or pharma rep." The power here came from mastering and delivering a story effectively as part of the process of fighting for reform.[37]

A filmmaker described another approach to storytelling, this one modeled on the educator Paolo Freire's ideas about participatory learning. Sharing one's experience with sympathetic but critical others was an opportunity to identify the structural forces that shaped those experiences. Stories here figured as material for political education. An advocate who worked with Latina women on issues of reproductive justice explained that the experiences shared by teenage mothers in the group became the basis for the group's agenda. When the young women recounted the injustice of high school athletes not being penalized for absences to attend games while they were penalized for missing school to care for their children, the group decided to fight for policy change on that issue. Storytelling was empowering insofar as it translated politically unrecognized needs into group goals.

How were these views of storytelling different from the ones on which I have focused so far? For one thing, they assumed a world in which the powerful and the powerless rarely shared interests. The advocates were on the side of the storytellers. Advocates did not rule out the possibility that storytellers might connect emotionally with their audiences, that policy makers might be persuaded by their accounts, or that donors might throw in their lot with the cause. But they did not assume common interests. Second, and I believe more important, there was a telos to the relationships forged in storytelling. People who told their stories then went on to present the group's demands. People who told their stories first in individual terms went on to explore their experiences in more structural terms. People who told and heard stories then turned those stories into an agenda for action.

As I said, interviewees who articulated these views of personal storytelling tended to be community organizers or people familiar with Freirian popular education. It makes sense that those working in communication and fundraising, by contrast, were more comfortable seeing a communicative form on its own as capable of forging a solidary relationship. And indeed, an organizer contrasted storytelling's use "as a tool in organizing versus being used as a tool in communicating publicly." That said, the line between the two views was not bright. Organizers also sometimes invested storytelling with the power to overcome barriers of wealth and power. This suggests to me the operation of a wider discourse about personal storytelling, part of an even wider discourse about the power of rationalized communicative forms to forge relationships of egalitarian solidarity by way of intimations of intimacy.

CONCLUSION

The experts in public engagement that I described in the last chapter and the advocates that I described in this one turned the values of egalitarian intimacy into a model for solidarity across difference. That they were able to do so is surprising. After all, among the challenges they faced was that the people whom they sought to connect had vastly different amounts of political power. Dialogue and deliberation specialists aimed to connect ordinary citizens to political decision making, but they did so with the knowledge that decision makers were under no obligation to accede to citizens' recommendations. Advocates for the homeless and the victims of trafficking aimed to build a relationship between people affected by the issue and those with the political influence and economic resources to help them, but to do so without exploiting people who had already suffered.

These were difficult, perhaps impossible, tasks. And yet experts in dialogue and deliberation and in personal storytelling managed to turn them into technical and solvable ones. They did so by way of their expertise in distinctive forms of communication—of talk. If done right, they argued, talk could forge relationships across differences of experience and opinion, as well as differences of power and status. As Caroline Lee observes with respect to dialogue and deliberation specialists, a true belief in the civic power of deliberation was precisely what allowed deliberation specialists to sell their services to corporations and municipalities. The champions of advocacy storytelling who featured in this chapter believed just as firmly that encouraging victims to tell stories of hope and barely betrayed pain empowered them as much as it appealed to donors. Like specialists in deliberation, they believed in the authenticity of relationships as a bulwark against manipulation. And like those specialists, they treated authentic relationships as ones that could be crafted following a set of prescribed steps. Advocates learned how to produce something like an aesthetic representation of authenticity. They produced victims who displayed just the right amount of agency to seem dignified, just the right amount of suffering to need help without being off-putting, and just the right amount of hope to make audiences feel that their help could make a difference.[38]

But I have identified liabilities, both narrowly practical and more broadly ethical, in the schemas of political relationship that figure in public deliberation and advocacy. A schema of partnership made it difficult to leverage the power of the deliberative forums. An insistence on stories' intrinsic persuasive power discouraged advocates from assessing just how effective storytelling was. More generally, I disputed the notion that deliberation organizers were empowering participants by representing them as unified around priorities that happened to mesh with those of potential investors. And I disputed the notion that advocates were empowering storytellers by representing them as equal and intimate with potential donors. In each case, a relationship of equality was artfully rendered rather than interactively arrived at.

In the end, a communicative style is not equipped on its own to forge egalitarian political relationships. Simply becoming expert in storytelling is not enough to equalize the relationship between rich donors and the people who appeal to them for money and support. It is not enough to protect the people who tell their stories from feeling exploited or used. A solidary relationship needs to extend in time. And an egalitarian relationship needs to be actively worked out rather than simply depicted.

CHAPTER SIX

Solidarity without Intimacy

Most of the time we understand each other quite well; we just don't agree.
JOHN DURHAM PETERS, *Speaking into the Air* (1999)

In previous chapters I criticized the idea that we can best build solidarity by encouraging people to share their stories, recognize their commonalities, and become something like friends. This idea animates the intergroup contact initiatives that bring people together across lines of ethnic, religious, and political conflict. It underpins also the dialogue programs, deliberative forums, and advocacy storytelling I have described in previous chapters. While recognizing the appeal and, indeed, the virtues of such approaches, I have also faulted them for putting too much faith in the power of self-disclosing talk to erase long-standing inequalities and for providing an only momentary experience of intimacy without the possibility of developing an enduring relationship. I have also criticized them for operating on a model of politics in which people interact only as individuals rather than as members of groups. Other critics add that since intergroup contact initiatives are voluntary, they involve people who are already predisposed to want to connect with others across the usual divisions. They do little to break down barriers among the people who are most invested in those divisions.[1]

But there are other ways to build solidarity across difference. Rather than going small, one can go big. We need a stronger sense of our superordinate identities, in this view. If your and my Americanness felt truly central to who we were, more central than our partisan identities or our ethnicity or whatever identity it was that made us distrust or dislike each other, then those differences would not inhibit our sense of commonality. I will take up the solidarity-building promise of national identities in the next chapter. For now, I want to consider another answer to the question of how to build democratic solidarity. A perspective associated with the nineteenth-century writer Alexis de Tocqueville and the political scientist Robert Putnam today traces broad political solidarity to the voluntary organizations that are established for other purposes. Such purposes range from worship to neighborhood improvement to, most famously, bowling. Voluntary organizations are integrated into people's lives rather than existing apart from them, authors in this perspective point out. In such organizations, people develop skills of civic engagement. But they also develop the trust in people outside their circle of intimates that, in turn, forms the basis for more generalized trust: trust in other citizens, groups, and political institutions. The solidarities forged in civil society thus produce solidarity in the first, Durkheimian, sense in which I have used it: a sense of shared obligation to the laws, norms, and institutions of the society.[2]

There are problems with the argument. For one thing, the organizations that people join on their own tend to expose them to people who are like them, which does not do much to increase their trust in diverse others. This is why Putnam and other scholars emphasize the importance of bonding ties with people similar to oneself and bridging ties with people who are different. The second is as important as the first in producing norms of reciprocity and trust in diverse societies. Creating bridging ties is easier said than done, though, especially in a society, such as ours, that is segregated by ethnicity, race, class, and now political partisanship. Moreover, as I suggested in the last chapter, what may seem like a bridging tie to me, a tie highlighting your and my fundamental sameness, may seem to you like one more effort to deny our differences under the guise of a superficial amity. Still another problem lies in a preoccupation with the socializing functions of voluntary associations. The emphasis is on building citizens' trust in their political institutions, not in building their capacities to transform those institutions. But the challenge of developing broader solidarities may not be easily detached from the challenge of developing responsive political institutions. To the contrary, citizens' trust in government may depend on winning reforms that make government more responsive and fairer. Citizens' trust in their fellows, for its part, may depend on reforms making their status more equal.[3]

All that said, I do believe that we can learn something about the conditions for solidarity by paying attention to the internal life of voluntary civic organizations. But it is not the character of the bonds that occur naturally among members that is important, in my view, so much as the norms that are communicated for members' interactions with each other and with people outside the group. Some organizations may promote schemas of civic relationship that are more egalitarian and more committed to unity-with-difference than is typical. Indeed, and contrary to the Tocquevillian perspective, group members may not even need to have direct contact with people outside the group to begin to imagine new ways of treating them. Organizations may also produce new schemas for the appropriate relationship between citizens and their political representatives.

Importantly in this regard, relationship schemas as I understand them bridge the real and the imagined. People can start out with an imagined relationship schema and strive to put it into practice in their everyday interactions. Or their everyday encounters may give rise to a new relationship schema. In the course of their interactions, they develop new expectations about what is owed to those interacting, new notions about how the obligations of the relationship should change over time, new customs for dealing with difference and conflict, and new ideas about what equality or political representation more broadly might mean. In this chapter I show these things happening. I discuss union members who supported economic redistribution, congregations that admitted gay and lesbian members, volunteer groups that built lasting ties across boundaries of class and race, community organizers who taught people to confront power, and activists who created radical democracies within their own organizations. I also describe aristocrats who came to enjoy equality and work teams that began to genuinely cooperate—not civic associations, but still revealing something important about the kinds of voluntary interactions that build solidarity.

In each case, people imagined and acted on ties that were, variously, more inclusive, empowering, egalitarian, and cooperative than usual. They did so, however, not by talking the way intimates do. They did talk—in fact, they talked a lot—but in genres and registers different from those we associate with intimate relationships. Rather than personal self-disclosure, they engaged in serious reflection about group responsibilities, status-leveling humor, and direct challenge. There was nothing especially easy or natural about the relationships they forged. Their newness made them difficult to practice; it certainly made them difficult to sustain. Accordingly, I pay attention not only to the conditions in which groups arrived at new relationship schemas, but also to what made it possible for those schemas to guide other people in other interactions. I will talk about the contrasting virtues of play and reflection in forging new relationship schemas, and also about the power of collective rituals in sustaining them. Durkheim argued that rituals reinforce solidarity by taking individuals out of the routines of daily life and reenacting their essential groupness. I argue that rituals can work to reinforce new solidarities well as old ones, infusing new relationship schemas with a power and appeal that transcend narrow calculations of interest. Such rituals can take diverse forms, as I will show, including even processes as seemingly prosaic as collective bargaining. In some ways con-

trary to Durkheim, moreover, I argue that rituals can reinforce forms of solidarity that emphasize difference alongside sameness.[4]

SOLIDARITY IN UNIONS, CHURCHES, AND VOLUNTEER GROUPS

Why are the citizens of some countries more supportive of redistributive
policies toward the poor than others? The political scientists Nadja Mossiman and Jonas Pontusson seem to take a page from Putnam when they argue that we should look neither to self-interest nor to citizens' commitment
to principles of equality, but rather to voluntary institutions—in this case,
unions—to better understand the conditions in which people develop a
wider sense of solidarity. Previous research had shown that union members
are more supportive of redistributive policies than nonmembers but tended
to attribute that difference to the idea that unions provide people information on what their material self-interest is. Mossiman and Pontusson argue
something different. Unions that organize mainly low-wage workers usually
have as a central policy commitment the compression of wage differentials.
Those unions communicate to their members norms valorizing equality,
the authors theorize. Union members then draw on those norms when they
assess the government's proper role in responding to inequality. Note that
high-wage workers should also encounter and adopt these norms. And note,
too, that the norms' effect does not depend on direct contact between high-
wage workers and low-wage ones—here, the authors depart from Putnam.
The policies pursued by the union are invested with, and sustain, a schema
of what—of *who*—the union is. High- and low-wage workers are exposed to
that schema, and the normative commitments that come with it, when they
hear about union policies and the reasons for them.[5]

Supporting the argument, the authors find across twenty-one countries that union membership is associated with support for redistributive policies, and that the union effect is stronger for high-wage workers.
That is, high-wage workers in nations that focus on organizing low-wage
workers are more likely to support redistributive policies than those in nations whose unions organize primarily high-wage workers or those whose
unions organize both. None of the factors that we usually rely on to explain
people's willingness to act on behalf of others—namely, their self-interest,
their commitment to principle, or their direct solidary ties—explain the
union effect on high-wage workers. Instead, in my terms, union policies
communicate an imagined relationship, one in which workers are more or
less equal. High-wage workers, like low-wage ones, use that relationship to
think with—in this case, to think about national welfare policy.[6]

We can see a similar dynamic in some American churches. When have Protestant churches opened their doors to gay and lesbian members? Few denominations provide guidance about membership for gays and lesbians at the congregational level, and surveys suggest that Americans remain ambivalent about homosexuality. Clergy, for their part, often avoid what they see as a politicized issue. Which congregations, then, define that which binds them in a more inclusive way? A national survey of fifteen hundred congregations found, predictably, that congregations with more liberal traditions (that is, not operating on the principle of biblical inerrancy) and with more highly educated members tended to welcome gay and lesbian members. Even taking account of these other factors, however, congregations that engaged in interracial worship were over one and a half times as likely to offer membership privileges to gays and lesbians. Why? The sociologist Gary Adler argues that such congregations had customs of bridge building—interracial worship was one such custom—that encouraged engagement with multiple forms of difference. Adler's argument is not that adopting interracial worship activities led directly to congregants' openness to lesbian and gay members. Rather, they both reflected a congregational model, a sense of who members were as a congregation. Again, in my terms, that relationship schema of congregation was enacted in practices and rituals such as interracial worship and extended to include gay and lesbian members.[7]

Studying not congregations, but congregation-based organizing coalitions (I will describe these in more detail later), the sociologist Ruth Braunstein and colleagues probed how coalitions dealt with the challenges posed by differences of race, ethnicity, and class among their members. The authors' national survey showed that coalitions facing such challenges were significantly more likely to rely on interfaith prayer vigils than those that were not. The authors observed these vigils in one coalition, which included people of multiple faiths, income level, race, and ethnicity. Clergy from different faiths led prayers together, often in more than one language. Sometimes clergy pointed out commonalities among the various faiths; sometimes they celebrated differences; and sometimes they combined and synthesized prayers, drawing from multiple holy writings. Members, for their part, were taught the rituals of other traditions: learning, for example, how to pray toward Mecca. The prayers often involved physical actions: members were asked to sing, hug, hold hands, learn new postures. The rituals helped to build a sense of solidarity that was based at once on sameness—communicating the message that members were all people of faith—and on difference, communicating the message that members were made stronger by the differences in their faiths. Ritualized practices enacting an inclusive understanding of the group's identity were thus important in fostering a wider solidarity. Note that these practices did not simply celebrate a superordinate group identity: we are all workers, we are all Christians, or we are all people of faith. To use Braunstein and colleagues' phrasing, group rituals *organized* differences rather than suppressing them.[8]

In an ethnography of church volunteer groups seeking to build just the kinds of bridging ties that Putnamesque scholars recommend, the sociologist Paul Lichterman similarly noted the role of group customs and rituals. Lichterman followed eight middle-class Protestant groups in a midwestern city who sought to respond to the Clinton-era welfare reforms by building solidarity with poor people. One group was a coalition of congregations, social workers, county welfare agency staff, and the directors of homeless shelters and food pantries. Worried that people on public assistance would lose what safety net they had, the coalition sought not only to coordinate efforts but also, in the words of its charismatic leader, Donald, to "rebuild the caring structures of our community." A smaller group of church volunteers launched a series of Fun Nights to prevent at-risk teens from falling prey to drugs and violence. An evangelical group formed an Adopt-a-Family program to connect middle-class church families with families whose breadwinner was making the transition from welfare to work. Other groups similarly identified problems that they could tackle by working directly with the city's poor.[9]

Of the eight initiatives Lichterman studied, seven failed. Either the group disbanded altogether or gave up the effort to create wider civic bonds. This was not because volunteers lacked commitment or energy. And insofar as all were church members, they participated in prayers emphasizing their fellowship with others. Rather, the problem lay in customs that were distinctive to each group. It lay in ways of interacting and especially, norms of talk, that defined the group. For example, Donald, the minister who encouraged his coalition to transform the landscape of civic life, actively stopped anyone in meetings from reflecting out loud about what such a transformation might look like. When coalition members tried to get the group to talk about their larger purposes, Donald cut them off by asking whether they had an "action proposal"—what the speaker wanted people to *do*. His relentless orientation to action over talk—a "do, don't talk definition of civic action," Lichterman calls it—led the coalition quickly to retreat to a familiar style of operating, in which groups simply reported on the initiatives they were pursuing and then discussed logistics of how to supply volunteers, coordinate timetables, and so on. There was no reason to have those discussions in such a large group, though, and the coalition foundered. (Interestingly, Donald did encourage talk in the monthly "dialogues" he sponsored, which were intended to build ties between liberals and conservatives. But there, Lichterman observes, the talk "was personal, confessional, biographical—about people's formation as individuals, not about how a group might form itself in relation to its civic context." In my terms, egalitarian intimacy provided inadequate basis for solidarity among groups.) Meanwhile, Adopt-a-Family volunteers were discovering that relating to families in poverty was more difficult than they anticipated. Just as the coalition's style of privileging action over talk kept them operating within existing grooves, the Adopt-a-Family volunteers clung even more firmly to their idea of a relationship of "Christlike care" in the face of difficulties and then, still frustrated, began to drift away from the program. Over and over again, volunteer groups' customs—in particular, styles of talk reflecting the group's sense of who it was—limited their ability to forge enduring connections with a larger circle.[10]

The one group that succeeded in building civic ties volunteered in a low-income, multilingual, mixed-race neighborhood. When they began their work, volunteers planned simply to do what the neighborhood social worker told them to do. But over time, they decided they wanted to put in place more enduring resources: to hire a public nurse to serve the neighborhood and create an eviction-prevention fund that would help people at risk of losing their homes. In figuring out how to do these things, volunteers began to wrestle with how they as a group could work most effectively with people and agencies in the community. Their efforts paid off. Neighborhood residents joined the group, including one who became the group's facilitator, and the original volunteers took turns serving on the steering committee of the neighborhood center. These were the kinds of enduring ties that all the groups sought. But only this one succeeded. Why? Because of their custom of what Lichterman calls "social reflexivity"—"reflective talk about the group's concrete relationships in the wider social world." This group spent a lot of time talking, often in ways that were difficult and faltering. They spent long meetings figuring out how to deal respectfully with the prickly neighborhood-center director and how to reconcile what ministers were telling them residents wanted with what the neighborhood social worker was saying. They pushed themselves to remember that people in the neighborhood often knew residents' needs better than they did. But they also cautioned against an unquestioning deference. When the African American public nurse they hired said that she would use "culturally appropriate" methods for ministering to the needs of Spanish-speaking and Hmong residents, they insisted that she describe in detail just what that meant.[11]

The talk that allowed this group of volunteers to build solidarity was not the kind of self-disclosing, intimacy-aspiring talk that figures in Giddens's pure relationship or in the dialogue, intergroup contact, or story-sharing initiatives I have described. If not especially fractious, it was nevertheless full of conflicts that were acknowledged rather than submerged. Most important, it was talk about volunteers' relationship with other groups, not just individuals. Volunteers wanted to build relationships with particular people, certainly. But figuring out their relationship with the community sometimes meant figuring out whether their loyalty should be to ministers or to the social worker—and this apart from any feelings they might have about the person occupying each role—and figuring out whom to target if they wanted to create ties with a multiethnic neighborhood. If group members became something like intimates with each other, it was not because they exposed their personal drives and demons, but rather because they helped each other to engage in critical self-reflection about their group's purposes and how they should pursue them.

Contrary, then, to the notion that building ties of individual friendship in a space removed from decision making can scale social divides, this group succeeded when it did not try to treat community members as potential friends. It was members' determination to think carefully about the kinds of relationships they wanted to create in and with the community that allowed them to build enduring bonds. The larger point is that groups can deliberately create new schemas for what is owed to known and unknown others. Indeed, in societies where bridging ties do not come naturally, unfamiliar, even unnatural-seeming, modes of interaction may be essential to democratic solidarity.

DEVELOPING RADICAL EQUALITY IN SOCIAL MOVEMENTS

Worlds away from midwestern church volunteers are the activists who strive to enact radical democracies within their own movements. I have in mind the 2011 Occupy activists and the Spanish 15 May activists who made decisions about how to operate their encampments in giant open-air general assemblies, in which anyone who wanted to participate could do so and which carried on until the group reached consensus. Before Occupy, global justice activists used consensus to mobilize direct-action protests against international trade summits. And today, many groups in the broad penumbra of the anarchist Left operate without hierarchies and with some version of consensus.[12]

These activists may spend just as much time in circular, tentative, and often frustrating talk as the members of the successful church volunteer group, but their aims are different. They seek not to forge ties with government bureaucrats and churches in a single neighborhood, but rather to enact in the here and now alternatives to polities they see as democratic in name only. Whereas the neighborhood volunteers placed a premium on accomplishing practical objectives, champions of leaderless organizations are often criticized for their indifference to practical effectiveness. After all, activists are sometimes in a position to have an impact that is felt beyond their organizations, yet they seem willing to squander that opportunity in favor of perfecting consensus within a cluster of like-minded others.[13]

But I see in their activism a similar effort to build forms of solidarity that are not based on emotional intimacy. I am struck by activists' experimentalism: their effort to develop not just new rules for doing democracy, but also new schemas of democratic relationship, ones based on activists' evolving understanding of equality and solidarity. They style their radical democracies on friendship, but on a distinctly nonexclusive form of friendship, as well as on online networks and affinity groups. They seek to "prefigure"—to show the viability of—a radically egalitarian society; but their more tangible accomplishment may lie in creating forms of solidarity that diffuse across activist circles and possibly, movement generations.[14]

As I noted in chapter 1, activists in the women's liberation movement in the 1960s often found themselves frustrated in their efforts to build leaderless organizations. It was not only the inefficiencies that bothered them, but the fact that their groups seemed to reproduce precisely the inequalities they were trying to overcome. The feminist Jo Freeman famously called it the "tyranny of structurelessness": in the absence of formal rules, decision making ended up being dominated by cliques. Yet some groups did try to implement formal rules: lot systems, for example, which distributed tasks randomly; disk systems, which prevented any one person from monopolizing the discussion; and more radically, efforts to divide large collectives into multiple collectives, again randomly. These failed, members said later, because they felt artificial. The problem, I argued, was that friendship is by definition inimical to formality. Collectives' dependence on relationships of friendship made it difficult to adopt the kinds of formal mechanisms that would have equalized power, even as activists recognized the liabilities of their failing to do so.[15]

Some women's collectives disbanded. Others, especially rape crisis and domestic abuse centers, adopted formal structures such as boards of directors and executive decision making. But more radically egalitarian forms of organizing did not disappear. Some feminist collectives continued to operate without formal leaders, chains of command, or voting. Subsequent waves of activism, including the American antinuclear movement, Latin

American protests that relied on "horizontalist" alternatives to top-down leadership, and a resurgent anarchism all developed new tools for consensus decision making. Anarchists played key roles in the movement challenging corporate globalization that came to international attention in 1999, with direct-action protests in Seattle and the first World Social Forum held in Porto Alegre, Brazil. Anarchists were also involved in the anti-austerity and pro-democracy protests, including Occupy and the 15 May movement, that gained international attention in 2011. Activists shared an increasingly sophisticated repertoire of tools for radically egalitarian decision making: hand signals, provisions for modified consensus, a "progressive stack" that put the voices of marginalized groups at the head of the speaking queue, and the positions of facilitator and vibes watcher, who were responsible for alerting the group to imbalances in speaking patterns.[16]

Along with decision-making tools, activists also worked to develop egalitarian relationships. The insight, and I believe it was a good one, was that, contrary to Freeman's argument about the need for formal rules, there can never be enough rules to sustain an organization. Decision making relies not only on formal rules—for instance, parliamentary procedure or strict or modified consensus—but on countless informal rules about what kinds of issues are appropriate for group discussion and how to raise them, how to formulate and assess deliberative options, how to deal with breaches of the rules, and so on. These informal norms help to create the interpersonal trust that fills in the gaps between the rules and that leads people to assume that the rules' ambiguity owes to their misinterpretation rather than their indeterminacy.[17]

The task for activists was to build these norms rather than relying on those that arose naturally from friendship. At the same time, activists' understandings of equality and unity were also evolving. Equality was no longer seen as a matter of allowing everyone to participate, as it had been for activists in the 1960s and 1970s. Activists now were attuned to the subtle ways in which privilege could shape even professedly egalitarian interaction. Along with mechanisms such as the progressive stack and using male and female teams of facilitators, activists also sought to develop relationships of what the sociologists Christoph Haug and Dieter Rucht call "non-exclusive friendship." Among German autonomous activists in the women's, antiracist, and global justice movements, the sociologist Darcy Leach found a "fight culture" (*Streitcultur*) that produced norms of "dissent, collective reflection, not taking oneself too seriously, the sharing of knowledge and skills and an etiquette of 'giving up power.'" In her study of eight groups that relied on consensus decision making, Leach found that those that had explicit discussions about the distribution of power in the group were more efficient in making decisions than those that did not. Presumably, this was because they lost less time either to domineering speakers or to disputes about speakers' domination.[18]

American activists similarly put a premium on "calling out White privilege" or "male privilege" in meetings. The anarchists active in movements against home foreclosures, land rights, and immigrant rights whom my student Kathryn Hoban interviewed were determined to confront inequalities within the group. One observed, "The power of consensus decision-making when it's done well is how it makes power explicit, how it makes social dynamics explicit, and therefore able to be dealt with." As in the German groups, the key was figuring out ways to lodge and respond to those challenges without derailing the group's ability to make decisions.[19]

Proponents of consensus in the 1960s and 1970s often strove for the single best decision, one with which all participants would agree. Activists today do not. Partly as a result of their interaction with groups from the global south in the 1990s, northern activists became sensitive to the dangers of steamrolling over other groups' priorities in the name of supposed unity. They came to believe that differences of agenda, tactical preferences, and experience had to be continually recognized. Again they responded practically by developing both formal mechanisms, such as the use of modified consensus for some issues, and new relationship schemas. The anthropologist Jeffrey Juris argues that the horizontalist forms of decision making developed in the global justice movement were self-consciously modeled on online networks. Networks served as a practical metaphor for how to do radical democracy. Autonomy was valued over unity, and coalitions were temporary: they could form, dissolve, and reform. The image of autonomous groups linked along the lines of a virtual network pointed to a new understanding of democracy as well as new forms of solidarity: ones with no political center, and in which any unity was self-consciously provisional.[20]

Another relationship schema was the *encuentro* or encounter, introduced by the Mexican Zapatista movement and adopted by the World Social Forum, in which diverse groups would meet and share strategies, tactics, and ideas, without any expectation of taking joint positions on issues. "Affinity groups" were adapted from Spanish anarchism by the antinuclear and peace movements of the 1970s and then by the global justice movement. They are made up of five to fifteen people joined by a shared ideological or tactical commitment. Affinity groups began as way to provide support and protection for people during direct actions, but they evolved into a decision-making unit. Affinity groups communicated with other groups in clusters and in spokescouncils, but they made their own decisions. Later in the global justice movement, affinity groups evolved into "working groups" covering communication, first aid, legal assistance, blockading, police relations, and so on. The goal was to foster people's autonomy and initiative, since anyone could join a working group, and the groups largely made their own decisions. Larger meetings—which came to be called general assemblies—were reserved for sharing information.[21]

Many activists complained after Occupy that that movement had reversed the roles of working groups and general assemblies, with the latter making decisions rather than only sharing information. The point of the new arrangement was to enact in as public a way as possible the movement's commitment to radically egalitarian decision making. But for many there were costs not only in time and energy, but also in genuinely democratic participation, since practical decisions ended up being made behind the scenes. Several years after Occupy, activists were critical not only of general assemblies, but also of fetishizing consensus. One activist interviewed by Hoban described "a very practical shunning of spiritual purity." Said another: "It's all trial and error. Every organization can be seen as a social experiment . . . but it's not scientific. . . . It's messy." Interviewees praised groups that had "creatively altered" the process, especially in ways that made it accessible to people without long experience of the form. The activist and scholar Marianne Maeckelbergh draws attention to the same process of creative adaptation. In the 15 May movement in Barcelona, she saw the same "inter-barrio" meetings that activists had used to share information at global summits in the 2000s. But in Barcelona they became something much more practical, for the barrios were made up of people who lived and worked in the neighborhood and were therefore able to draw on the resources of existing relationships. As the movement continued, activists experimented with a range of other forms, seeking in particular, as two observers put it, to integrate vertical and horizontal political logics.[22]

Activists' development of new kinds of cooperative relationship has helped combat some of the old problems of radically democratic decision making, notably the risk that in the absence of rules power operates without accountability, and that consensus prove coercive. Unsurprisingly, perhaps, the solutions have created their own problems. I noted Darcy Leach's finding that groups that relied on a lot of rules to make decisions were not more efficient or fairer than those that did not. However, the groups that were most efficient did tend to be steeped in the practice of collectivist decision making. They lived in cooperative housing, had their children in cooperative daycare, and bought their food from cooperative markets. The larger point is that deep familiarity with the norms of radically democratic decision making makes it easy to practice but may also render it less accessible to those without that level of familiarity. And in fact, with important exceptions, anarchist groups have been much less effective in building cross-race and cross-class coalitions than the community organizers I describe below.[23]

There is another problem. We can think of consensus-based decision making as a ritual that reinforces activists' distinctive understanding of solidarity as radically egalitarian, respectful of difference, and constantly evolving. But the ritualistic aspects of the form militate against the experimentalism that activists also prize. Finally, activists' insistence that representation is by definition undemocratic seems to foreclose the possibility that activists might experiment with what genuinely democratic representation would look like. After all, as the political theorist David Plotke, whom I cited in chapter 4, points out, the opposite of representation is not participation. If the problem with current democracies is that they are unresponsive, then the solution should be to make democratic representation more truly representative, not to reject it altogether.[24]

These limits notwithstanding, activists' efforts to build forms of solidarity in which equality and unity are actively negotiated seem to me to be important. Modes of interaction and relationship schemas that are developed in one movement are taken up by activists in other movements and modified as activists struggle to balance the demands of collective action with those of radical equality. More than their rules for consensus decision making, I believe, it is their approach to building new forms of solidarity that may well be utilizable by groups outside radical activist circles.

DEVELOPING LEADERSHIP AND ACCOUNTABILITY IN COMMUNITY ORGANIZING

Community organizing groups, often based in congregations, seek to advance the self-identified interests of working-class and middle-class people. Whereas once their purview was only local, today networks of community organizations also press for state and national policy around universal health care, a minimum wage, home foreclosures, immigration, and racial profiling. Like radically democratic direct-action groups, community organizations see themselves as challenging entrenched structures of power, and they often rely on tactics of direct action. But they reject anarchist groups' concern with process over outcomes, as well as what they see as the overwhelmingly middle-class and White character of such groups' membership.[25]

The contrast between the two forms of collective action is perhaps sharpest in their meetings. For community organizing groups, meetings emphatically are not places for experimenting with new forms of solidarity. Instead, they are carefully choreographed performances in which political officials are asked to commit their support to a policy or plan the group is seeking before an audience of hundreds and sometimes thousands of members. After a prayer and rousing introductions of the groups in the coalition, several individual members testify to their experiences with the issue in question. They relate what it has been like to go without health insurance or to survive on a job that does not pay a living wage (I described this kind of storytelling in chapter 5). Another member presents the results of group-produced research on the issue in question and what they propose to address it. Then the public officials present are "pinned" by an organization member: asked directly, one by one, whether they will help pursue the group's goal, by introducing or voting for legislation, committing funds, or some other measure of support. Actual negotiations over what the officials will commit to, as well as decisions about the group's plans of action, take place outside these meetings. The meeting itself is a kind of ritual for communicating the power of the people against that of public officials. It celebrates a relationship schema in which ordinary people have a claim on the powerful by virtue of their unity, numbers, and organization.[26]

Most of the work of relationship building occurs outside these meetings and centers on training people to become leaders. In the ideology of community organizing, power is built on webs of relationships. This is true of the power that is the status quo and the power that seeks to change it. Leaders, in community organizing parlance, are people who can motivate others to turn out for actions; they are not necessarily people with spiffy educational credentials, money, charisma, or political experience. This is the understanding of leadership that the SNCC organizers I described in chapter 2 slowly arrived at, and it is a radical one. A middle-class leader in San José, a technical writer with a graduate degree, described another leader admiringly, a monolingual Spanish-speaking woman with a fifth-grade education: "Maria is a really powerful leader. She'll easily bring eighty people to a meeting." People are also called leaders before they have developed the skills to recruit people they do not know, strategize, coordinate actions, and negotiate with officials. Calling them leaders is prefigurative in the sense that it treats people as what they will become. But note that there is a clear understanding of how one gets from here to there: from potential leadership to leadership. This is the telos of relationship that I argue is missing from the civic initiatives I described in earlier chapters.[27]

Organizers meet with leaders regularly, from the first "one-on-one meeting," where they gauge potential leaders' commitment, through the steps of recruiting members, crafting group goals, developing an action plan, coordinating public actions, negotiating with power holders, and, at each step of the way, reflecting on the success of the effort and what might have been done differently. Perhaps most important, organizers teach organization members to interact with each other and with people outside the organization in ways that are deeply unfamiliar. From the very beginning, organizers ask leaders to commit a certain amount of time to the group, and they teach them to demand similarly quantifiable commitments from the members they recruit. This is hard to do. As an organizer interviewed by the political scientist Hahrie Han explains, "It's just challenging for some of the organizers to push people in that way. . . . It's not what we're taught. . . . To actually like commit to it and to hold somebody accountable to it." Leadership also entails a willingness to confront officials. The public meetings dramatize this most clearly. They are polite and orderly, but they are clearly intended to put officials on the spot. At a meeting with California legislators before an audience of two thousand members of the Pacific Institute for Community Organization (PICO; recently renamed Faith in Action), a speaker described San José's failing schools and then invited legislators to respond. "If we hear finger pointing from our legislators," she warned, "I will stop you. I will interrupt you. Assemblyman, you have five minutes." For the audience, the speaker's forceful delivery made clear that representatives would not be able to maneuver their way out of taking a stand. The person who is tasked with pinning an official or other target learns how to prevent him or her from giving any answer other than a clear "yes" or "no." The theory is that a "no" is better than an ambiguous answer, since it both prevents the official from getting off the hook and may reenergize members with a sense of indignation. The ritual aspect of pinning also legitimates a kind of combativeness that, in other circumstances, might be perceived as uncivil.[28]

Indeed, for many members, and especially for clergy, the combative character of Alinsky-styled organizing is challenging. The sociologist Heidi Swarts describes a St. Louis priest's dismay after audience members at a public meeting he was chairing angrily booed the speaker, a senator's staff member. The senator himself had been invited but had sent only a low-level aide who knew little about the issue. Still, to the priest's mind, the audience's reaction was plainly uncivil, and even worse was that organizers in the post-meeting evaluation praised the audience for having sent the message that they would not be ignored. The interfaith organizing group that the sociologist Ruth Braunstein studied likewise abjured confrontation. The lead clergyman in the group refused even to use the term "target" to describe officials, explaining, "*Target* means you're going to shoot them, and I don't like that." That stance may have cost the group strategically, however. It decided not to ally with a powerful union in pressing a congressional representative to support health care legislation because it disliked the way union representatives had pressured the congressman. "We're not here to bludgeon," insisted a group member. "That is against our values." Participants' values centered on bringing morality into politics, they said. They saw citizens "as potential partners with stakeholders, seeking the common good rather than facing off in a zero-sum battle over opposing interests." This is the language of partnership that I described in chapter 4. Community organizers in the Alinsky mold would counter that sometimes the interests of the powerful and the powerless simply are opposed. The battle is indeed zero-sum, and ignoring that fact works to the interests only of the powerful.[29]

Practically, organizers insist that there is a difference between the public office and its occupant. While an official may be personally sympathetic to the group, she is also likely to be under pressure from other parties: from developers, perhaps, who want tax breaks, or from those who have donated to her election campaign. The community needs to serve as its own source of pressure. One organizer described politicians' efforts to curry favor with her: "Oh, I mean, flattery and nice things by politicians. Personalizing things, like 'Oh, you wouldn't be mean to me, would you?' Oh no, I'll be mean to the office! (laughs) You just happen to be the person holding the office at the moment!" The PICO coalition's standard question, "Who do you love?" emphasizes participants' allegiance to their families and congregation. Slyly alluding to that question, an organizer in a meeting asked pointedly, "Who do we love? People with titles?" A community organization may work out a relationship of mutual trust with a particular official over time as the organization recognizes that the official makes good on her promises and the official sees that the organization's demands really do promise to help the community. But a relationship of trust only extends as far as the official's actions are consistent with the organization's interests. As a New York organizer put it, the goal was a "public relationship, where there was mutual respect, mutual understanding, some agreement, some disagreement, and the right amount of tension and formality, engagement and distance . . . an intricate and long-term public relationship."[30]

This characterization, to be sure, points to the challenge of forging such a relationship. Finding the sweet spot between agreement and disagreement, formality and informality, engagement and distance, tension and cooperation is surely difficult, made even more so by the fact that there are multiple public officials, all of whom will cycle out of office. Some critics of community organizing's confrontational style argue that focusing from the outset on points of common interest with officials—*beginning* with a relationship of partnership—is more likely to build the sense of common purpose that can actually get things done. More commonly, though, the objection is moral. Braunstein argues that the interfaith coalition she studied was not unusual in its antipathy to confrontation and may reflect a deeper divide in the world of faith-based organizing. Her research suggests, however, that clergy members' opposition to confrontation may also reflect their commitment to norms of politeness. Either way, community organizers face an uphill task in winning acceptance for a schema of political relationship in which accountability sometimes demands overt confrontation. To return to the critique of the Tocquevillian argument, solidarity in civil society is not good for much if it exists alongside unresponsive political institutions. But transforming political institutions requires that citizens create new kinds of relationship with political officials as well as with one another.[31]

DEVELOPING EQUALITY IN PLAY

Rather than intimacy, the groups I have described so far aimed for relationships, variously, of solidarity across difference, of radical equality, and of accountable leadership. To create those relationships, groups relied on forms of talk that were different from mutual self-disclosure, including extended joint reflection, prayer, and confrontation, sometimes in ritualized form. The register in each was earnest and serious. And yet, new schemas of relationship have also been forged in unserious settings; indeed, in play.

The historian William Sewell makes this point in accounting for the rise of our modern understanding of equality. He begins with a puzzle. Eighteenth-century France was a society organized around hierarchical principles of aristocracy, privilege, status, and deference. Why would such a society produce a belief in the equal rights of men, and indeed, a revolution based on that belief? The standard answer among historians today, Sewell observes, is a Marxian one. The Enlightenment and the revolution that followed it were bourgeois projects. Members of an emerging capitalist class wanted the freedom to pursue their interests, and they dressed their interests up ideologically as a stake in equality. Yet, key Enlightenment figures—and, crucially, the ones who made the press for equality the revolution's guiding force—were aristocrats and clerics, not members of the bourgeoisie. Why would aristocrats suddenly begin to see commoners as equals? The answer Sewell gives is capitalism. But what capitalism produced was not so much a set of new interests as it was things—commodities—and something else: a new appreciation for the relations of equivalence that were characteristic of the market.[32]

Sewell's alternative account turns on the explosion of commerce in the mid-eighteenth century. The Parisian market was flooded with newly cheap textiles, clothing, carriages, snuff boxes, accessories, and baubles. These were fashions that, for the first time, ordinary people could afford. Commoners eagerly purchased the finery and then proceeded to parade it, first in parks that were open to those who looked and acted well-bred, and then in boulevards that were truly open to all. In these spaces of leisure, people of low and high breeding encountered one another in a way they did not in the rest of their lives. Their experience of equality within the bounded space of the promenade made it possible for them to begin to envision a similar relationship outside the promenade. The relationships of equivalence that characterized the exchange of commodities became a model for egalitarian civic relationships.

It is tempting to explain what happened in the parks and promenades as face-to-face contact producing intimacy. This would be the preferred interpretation by champions of intergroup dialogue, public deliberation, and advocacy storytelling. In this view, as nobles encountered ordinary people they came to see them in their humanity. They began to understand that shoemakers, maids, and fishmongers were not so different from them, and their experience of egalitarian intimacy led to their embrace of equality more generally. But that is not what happened. Nobles never saw commoners as equals. That is why they were not threatened by the fact that commoners could pass themselves off in the park as being like themselves. Commoners remained commoners, *except within the delimited space of the park and promenade*. It was not intimacy but abstraction that was made possible by nobles and commoners commingling within that bounded space. Nobles came to see that people could be considered equal abstractly within a bounded space—whether it be geographical or political—without its threatening the prerogatives of their own power and status. Certainly, this points to one of the serious problems with equality understood in abstract terms; namely, that it does not do nearly enough to combat substantive disparities of power and privilege. Still, encounters along the promenade made French nobles and aristocrats surprisingly amenable to the relationship of civic equality championed by the *philosophes*.

If encounters between nobles and commoners were unthreatening because they posed no threat to nobles' intrinsic superiority, they were appealing because they were fun. Accounts of these meetings evinced a playful, lighthearted tone. The experience was one of amiable discovery. For example, the Baroness d'Oberkirch wrote of accompanying her companion, the Princesse de Condé, to the Boulevard du Temple, where they visited an all-night theater and thoroughly enjoyed themselves observing drunken soldiers flirting with a young woman. Accounts of these and other encounters emphasized a delight in transgression, an appreciation for playing at new roles. Writers effectively counseled their readers that they should enjoy the experience of civic equality, that it was a pleasure rather than a threat.[33]

I criticized public deliberative exercises for being removed from the messy politics of actual policy making. Yet, there are definitely benefits to that separation. As I noted, it is easier to cast a forum's recommendations as reflecting the will of the people if the forum is seen as operating independently of the political agencies and groups that have a prior stake in the issue. I wonder, too, if the fact that the New York City forums took place on the weekend and evenings and were seen as separate from the everyday work of policy making made them seem more interesting and even fun, and if that in turn made it easier for people to experiment with new relationships in the forum. In settings of recreation or leisure, or that are outside politics or work, places where there seems to be less at stake, people are freer to interact in new ways. Not only can they subtly mock established hierarchies and violate the usual norms of deference; they can play at, play-*act*, alternatives.

The prefigurative dimension of play has been tapped by many movements. As the scholar and activist Benjamin Shepherd and his colleagues write, playful protest—the use of puppets, games, satirical songs, and so on—is a way to elude police repression during demonstrations and to invite bystanders into the movement. But play also reveals new possibilities: new ways of occupying spaces, of living and working cooperatively, of relating to the state, and of forging solidarities across difference. For example, Critical Mass bike rides today involve hundreds of bike riders, often costumed and with musical accompaniment, riding slowly through cities at rush hour and, by their sheer numbers, forcing cars to make way for them. When the group nears a busy intersection, several members bike ahead and plant themselves in front of oncoming traffic so the group can slowly ride through against the light. The experience is heady: participants have the experience of defying the rules, but also of democratic self-organization by hundreds of people.[34]

Precisely insofar as such activities are unserious, however, and outside the "real" work of politics, the experimentation they encourage risks being seen as properly temporary, a break from politics rather than a viable model for it. Perhaps another step is required for the new ways of interacting in play to become something like relationship scripts outside play. Aristocrats' interactions with commoners in parks and boulevards would have remained just a pleasant diversion had not the *philosophes* named that interaction "equality" and then turned it into a rallying cry for revolutionaries determined to transform political and legal structures. If play makes it possible to bracket the usual relationship schemas, the experience of alternatives must be translated into interactional norms that extend beyond the particular encounter. A first step may be that the relationships are named; perhaps a second that they are ritualized.[35]

Consider, in a very different time and place, the sociologist Katherine Kellogg's ethnography of two hospitals that sought to limit the number of hours interns worked. After a national scandal in which overworked interns were held responsible for a young woman's death, hospitals were required to adopt reforms. Both the hospitals Kellogg studied hired a floating team of surgical residents for the night shift, making it possible for interns to leave earlier in the evening. But the interns were unwilling to take advantage of the new system in either hospital, instead staying late to complete the routine scut work that had traditionally been required of them. Loyalty to an "iron man" view of the physician's ability to handle long hours initially led senior residents not to cooperate and interns not to assert themselves. That did eventually change in one hospital, however, and Kellogg's explanation is interesting. Afternoon rounds in that hospital were conducted in spare rooms rather than in the residents' lounge. Away from the scrutiny of other residents, many of whom opposed the new system, surgical team members who favored it were able to figure out with the interns on their team how to make the system work. As a result, they began to adopt it.[36]

Critical to the change, though, was that residents began to refer to their relationships with interns and with each other differently. They began calling senior residents "coaches" rather than "commanders," day residents "team players" rather than "wingmen," the new night residents "members of the team" rather than "stopgaps," and interns "rookies" rather than "beasts of burden." Once interns were "rookies," they were more like students or apprentices. They were naive, certainly, and still had the obligation to prove themselves to more senior residents; but the term implied that they would eventually become senior residents themselves rather than existing only to be exploited, as "beasts of burden" had been. Residents' relationship with a rookie had a telos. Naming the new relationships was important in creating relationship schemas and that, in turn, ensured that cooperation did not end with the interaction of the particular team.[37]

BUILDING UNFAMILIAR RELATIONSHIPS

The initiatives I have described in this chapter sought to build unfamiliar relationships. They sought to build relationships of solidarity among people divided by race, class, sexual orientation, and religion. They sought to build relationships of equality that went beyond formal rules. They sought to build relationships of accountability between citizens and policy makers.

And they sought to build relationships of cooperation among people with traditions of competition. None of the initiatives I profiled did so by modeling such relationships on intimacy. They did not help people to get to know each other in all their individual uniqueness by sharing their personal stories, with the assumption that this kind of mutual revealing would produce solidarity.

For the unions, congregations, and faith-based community organizing coalitions I described, the solidarity they sought needed to extend beyond people who knew each other, let alone knew each other intimately. For the church volunteer group, success meant creating ties between themselves as a group and a community, not ties between individuals. For radically democratic movement groups today, intimacy is dangerous insofar as it conceals inequalities among those in the group and excludes those not in the group. For community organizers, the telos of intimate relationships is counterproductive. In developing leaders, organizers hope to make themselves eventually unnecessary, not, as in an intimate relationship, to deepen the mutual interdependence of the relationship partners. Finally, the relationships in both the eighteenth-century Parisian promenade and today's Critical Mass bike rides are unlike intimate ones because they involve little in the way of authentic self-revelation. People are often costumed (and therefore not their authentic selves), relationships are fluid, and talk is unserious. But those very features make it possible to experiment with alternative relationships and to glimpse possibilities for new modes of interaction.

I have also asked when new ways of interacting stick—that is, when they produce norms that are capable of guiding interactions between other people at other times. Rituals, I have suggested, can make normative the behaviors associated with new political relationships. Whereas a rule influences people's behavior in part through the existence of penalties for the rule's violation, and a relationship influences people's behavior through mutual norms of obligation, a ritual endows actions and interactions with a kind of sacred character. Community organizing's challenges to public officials are rituals: they occur in a special time and place separate from regular activities, they involve the group in practiced actions, they inspire high emotions, and they communicate the group's collective identity as unified and powerful. Similarly, the interfaith prayer rituals that such groups engage in do not deny participants' differences—do not say simply, we are all children of God—but instead turn the group's embrace of differences into a statement about who the group is. Decision making is a ritual for horizontalist movement groups, which also embrace an identity as simultaneously unified and internally diverse. In each of the initiatives I have described, rituals have served to bind participants in a new and unfamiliar kind of solidarity: one that challenges authorities, that includes people usually outside the circle of faith, that is between groups rather than only between individuals, and that refuses to ignore asymmetries of power.[38]

This is not to say that rituals represent a surefire formula for success. Rituals are hard to engineer. We may know that someone at some point created the ritual, but for it to be effective, its authorship must be obscured. Rituals are experienced as acting on the group, not created by it. Moreover, once certain group practices become ritualized—come to be seen as reflections of who the group is—it becomes difficult to revise them. Activists committed to horizontal direct action thus struggle to balance the experimental character of their decision making with its ritualized character. Likewise, if public officials refuse faith-based coalitions' demand for their support, organizers have to decide whether to dispense with a ritual that still serves solidarity-building functions. Finally—and this is true in all groups—rituals that seem essential to longtime members may seem bizarre and off-putting to newcomers.[39]

Given all these difficulties, it might seem more sensible to simply choose to act, to commit to a project that is in the interests of the multiple groups one believes should be included in the circle of solidarity with the idea that in working jointly, common bonds will be created. Perhaps *not* being self-conscious about how people are interacting, *not* endlessly talking about what this relationship is and where it is going, will allow those things to be worked out on their own. There is merit to this view. The danger, though, is that people fall into the old grooves of acting and interacting. This is what the sociologist Kathleen Blee found in her ethnographic study of dozens of new movement groups in Pittsburgh. Groups were launched with boundless energy and creative ideas for how to tackle issues ranging from local gun violence to global climate change. Soon, however, that creativity dissipated as activists retreated to familiar modes of action and familiar modes of interaction. When internal strains became impossible to ignore, groups responded by recommitting themselves to action. Of the 295 meetings that Blee's team observed, there were fewer than a dozen explicit discussions of how group members got along. Over and over again, groups emphasized doing rather than talking. The emphasis on doing, however, did not solve the internal problems, nor did it help groups to regain the initiative they had had at the start.[40]

Recall Donald, the minister whose "do, don't talk" mantra made it difficult for a coalition that was dedicated to rethinking the structure of social welfare to actually do that rethinking. Recall the feminist collectives, for whom modeling decision making on friendship was natural but made it difficult to create more formal mechanisms for guaranteeing equality, even when members knew they needed those mechanisms. And recall the faith-based organizing coalition leaders, whose opposition to a more confrontational stance may have reflected their fear of being impolite more than it did a moral principle. These examples suggest that familiar modes of interacting may undermine people's ability to forge democratic organizations, movements, and polities. They suggest that real political change may depend on making familiar new modes of interaction and creating new relationship schemas.

I described such schemas emerging through *play*, through people's deliberate *reflection* about the relationships they wanted to create, and through their *ritualizing* of the new kind of relationship. Is one of these better than the others? Certainly, play makes it easy to experiment in a way that reflection and ritual do not. Reflection is necessary to turn possibilities arrived at unexpectedly into longer-term commitments to acting differently. And ritual turns those normative commitments into familiar practices, which neither play nor reflection do. I am not sure that all three are always necessary to producing new solidarities, but it would be worth finding out.

Is there any reason, finally, to believe that such relationship schemas might generalize beyond the organization or movement? After all, the Tocquevillian brief for the ties naturally formed in voluntary organizations was that such ties would produce a more generalized trust. Why should we believe that the affinity groups and *encuentros* of anarchist social movements or the accountable leadership of faith-based organizing should influence anyone outside the organizations in which they are practiced? I have two answers to the question. One is that people who experience these modes of interaction may carry them into other settings. In fact, movements have often had an impact by pioneering new relationships and associational forms. Domestic partnerships, minority group allyship, consciousness-raising groups, cooperatives, collectives, and consensus management each began in a movement, but outlived the movement in which it originated. One can imagine that some of the relationships and interactional styles pioneered in the movements I have described might also endure.[41]

My second answer is that voluntary organizations' efforts to reimagine the ties that bind at the meso level suggest that it may also be possible to reimagine the ties that bind at the macro level. Just as voluntary organizations reflected on and ritualized new schemas for membership, might governments do the same for new schemas of membership in the nation? This is the question with which I begin the next chapter.

CHAPTER SEVEN

The Uneasy Balm
of Communication

*Providence has been pleased to give this one connected country to one
united people—a people descended from the same ancestors, speaking
the same language, professing the same religion, attached to the same
principles of government, very similar in their manner and customs.*

JOHN JAY, *The Federalist Papers* (1787)

*What if they are the true dwelling of the holy, these
fleeting temples we make together when we say, "Here,
have my seat," "Go ahead—you first," "I like your hat."*

DANUSHA LAMÉRIS, "Small Kindnesses" (2019)

Very little of what John Jay wrote was true even when he wrote it. At the
time, barely 40 percent of the U.S. population spoke English as their primary language. Today the idea that solidarity at the level of the nation must
or should be built on shared ancestry, religion, customs, even language is
largely unappealing. On what, then, should it be built? Some scholars reject
the virtues of national solidarity altogether. In a world threatened with ex-
tinction, we cannot afford obligations only to the nation. Our bonds must
extend wider; our solidarities must be cosmopolitan. Other scholars have
pointed out that such solidarities are difficult to forge in the absence of
international institutions and imaginaries in our everyday lives. By contrast,
allegiances to the nation are familiar, enacted in diverse institutions, emotionally powerful, and capable of motivating real sacrifice. We also know,
however, that national identities have been invoked to exclude and margin-
alize. They have been defined in ways that motivate bellicose international
policy and stingy domestic policy. The question, then, is whether there are
kinds of nationalism that are inclusive. Can the imagined community of the
nation be made to welcome newcomers? Can it motivate a willingness to
sacrifice on behalf of those in need?[1]

Beginning with the political scientist Hans Kohn in the 1940s, scholars have distinguished between ethnic and civic nationalisms, if as much to challenge the distinction as to uphold it. Ethnic nationalism claims a prepolitical shared past of kinship or quasi-kinship. Civic nationalism instead locates solidarity in a shared commitment to liberal norms and institutions. Although Kohn associated the types with actual nations, scholars since then have argued that most nationalisms incorporate some version of both, along with clusters of beliefs that are not reducible to either one. In the United States, for example, the political scientist Rogers Smith identified three forms of nationalism in legal rulings from colonialism to the Progressive Era. Smith found the liberal nationalism that has been celebrated by countless writers, the "American creed" of freedom, liberty, and equality, along with a penchant for limited government and individual enterprise. Often intertwined with that liberal vision, he found a civic republican belief in self-government and in the virtues of political participation. Just as prominent as those two traditions, however, was an ethnocultural one that vested identity in ascriptive criteria. "American" was White, English-speaking, Protestant, and of northern European ancestry.[2]

In public discourse, but also in survey data and focus groups with ordinary Americans in the early 2000s, the political scientist Deborah Schildkraut found four conceptions of American citizenship, not three. Alongside ethnocultural, liberal, and civic republican conceptions was an incorporationist one, which viewed American identity as grounded in its immigrant legacy and which prized the contributions of diverse ethnoracial groups. This perspective saw America's unique strength as lying in the balance it struck between assimilation and difference. Importantly, Schildkraut found that these different conceptions of national identity did not map neatly onto demographic groups. Older and less educated respondents were more likely to hew to an ethnocultural vision, and recent immigrants were somewhat more likely to embrace an incorporationist vision, but all four traditions were embraced by Whites, Nonwhites, people who had immigrated recently, and those who had not. In fact, immigrants were more likely than the native-born to endorse the civic republican view that being American required involvement in local and national politics. Another view: According to the sociologists Bart Bonikowski and Paul DiMaggio, almost half of Americans surveyed in 2004 either embraced elements of both liberal and ethnocultural traditions or expressed little in the way of national pride, identity, or investment in restrictions on membership at all.[3]

Other studies have suggested that even the same people invoke elements of multiple traditions, along with a mix of historical figures, objects, activities, and political institutions to define national identity. Liberal and ethnocultural nationalisms were thoroughly mingled in the everyday talk and action of the residents in a Transylvanian town studied by the sociologist Rogers Brubaker. The British nationals interviewed by the psychologist Susan Condor talked about national identity in terms of common origin and shared commitment, but also as lying simply in the fact of temporal-spatial co-presence—that people lived in the same place at the same time—and in terms of common fate.[4]

The fluid and syncretic character of people's ideas about national identity suggests that keying different dimensions of that identity may produce different ideas about who belongs. This is easily missed by surveys that ask people about appropriate criteria for membership in a bounded community. Thus, in the United States surveys ask respondents to identify the traits and behaviors that make people "truly American." Unsurprisingly, people who identify on the basis of an ethnocultural understanding of citizenship tend to have negative views of immigrants and racial minorities and to oppose generous welfare policies. But we can also see in ethnocultural, liberal, civic republican, and incorporationist traditions, as well as in the other materials that people draw on to imagine what it is to be American, ideas about the *character and dynamism of people's bonds* as Americans. The emphasis here is not on what defines someone as properly a member of the national community, but on what kind of community it is. The fact that people can imagine the community in different ways, I believe, means not so much that they can draw the boundaries between insiders and outsiders in different places as that they can see those boundaries as being more or less central to who they are, with important consequences for their views of domestic and foreign policy.[5]

Two sets of experiments will help to clarify my point. Shortly after the attacks of 9/11, the psychologists Qiong Li and Marilyn Brewer primed subjects to think about the bonds of American community in one of two ways. Some subjects read a statement that 9/11 had united Americans by reminding them "what we have in common as Americans . . . the core essence of what it means to be American." Li and Brewer anticipated that the statement would prime a familiar view of groups as cohering around members' similar and fundamental attributes, attributes that endow the group with a timeless essence. For members of this kind of group, the authors hypothesized, differentiating the group from outsiders would be especially important. Boundaries would be seen as essential to maintaining the integrity of American identity. Other subjects read a statement that 9/11 had united Americans by giving them "a common purpose to fight terrorism in all of its forms and to work together." The authors anticipated that this statement would prime a different but also familiar view of groups cohering around members' efforts to solve a common problem or pursue a common purpose. Unity here would be seen as dynamic and temporal rather than fixed and timeless. Maintaining boundaries between the in-group and the out-group would be less important than ensuring that members of the group were able to cooperate effectively. When, after reading one of the statements, subjects answered questions designed to measure their attachments to the nation and their views of minority groups, the authors found that in the first, essence-based group condition, higher levels of national identification were associated with cultural intolerance and more restrictive understandings of American identity. In the purpose-based group condition, that was not the case. Thinking about the imagined community as bound by common purpose led people to be more concerned with what group members needed in order to be able to work together. The boundary between in-group and out-group simply was not emotionally charged.[6]

Another set of experiments focused not on boundaries within the nation, but boundaries between nations. The political scientist Kathleen E. Powers sought to prime an understanding of the nation as characterized by peer relationships of equality rather than relationships of communal sharing. Recall Alan Fiske's argument, on which Powers draws explicitly, that these two relationship schemas are deeply familiar to most people: an equality-matching schema characterizing work groups and neighbors, and a communal-sharing schema characterizing families, friends, romantic partners, and, in weaker form, nations. What would it mean, though, to think about our national identity instead in terms of equality-matching relationships? Powers asked subjects to imagine themselves citizens of a fictional country that had suffered internal conflict in the past but no longer did. Some subjects read about current group relations characterized by communal norms of exchange, decision making, and identification (with language such as citizens are "unified as a community" and "have similar values"). Other subjects read about current relations operating on the egalitarian norms of Fiske's equality-matching relationship (citizens "differ in many ways, but . . . generally think of one another as equals"). Asked subsequently how the country should respond to a three-part foreign policy crisis, subjects in the equality-matching condition were significantly less likely to endorse a militaristic response. Interestingly, these subjects did not score lower on measures of national chauvinism. Rather, Powers speculates, they saw their country's superiority as lying in its egalitarian, peer-like relations rather than in its shared primordial past. In a second experiment in which the country was the United States, Powers again found that priming equality-matching relationships diminished the bellicose dimensions of nationalism.[7]

Note that both sets of experiments drew on understandings of solidarity that are familiar to Americans. We have ready referents for groups that are unified around members' common purposes rather than their sameness, and referents for egalitarian peer relationships as distinct from communal-sharing ones. People may not call these relationships to mind immediately when they think of what binds co-nationals, but as these experiments suggest, they can do so pretty easily. And doing so leads them to endorse policies advancing an inclusive national solidarity and one that does not assume antagonism with other nations.

The political theorist Iseult Honohan similarly turns to the metaphorical power of familiar relationships as an alternative to civic and ethnic nationalisms. Whereas ethnic nationalism imagines citizens as something like kin or close friends, she observes, civic nationalism imagines a loose grouping of strangers. Both pose problems. It is hard to see how a relationship of kinship or close friendship would extend to people whom one doesn't know intimately. But it is also hard to see how one could legitimately expect more than minimal courtesy from a group of strangers. Furthermore, while kinship is not chosen, friendship and a shared belief in democratic principles are. How does one reconcile this voluntary view of civic bonds with the fact that most of us do not choose our citizenship? Honohan suggests that we might think of our fellow citizens instead as something like colleagues. Honohan is Irish; I believe that for Americans the term *co-worker* might be more appropriate. We do not choose our co-workers, and yet we recognize that we are in some respects interdependent with them. If our company fails, for example, we will all be out of a job. We also have certain obligations to our co-workers, obligations that do not depend on our intimacy: obligations of communication, consideration, and trust. Our experience of solidarity as co-workers does not depend on our antagonism toward an out-group, and it can be expanded to include co-workers whom we do not know at all.[8]

A metaphor of citizens as co-workers has even more to recommend it. According to the political scientists Diana Mutz and Jeffrey Mondak, the workplace is where Americans are most likely to talk about politics with people who have different views from theirs. There is an openness that is born precisely of the fact that we do not choose our co-workers, nor they us. We do not risk losing an intimate relationship by professing views at odds with theirs, but we also know that we cannot antagonize them so much that it becomes impossible to work together.[9]

My point is not that the metaphor of the co-worker is necessarily the best one for conceptualizing the bonds of national identity. Rather, it is that metaphors of relationship may offer a fruitful way of thinking about what binds us. Recall the messaging consultant I quoted in chapter 5, who complained that a transit union had sought to gain public support by depicting striking workers next to their trains "rather than showing them with their families or coaching Little League or whatever it is they authentically do." I objected there to the notion that operating trains was not what train workers authentically did. But the consultant was probably right that portraying the striking workers with their families or coaching Little League had a better chance of eliciting audiences' support. One message for the audience would have been that the workers were people like them. But more interesting to me, Little League coaches would also have been people audiences might have known. Their bond would have been based not on imagined similarity but on imagined contact—contact that was casual but also recurring. Recent research on intergroup contact has shown that if people from a majority group are encouraged to imagine a positive or even neutral interaction with a person from a minority group, they become more favorably inclined toward the group. They do not have to imagine the interaction in detail, nor do they have to imagine themselves as having anything close to an intimate bond with the stranger.[10]

There may be power in imagined relationships that are distinctly quotidian. What joins us as Americans may be the fact that we live in the same place at the same time and struggle to raise our children as happy and responsible adults, as well as—and this is the key—encounter each other, or can imagine encountering each other, in the school pick-up line, the supermarket, and the PTA. Perhaps it is in the moments the poet Danusha Laméris describes—when the waitress refilling your coffee calls you "honey" or the passerby says "God bless you" after you sneeze—that we experience American "temples of the holy." Perhaps we are bound less by our common past or shared aspirations than by the relationships we can imagine having along the way.[11]

Of course, our common past—or, better, the stories that have come to be accepted as our past—remain important in defining the boundaries and obligations of citizenship. Accordingly, we might also reflect on and add to the relationships that figure in what the political scientist Rogers Smith calls our "stories of peoplehood." In the American story, we might recount episodes of cooperation alongside those of competition and conflict, but cooperation among groups, and cooperation that has produced enduring institutions rather than only short-term alliances. We might supplement the familiar image of the community barn raising—Americans pulling together voluntarily, outside government—with episodes in which government has been, variously, the target of collective action, the setting in which the metaphorical barn raising took place, or a vital actor in the process. Our stories of American peoplehood might combine civic republican, liberal, and incorporationist visions of citizenship by featuring the immigrant groups whose political struggles to make America their home led to legal rights and institutions that we take for granted today, such as the eight-hour workday.[12]

Along with celebrating diverse peoples' contributions to American institutions, we might plumb American history for the relationship schemas that underpin current ideas about who we are as a nation, as well as for viable alternatives. I have in mind something like what the historian Paige Raibmon does in reexamining the history of the Canadian province of British Columbia. Raibmon was asked to review a fourth-grade textbook that had been overhauled to reflect the role of indigenous peoples (in Canadian parlance, First Peoples) in the province's history. The new version of the textbook provided rich accounts of influential indigenous figures and ordinary people's lives, and it did not shy away from covering controversial episodes such as the British governor general's recommendation in 1763 that indigenous peoples be sold blankets infected with smallpox. But Raibmon was struck by the way in which tendentious points of view were still embedded in seemingly neutral language. For example, after reprinting the governor general's letter, the text went on: "European blankets, given in trade, were thought to be one way that First Peoples caught the deadly smallpox virus." Aside from the fact that the use of the passive tense concealed the agency involved (who gave them the blankets?), the text turned a relationship of warfare into a peaceable and reciprocal relationship, since the blankets were "given in trade." Raibmon's alternative wording made the historical relationship clear: "British traded blankets infected with smallpox in order to spread the disease among their Indigenous enemies."[13]

Another example of concealing and revealing relationships: Several passages in the text praised First Peoples' use of "natural resources." Again, though, the phrasing made natural a European relationship to animacy, kin, and utility. "The term 'natural resources' implies that everyone who looks at a tree wants to make a dollar off it," Raibmon writes. She quotes the Potawatomi botanist Robin Wall Kimmerer: "In the settler mind, land was property, real estate, capital, or natural resources. But to our people . . . it was a gift, not a commodity." The difference was more than one of semantics, Raibmon points out: "Commodity exchange marks the end of a relationship, whereas a gift exchange perpetuates it." The point of Raibmon's rephrasing of the story of Canadian peoplehood was not to produce an anodyne historical account with which everyone could agree. It was to make clear that trade was a euphemism for war and utility a euphemism for exploitation. And, just as important, it was to provide the materials for conceptualizing alternative relationships—here, relationships among groups living on (with) the same land.[14]

The historian Teresa Bejan's reinterpretation of the thought of the American theologian Roger Williams does something similar. Williams, who founded the colony of Rhode Island for religious dissenters, is often taken today as a champion of the virtues of mutual respect, trust, and goodwill among those of differing views. That characterization is dead wrong, Bejan observes. Williams argued fiercely against a notion of civility that, he said, built Christian values of charity into its very definition, thus making it impossible to have any kind of relationship with non-Christians. The task, Williams believed, was to enact the "mere civility" that would allow people to converse with those whose views they impugned. Far from being the multiculturalist *avant la lettre* that some contemporary philosophers have made him out to be, Williams shared his contemporaries' views of Native Americans as barbarians and Quakers as devil worshippers. But he believed that they could be converted to the Protestant faith. Toleration, and a kind of toleration that brooked noisy argument, was necessary, Williams believed, because it offered the best hope for showing non-Protestants the error of their ways.[15]

Williams's drive to convert those whom he perceived as faithless hardly seems to offer a model for how to live together. But there may be virtue, and indeed practical possibility, in Williams's idea of relationships based on talk that is contentious but accepting of certain basic norms (surely "mere civility" should include the expectation that speakers not knowingly lie or misconstrue evidence), talk that always holds out the possibility of agreement, and, most important, talk that is ongoing. Recovering an American history of solidary relationships—and the kinds of talk that have accompanied them—may yield other promising schemas.

Ideas about the nation are communicated in countless ways: in commemorations and museums, textbooks and sports, the names of buildings, parks, and streets, television ads and game shows. In addition, as much as government policies reflect preexisting solidarities, so too do policies *produce* beliefs about one's obligations to the collective. For example, research shows that citizens in welfare states tend to support more generous policies toward the disadvantaged. This is not because they are born with more encompassing allegiances than the citizens of other states, but rather because once policies are in place, they engender not only consent but rather an appreciation for the principles and promises that are embedded in them. In this view, generous policy leads to more expansive solidarities as much as the reverse.[16]

The ideas that are communicated by means of policy are varied. As the political scientist Peter Hall argues, existing policies around welfare probably communicate to citizens ideas about the role of effort relative to that of sheer luck in upward mobility, and those ideas then shape people's preference for more generous or less generous policies. But among the ideas embedded in and promoted by national policies, I argue, are metaphors of relationship. Those ideas are often familiar ones, but not always. In Hall's recounting of the origins of Sweden's welfare state, a new metaphor of relationship was at the center of Social Democrats' egalitarian agenda. In a country whose population was mainly agrarian, party candidates could not appeal to class solidarity. Instead, the party's leader, Per Albin Hansson, described its goal as one of creating a "people's home" (*folkhemmet*). "The good home," Hansson declared, "does not recognize any privileged or neglected members, nor any favourite or stepchildren. . . . Applied to the great people's and citizens' home this would mean the breaking down of all the social and economic barriers that now separate citizens into the privileged and the neglected, into the rulers and the dependents, into the rich and the poor, the propertied and the impoverished, the plunderers and the plundered." The metaphor of the "people's home"—again, perhaps somewhat odd sounding to American ears—was retained once the Social Democrats won electoral power, and it remained important in the party's subsequent governments.[17]

Like the Social Democrats in Sweden, political movements in this country have been carriers of new schemas of political relationship. The sociologist Irene Bloemraad points out that policies supportive of immigrants today were won by earlier movements on behalf of African Americans and other native-born racial minorities. The currency of an incorporationist conception of American identity also owes its existence to those movements. Perhaps community organizing groups like the ones I described in the last chapter will help us to rethink how we are bound not only to each other, but also to those who represent us politically. Perhaps the people who experienced consensus-based decision making in Occupy and other movements will carry into settings outside movements not necessarily an insistence on consensus, but rather an understanding of solidarity as requiring effort to tackle persistent inequalities.[18]

In sum, metaphors, stories, policies, and movements may all be the vehicles of schemas of national belonging that are more inclusive than the ones we have now. In a moment, I will return to such schemas as an alternative to the ideal of egalitarian intimacy that operates in civic efforts today. First, though, I want to recap some of the ways in which people have invented relationships to deal with the standard challenges of solidarity.

What can we learn about how culture operates more broadly by paying attention to such efforts?

STRUCTURE AND CULTURE, CREATIVITY
AND CONSTRAINT

Sociologists of culture recognize that culture both enables and constrains. Culture helps us to deal practically with the situations we confront daily and it sometimes enables us, individually and collectively, to envision new possibilities. At the same time, culture also limits our ability to act on those possibilities and sometimes even to envision them. The challenge for scholars has been to capture culture's enabling and constraining dimensions at the same time. We tend instead to emphasize one or the other. As a result, our accounts risk either downplaying the specifically cultural, rather than material, obstacles people face, or, contrarily, minimizing their capacity to think their way around those obstacles. This has been the case in studies of the operation of institutional schemas. From a macro perspective, scholars have shown that schemas, variously, of organizational form, personhood, and rational policy, diffuse across organizations and even nations in a way that makes organizations in an industry or nations in the modern world polity look increasingly alike. The emphasis in these institutionalist accounts is on conformity. But from a micro perspective, scholars have shown people variously resisting, ignoring, combining, and transforming institutional schemas. The result, they say, is that organizations and nations actually look very different from one another, and institutional scripts like "bureaucracy" actually take diverse forms.[19]

Viewing the local as the site of improvisation and creativity, viewing personal relationships and interactions as negotiated rather than imposed, and viewing top-down constraint as modified by bottom-up agency all have real analytical value. But they risk missing the extent to which the local is also structured by norms whose source lies outside the local and the extent to which even personal relationships are shaped by scripts that predate people's interaction. The task, then, is to capture both the fact that people can transpose operating logics from one sphere to another and that those logics constrain subsequent action.[20]

I have argued that paying attention to the relationship schemas on which people draw can help us to do those things. Again, whereas relations are structural ties and relationships are individual and idiosyncratic, relationship schemas are collective cultural constructions. Friendship today means something very different than it did in ancient Greece or in industrializing Europe. Relationship schemas come in many versions. The schema for men's friendship is different from that for women, that for older women's friendship is different from that for young women's friendship, and that for work friends is different from that for Facebook friends. As the latter suggests, new schemas come into being and old ones disappear. And any enactment of a relationship schema is unique. As many marriages as I have observed among friends and family, as well as in books, films, and television shows, my marriage is different in ways that seem to me to be vital. Still, the power of relationship schemas lies in their familiarity. In new settings and new encounters—situations that are rife with uncertainty—relationship schemas provide some stability of expectation.[21]

Say you are in a deliberative forum for the first time. You will probably struggle to make sense of what this group of strangers is. You will recall other groups you have been in that bear some resemblance to this one: a jury, perhaps, or a PTA, or an organizational development workshop at work. You will probably treat others in the group, initially at least, in a way that is familiar from those other relationships. As you continue to interact with the group, the relationship schema on which you rely (and the one on which others rely, which may or may not be the same) may change. You rely on the schema less as you come to develop expectations about each participant based on your knowledge of him or her. Or cues from participants or from the forum's organizers may lead you to shift schemas, and you may begin to treat participants more like members of a therapy group than a jury. You may combine schemas, listening empathetically to participants' experiences with traffic downtown and then shifting gears to a bargaining relationship try to negotiate a compromise in what participants want from a new downtown plan. As scholars argue with respect to logics of organizational form or national policy, people are able to adapt, combine, and modify logics of relationship.

Relationship schemas' capacity to inject familiarity into an interaction is the source of their creative power. We can transpose relationship schemas from one setting to another. We can treat strangers like friends, friends like children, employees like students, and customers like colleagues. We can treat people in terms of relationships we have only heard or read about rather than experienced ourselves. In previous chapters I showed people doing just those things to deal with some of the challenges of solidarity. The solidarity that operates within movements is of course different from that which operates in communities, and the solidarity that joins members of a civic group is different from that which joins members of a nation. My discussion has ranged across all four kinds of solidarity, identifying both challenges that occur in all of them and challenges that are distinctive to one or more. For example, the Durkheimian solidarity that is reflected in the laws and norms of the community obliges community members to abide by those laws and norms, even when they contravene members' self-interest. The solidarity of movements, by contrast, requires that community members be willing to challenge community norms. But self-interest again pulls in the other direction, in this case toward free-riding on the efforts of others. For the southern civil rights organizers I described in chapter 2, building Black residents' solidarity with the movement required that they overcome not only the pull of self-interest but also that of residents' obligations to their families, ministers, and other community members, many of whom, for good reason, counseled them not to participate in dangerous activism. The challenge here was that of competing solidarities. Where organizers were successful in competing with preexisting solidarities, it was by invoking the obligations of imagined relationships: the obligations of "first-class" citizenship (although the rights of such citizenship were not honored by the state), the obligations of membership in a South-wide movement (although for those living in the rural areas of the Deep South, the movement was remote), the obligations of parenthood (to young organizers who were not their children), and the obligations of leadership (although it meant defying the counsel of recognized leaders).

Had the debtors I described in chapter 3 been motivated solely by self-interest, they would have chosen to try to renegotiate the debts they had the best chance of lowering without incurring lasting penalties. But they were motivated also by their solidary obligation to the norm that one should repay one's debts in full. They were not comfortable striving to cut the best deal they could with anonymous creditors. Instead, they imagined themselves to be in a reciprocal relationship with creditors, whom they viewed as people rather than impersonal organizations. Choosing to pay back their debt in full was an acknowledgment of the service they had received; choosing to try to renegotiate the debt was to signal the inadequacy or triviality of the service. In the process, debtors often chose to renegotiate debts that came with penalties for doing so. But acting on the basis of imagined relationships allowed them to preserve some sense of moral agency. Debt-settlement agents, for their part, were self-interested in wanting to keep their jobs but shared the moral belief that one should not exploit people. Faced with that challenge, they recast their relationship with clients. It was one not between salespeople and vulnerable consumers, but between financial educators and their students. Again, the relationship was imagined, but it allowed agents to convince themselves that what they were doing was fair.

If in these cases imagined relationships helped people to balance their competing loyalties—to their own self-interest and/or to the other groups of which they were members—in other cases imagined relationships helped in a different way. People sometimes transposed the norms and expectations of a culturally familiar relationship so as to know how to act on solidary obligations that were abstract or otherwise ambiguous. This was true of the 1960s activists who committed to running their organizations as radical democracies but had little in the way of guidance on how to do that. Treating each other as friends made it easy to allocate tasks and arrive at decisions in an egalitarian fashion. It was also true of the forum participants I described in chapter 4, who were instructed to discuss plans for Lower Manhattan. Lacking experience of public deliberation, they drew on models of cooperative bodies with which they were familiar: focus groups, advocacy organizations, block associations, and the United Nations. Especially interesting was participants' sense that they were collective political actor. This helped them to handle a challenge that is characteristic of solidarity as it figures in the sphere of civil society. For Tocquevillians, the trust citizens form in voluntary associations should extend outward to trust in other citizens and in political institutions. But if citizens' trust in government should rightly reflect the government's responsiveness, then the associations of civil society may need to press government more actively. The relationships that participants in the forum imagined had them doing that, refusing the line between civic engagement and political challenge that forum organizers may have been too willing to accept.

The advocacy groups I described in chapter 5 wanted people not affected directly by the issue they were tackling to contribute to the cause. They confronted a dilemma that many movements do. Solidarity, recall, is not charity. People in solidarity are willing to sacrifice for a group because they see themselves as part of the group. The challenge for advocates is to build that bond, but to do so without privileging the priorities of those with more power but less direct experience of the issue. The advocates I interviewed argued that when people affected by the issue told their stories, they built a relationship of intimacy, mutual respect, and reciprocity with their audience. The relationship was imagined, since in many cases storytellers never met their audiences. But advocates maintained that the relationship empowered the teller at the same time as it built support for the cause.

The challenge of difference is one facing many solidary groups. How much must group members share in order to cohere? Can diversity—and, crucially, a respect for diversity—coexist with solidarity? Appeals to solidarity at the level of the nation have always invoked "imagined communities," as the political scientist Benedict Anderson famously put it, binding citizens in relationships of comradeship with people they would never know. But scholars have argued that the bonds of imagined community depend on their exclusiveness. There must be outsiders for there to be insiders. As the examples I cited earlier suggest, however, not all relationships require that that boundary be a hostile one. People are capable of imagining their bonds as co-nationals in ways that are not focused on the boundary between us and them. That has made it possible for them to embrace diversity within the nation and more peaceable relations with nations outside it.[22]

In these cases and others, I have argued that people's capacity to act on relationships they only imagined allowed them to deal with standard challenges of acting in solidarity. Yet, in many of these same cases, people's inventive use of relationship schemas failed. Imagining relationships that were not there made it more difficult to act in cooperative and/or effective ways. Why? Sometimes reality simply intervened to discredit the relationship claims that people tried to make. In order to persuade Black residents to try to register to vote, southern civil rights workers claimed to have a relationship with federal officials. It was often painfully obvious, though, that even if organizers actually had that relationship with the government, it did little to protect residents from reprisals. And organizers were always vulnerable to charges that their outsider status gave them the luxury of leaving when things got tough.

Unsurprisingly, too, those with more power have often refused the relationship that those with less power have claimed. Debt-settlement clients imagined themselves in an equal and reciprocal relationship with their creditors, but their creditors did not see the relationship that way, and the creditors had the law on their side. People in the New York City public deliberative forums saw themselves as a collective actor and wanted the organizers of the forum to join them in advocating for the recommendations they produced. The organizers of the forum, however, were both aware of the dangers of their being seen as partisan and reluctant to breach the relationship of partnership they envisioned with decision makers. As a result, they refused to press decision makers publicly. Forum participants' belief that they were a collective actor meant little in the absence of anyone willing to treat them as one.

It was the otherwise powerless debt-settlement clients who had power when it came to the imagined relationship that women debt-settlement agents wanted to claim. Clients allowed male agents to style a relationship of financial educator and student with them, and as a result male agents were able to avoid the feeling that they were exploiting vulnerable people. But clients expected women agents to be more like therapists, and when women accepted that relationship schema, they felt sharply the wrongness of selling people a service they did not need. Many women agents either quit or accepted an otherwise less desirable job. The case suggests that relationship schemas are stratified by gender. They are popularly seen as either appropriate for men or appropriate for women, which makes it more difficult for people to use them creatively. In other cases the problem may be that a certain level of competency is required to enact a relationship schema. For example, as the communication scholar Fred Turner has documented, the currently popular schema of a collaborative peer network has its origins in the elite scientific teams that led post–World War II research and development. For all its egalitarian flair, the schema retains the expectation that participants be elite experts. Another example: many feminist organizations that adopted formal offices in the 1970s nevertheless strove to retain their collectivist commitments by encouraging consultation across levels in the hierarchy. They relied, explains the sociologist Rebecca Bordt, on the norms characteristic of professional colleagues. But one can see how people without the experience of professional colleagueship might find it difficult to gain voice or authority in such organizations.[23]

Finally, relationship schemas are constraining insofar as people's investment in the integrity of the schema—in what distinguishes this type of relationship from others—makes it difficult to modify the relationship. Again, in recognizing people's ability to transpose and combine institutional schemas, scholars have emphasized the practical and creative aspects of that ability. But the fact that we understand what certain relationships are in terms of their similarities to and differences from other relationships makes it unlikely that we would be able to modify them easily. We know what friendship is insofar as it is different from romance, acquaintanceship, and colleagueship. To be sure, some friendships are more like romances, and some friends are closer to acquaintances. And most relationships change over time, as parties renegotiate their obligations and expectations. Still, as the research I cited in chapter 1 indicates, the cultural norms governing different relationships are stable and strong enough that people experience real emotional distress when those norms are violated. Go back for a moment, then, to the hypothetical experience of a deliberative forum. If some participants in your group started talking too personally and emotionally about their experiences of your city's downtown, it might make you anxious. You might worry that the discussion was getting too close to a group therapy session. The confusion of two relationship schemas would create the feelings of anxiety I am hypothesizing you would feel.

Familiar relationship schemas made it difficult for radically democratic movement activists in the 1960s to modify the way they operated when it became clear it was not working. The original members of the group were friends, and their friendships made it easy to allocate tasks and reach decisions in a way that was both fair and efficient. When new members joined the group and felt excluded by preexisting cliques, groups sometimes responded by trying to create formal mechanisms of equality. Those did not work, however, because it was too difficult to formalize relations of friendship. It felt unnatural, activists told me later. In my terms, it felt like turning friendship into something it was not. In other cases, too, I have shown people struggling to modify the norms of familiar relationships. The organizers and sponsors of the New York City deliberative forums found it difficult to shift from a relationship of partnership with decision makers to something more contentious. As a staffer in one of the sponsoring organizations described it, her organization had a modus operandi of "a quiet relationship—influential board members talking to [decision makers]," and it was hard to abandon that MO. So too the clergy who led the community organizing coalition I described in chapter 6 recoiled from the prospect of publicly criticizing public officials whom they envisioned as partners. Certainly, in the first case sponsors had to make a strategic calculation of when to criticize decision makers and when to pull their punches. I wonder, though, whether something that was a risk was experienced as more of a taboo. In the second case, clergy said that attacking public officials was at odds with their efforts to bring morality into politics. The question there is whether under other circumstances clergy might not have defined polite challenge as immoral.

There is a more general cultural dynamic operating, I believe, and it is one worth exploring further. Just as the meaning of words is produced through symbolic oppositions and analogies, so too can we think of relationship schemas as having meaning in opposition and analogy to other relationship schemas. Similarly, we can think of modes of talk as having meaning against other modes of talk, organizational forms having meaning against other organizational forms, and styles of decision making as having meaning against other styles of decision making. Just as we know what business partnership is insofar as it is not acquaintanceship or friendship, we know what dialogue is insofar as it is not debate, what a collectivist organization is insofar as it is not bureaucratic, and what deliberation is insofar as it is not negotiation or bargaining. This makes it difficult to combine schemas or alternate among them: to shift from being a colleague to a friend, to shift from dialogue to debate, to implement formal rules without seeming to violate the tenets of collectivism.[24]

None of these is impossible, but they all require sensitivity and probably emotional work as well. In that regard, paying attention to relationship schemas alerts us to the likelihood that the difficulty in shifting among or combining institutional schemas of any kind is not only cognitive but also emotional. It often *feels* wrong. To recognize these kinds of cultural constraints thus requires that we pay attention to the symbolic structures of analogy and opposition that have often been conceptualized in cognitive terms while at the same time recognizing that those structures are sustained through emotional norms. Such norms are social even though the emotion itself is experienced as individual and spontaneous. We know too little, however, about the mix of cognition and affect through which we perceive boundaries between institutional schemas — relationship schemas or any other kind of schema — and act on those boundaries.

THE LIMITS OF EGALITARIAN INTIMACY

I have spent a lot of this book on a once-novel relationship schema that has diffused from the realm of private life to that of public life. I rehearsed Anthony Giddens's argument about the rise of an ideal of egalitarian intimacy in personal relationships in chapter 1, so I will outline it only briefly here. In the psychotherapeutic self-help literature of the 1980s, Giddens found not the depoliticizing preoccupation with personal relationships that so exercised critics, but rather the tools for interaction that was genuinely democratic. Relationships in that literature were considered to be only as good as they were effective in meeting partners' evolving needs, and their capacity to do that — to help partners both to know their needs and to satisfy them — depended on a continual opening to one another. That mutual self-exploration and trust both depended on and fostered equality. Giddens rejected the view that what took place in personal relationships was irrelevant to the public sphere; to the contrary, such relationships were both democratic in their own right and provided a model for what democracy in the public sphere might look like: "A symmetry exists between the democratizing of personal life and democratic possibilities in the global political order at the most extensive level."[25]

We can see evidence of the egalitarian intimacy Giddens describes in the public deliberation and storytelling initiatives I described. In both, a mode of communication privileging mutual self-disclosure and support is believed to build relationships that are egalitarian and cooperative. We can also see the ideal in the community dialogues around race that I described in chapter 4, in the nonprofit community empowerment projects that I outlined in chapter 1, and in some of the civility initiatives that have gained publicity since the 2016 election. I suspect that the approach has become a kind of go-to model for many civic actors seeking to build bonds of trust and common purpose among people from different classes, ethnicities, races, and political groups.[26]

Why has the ideal of egalitarian intimacy become so popular? I have not provided anything like a full account. Like Giddens and other authors who have described the rise and popularization of psychotherapeutic discourses, I see elements of a psychotherapeutic idiom in the initiatives I have profiled: for example, the emphasis on speaking as an "I" and on sharing feelings and personal experiences rather than opinions and arguments, as well as the injunction to listen empathetically. But I have been reluctant to characterize these initiatives as one more example of the so-called triumph of the therapeutic, for a number of reasons. One is my sense, following feminist critics, that the objection to bringing emotions and interpersonal relations into the public sphere often reflects an unwarranted fear of the feminine. I am also convinced that in some ways the problem lies in how the schema of egalitarian intimacy has been translated into the public sphere rather than in the schema itself (but also that, in other ways, the problem lies with the schema as it is enacted within both the private sphere and the public one). But I have also emphasized the intersection of a psychotherapeutic project with one of interpersonal communication. Dialogue and deliberation specialists have backgrounds in individual and family therapy, but also in facilitation, workplace coaching, organizational development, and management training, all areas of practice that depend on expert forms of communication. Some consultants come to advocacy storytelling by way of psychotherapy, but others do so by way of public relations and, in particular, an emerging field of public relations that caters to nonprofits. A reliance on rationalized modes of talk is a key feature of today's civic initiatives.[27]

I will summarize my objections to the idea that egalitarian intimacy and its associated mode of talk can serve as an effective basis for forging relationships of solidarity. But I should underscore the qualified character of those objections. In the preceding chapters and in this one, I often use phrases like "sometimes," "in some cases," "potential dangers," and my "concerns" and "worries" about an ideal of egalitarian intimacy, recognizing that the things I am describing are risks rather than certainties. And I am aware of the luxury I have to spin out the dangers of a particular approach to reform without having to come up with a practical alternative to it (and to do so quickly, cheaply, and in a way that passes muster with the other parties who together determine what civic reform looks like). The conceptual obstacles I describe exist in addition to those posed by deficits of time, money, and political clout. I do believe that the conceptual obstacles are worth paying attention to, and if in some places I have framed them sharply, it is simply because I have confidence in the capacity of the civic entrepreneurs I have interviewed—the dialogue and deliberation specialists, the storytelling consultants, the activists and community organizers—to confront them alongside the other obstacles with which they routinely grapple.

To frame my first concern sharply, then, it is that the mutually self-disclosing talk that is claimed to produce equality might instead serve only as a means of representing equality, with "representing" understood in an aesthetic sense. In other words, communication may be used not to move toward an egalitarian relationship but instead to suggest that it has already been achieved. The cause advocates I described in chapter 5 encouraged the people affected by sex trafficking or homelessness or poverty to tell stories emphasizing their resilience and agency. Doing so avoided exploiting them, advocates said, and instead put them in a position closer to equality with their audiences. But the equality was performed by one party more than it was enacted by two. Advocates' frequent references to story *sharing* implied that storytelling was reciprocal, despite the fact that it rarely was. But even had it been reciprocal, had both parties exchanged stories, that is no guarantee that the relationship would have been an equal one. As I noted, recent research on intergroup contact initiatives suggests that members of subordinate and dominant groups want very different things from contact. Insofar as storytelling is involved, members of subordinate groups benefit only if their stories are heard in the way they want them to be heard, not in a way that allows dominant-group members to easily identify with them. Again, my objection is to investing a form of talk—namely, mutual self-disclosure—with the power to remedy inequalities in power, status, and money.[28]

Return for a moment to briefs for the so-called sharing economy that I mentioned in chapter 1: initiatives ranging from Wikipedia and Creative Commons licensing, to Uber and Airbnb, to systems of local exchange in which people trade products like power tools and skills such as sewing or babysitting. At first glance, these initiatives do not seem to be characterized by mutually self-disclosing talk. Indeed, they do not seem to be about talk at all but about action, about exchanging goods and services in a cooperative and indeed anti-capitalist way. As the communications scholar Nicholas John points out, however, such initiatives do actually depend on mutually self-disclosing talk. Arguments for the sharing economy are compelling only because they confuse two very different meanings of the word *sharing*: sharing as an egalitarian distribution of goods, and sharing as self-disclosing expressive communication.[29]

What links Uber and Airbnb, which rent services, with community exchange systems is that they operate as loose, informal, minimally organized networks of amateurs and, crucially, that they depend on the Internet. As John shows, in 2005 Internet companies began using the language of "sharing" to describe online interaction. Prior to that the term had been used to describe the common use of a mainframe or disk ("time sharing" and "disk sharing") and to describe downloading copyrighted material ("file sharing"). Now, however, social media users were told that "Facebook helps you connect and share with the people in your life," that a social networking site was a place "where friends share their lives," and that they should "share what's important to you with the people you care about." Sharing now meant communicating one's experiences and values ("what's important to you") as a way to "connect" emotionally. As Mark Zuckerberg described Facebook when it went public in 2012, the goal was "to accomplish a social mission—to make the world more open and connected"; "people sharing more—even if just with their close friends or families—creates a more open culture and leads to a better understanding of the lives and perspectives of others."[30]

Insofar as the sharing economy depended on social media, it too was ascribed values of openness, collaboration, egalitarianism, and community. Indeed, the fact that people shared their experiences online was claimed to make sharing their goods and services natural, with no acknowledgment that the words meant different things. As one proponent put it in a popular TED talk, "We're at an inflection point where the sharing behaviors, through sites such as Flickr and Twitter, that are becoming second nature online, are being applied to offline areas of our everyday lives." There is little reason, though, that sending photos and videoclips to people whom one already knew should lead one to want to lend out one's possessions to people whom one did not know. The argument only made sense if sharing in the sense of expressive, self-disclosing communication was magically made the same thing as sharing in the sense of egalitarian exchange. Once again, emotionally self-disclosing talk was mistaken for an egalitarian and cooperative relationship. And the danger, again, was that forms of coercion and inequality might be concealed as a result.[31]

I want to be clear that talk undoubtedly is essential to forging democratic solidarity. But it must be a tool for negotiating equality rather than only a representation of equality. This kind of talk is often difficult. The activists I profiled in the last chapter who insist on radically egalitarian decision making often find themselves without time to do much of anything else. But they are committed to continually identifying ways in which people with the best of intentions can nevertheless reproduce the inequalities they renounce. The dialogue participants whom the political scientist Katherine Cramer Walsh studied arrived at genuine understanding when they ignored their facilitator's injunction to "dialogue, not debate" and instead challenged one another on how accurate or typical their accounts of their own experiences were. This led White participants in particular to recognize the ways in which African Americans' experiences were genuinely different from their own. Remaining in dialogue mode, by contrast, made it too easy for White participants to see everyone's stories as nicely matching and to preserve the comforting belief that "under the skin, we're all the same." To truly understand the ways in which race shaped people's experiences required that they break with that mode of sharing.[32]

My point is not that debate is more inherently egalitarian than dialogue or personal storytelling. No form of talk is inherently anything. Indeed, mis-recognizing that fact is what leads people to see the use of a certain kind of talk as the same thing as equality or the same thing as unity-with-difference. Again, since talk is a medium of relationship, using the talk associated with one kind of relationship can help to bring another one into being. But the talk on its own does not constitute the sum total of that relationship. Talking the way that equals do, but for a limited period and about some issues and not others, is not equality. By the same token, if I have criticized the claim that stories empower people from vulnerable groups by depicting them as agentic, hopeful, and restrained in their emotions—the claim, that is, that representing tellers as empowered is the same thing as empowering them—I have also described very different approaches to storytelling, ones that treated it variously as political education, a tool of agenda setting, or a step in the development of leaders. In these cases storytelling *was* empowering, not because of the form, but because of the purposes for which it was used.

Along with the danger that efforts to style democratic solidarity on egalitarian intimacy mistake a form of talk for a kind of relationship, in the preceding chapters I have registered two more objections to such efforts. With its emphasis on a bond that is based on individuals' uniqueness, a schema of egalitarian intimacy offers little guidance for relationships between groups or for relationships between people who are members of groups, as indeed, all of us are. In chapter 4, I described the common instruction in dialogue and deliberation initiatives to speak only as "I's." That injunction will be familiar to anyone with the experience of therapy or counseling, in which one is encouraged to claim one's feelings as one's own. Here the same injunction was used to encourage people to speak from their own experience rather than sticking to ideological talking points. Participants were encouraged to bracket their group memberships so as to be known by others.

An alternative, however, is for participants to serve as representatives in a more active way. They might be encouraged to seek out and bring into the discussion the opinions and experiences of other members of their groups: their families, friends, neighbors, co-ethnics, and so on. In the deliberative forums I studied, the fact that participants often saw themselves as representatives of groups led them to do the imaginative work of recognizing the limits of their own perspectives. It led them to appreciate that people with other group memberships might have different preferences and even, sometimes, that those groups had a greater claim to influence on a particular issue than did their own group. In the Grand Rapids planning process, members of a citizens' advisory committee convinced city planners that by actively engaging their friends and neighbors about their needs and priorities they could produce a set of budget priorities that more accurately reflected what residents wanted than a citywide survey had done. The fact that the plan produced by the committee met with little opposition despite being widely publicized suggests that they were right.

A schema of egalitarian intimacy also falls short when it comes to citizens interacting with those who hold political office. The community organizers I described in the last chapter argue persuasively that a script of egalitarian intimacy with officials is precisely what citizens should resist. It may lead them to let officials off the hook too easily, misreading an emotional bond for one based on common political goals. The alternative is a relationship schema that includes negotiation and contention as well as collegiality.

My third objection to a script or model of egalitarian intimacy as it has diffused from the sphere of personal life to that of political life is that it provides only an experience of solidarity without any indication of how that experience will lead to more enduring relationships of equality and political voice. The egalitarian intimacy that is striven for in the realm of personal life exists within an ongoing relationship, a relationship that should deepen over time. By contrast, the egalitarian intimacy that is forged in public deliberation, in efforts to connect advocacy efforts with distant donors, and in empowerment projects in low-income communities is often temporary. People are brought together for encounters in which the usual disparities of power, money, and access are suspended. But the encounter is delimited in time.

Again, there are practical realities standing in the way of creating more lasting civic bonds. In the case of public deliberation exercises, it would be expensive to hire professionals to structure a continuing relationship between citizens and political decision makers. In the case of advocacy storytelling, advocacy groups often have but a few moments to convince audiences to sign on to their cause. That makes it difficult to do anything like actually exchanging stories. The community development projects that produced more empowerment talk than actual empowerment were required to continually demonstrate their successes to the funding agencies on which their work depended. It makes sense, in that context, that staffers would call kids leaders well before they had exercised any kind of leadership.[33]

In each case, however, the obstacles to more enduring civic relationships were also conceptual. The relationships that professionals crafted did not have a telos, did not have, built in, any indication of where the relationship would go. The experience of one-on-one intimate connection was supposed to be enough. That experience was invested with the capacity to make people more politically involved, in the case of public deliberation, or more empowered, in the case of advocacy storytelling and empowerment projects. But just how that would happen was unclear.

The alternative is civic relationships that are intended to evolve and equipped to do so. Alinsky-styled community organizers, for example, envision leadership as something that is learned. They call people leaders who have leadership potential, prefiguring a relationship they hope to see. But they work closely with potential leaders to train them to recruit members, identify promising issues, coordinate actions, negotiate with officials, and so on. Leadership is something that is developed over time. Another example of a relationship schema with a telos was that animating the Grand Rapids planning process. City managers adopted a "50/50 rule": each stage of planning would include 50 percent prior participants and 50 percent newcomers. Prior participants would provide continuity and avoid reinventing the wheel; newcomers would bring new perspectives and capacities for problem solving. The political scientist Jane Mansbridge calls this kind of continuing back-and-forth "recursive representation." This is not the direct democracy that the anarchist activists I described in chapter 6 envision. Members of the public may demand justification for the policies that representatives adopt, but they do not have veto power. Yet recursive representation is unusual for routine politics both in that the back-and-forth is repeated and in that it involves parties' bringing to the discussion parallel discussions they are having with other residents, administrators, and elected officials. Similar to my point about people speaking as members of groups, recursive representation encourages members of the public to speak as "we's" who are developing their own perspectives in active discussion with their groups.[34]

At the other end of the temporal spectrum from the kind of civic engagement I just described are crowd-based approaches. The goal there is to capitalize on relationships that are ephemeral. Crowds are fun, electric; they convene, act, and then disperse. Crowd-based approaches may well attract the kind of people who do not usually participate in civic action, and for that reason alone they are worth experimenting with. But we need to know more about their potential for impact. It is difficult to see how crowd initiatives would allow participants to learn more about the issues or the policy process. Moreover, if the goal is for at least some citizens to move up the ladder of participation, going beyond providing public input to helping set agendas, craft and implement policies, run for political office, and so on, it is also difficult to see how participating in a crowd initiative would encourage that. Accordingly, if there is value in civic bonds that are temporary and intermittent, this does not negate the importance of schemas of civic relationship that envision people's deepening their involvement over time.[35]

CIVIC FRIENDSHIP

I quoted Hannah Arendt at the very beginning of this book, lamenting the lack of a conception of political friendship. Other scholars have similarly sought to reclaim an Aristotelian mode of civic friendship as the glue of democratic polities but have disagreed on just what that relationship would look like today. I believe it might look something like the initiatives I have described in this chapter and the previous one. In social movements, churches, unions, volunteer groups, and workplaces, people have developed new schemas of relationship as they have tackled the practical challenges of working together. New schemas have also emerged in the entirely nonpractical settings of play, where people have had the freedom to interact with one another in unfamiliar ways. In these settings, people have styled solidarity on relationships other than intimacy and arrived at by modes of talk other than self-disclosure. They have treated equality as actively negotiated and have sought to build ties not just between people in all their individual uniqueness, but also between people as members of groups and people interacting with political officeholders.[36]

In each case, though, turning those experiences into sets of interactional norms that might guide other people in other interactions has required additional work. I have drawn attention to the value of reflecting on or naming new relationship schemas: naming a schema equality, as did the *philosophes*; naming a new kind of leadership, as did southern civil rights organizers in the 1960s and as faith-based organizers do today; and naming affinity groups and *encuentros*, as did horizontalist direct-action groups. And I have drawn attention to the role of collective rituals in making new conceptions of political relationship normative. Such rituals include the public meetings in which community organizations pin public officials, enacting a conception of community in which accountability is expected. They include the collective bargaining processes in which unions' demands for wage compression enacted a commitment to equality that led even high-wage workers to value government redistribution to the disadvantaged. And they include the policy-making processes in which the metaphors politicians use to refer to the national "we" communicate important messages about the terms of political belonging. Meetings, collective bargaining, and national policy making are rarely considered to be rituals, but there may be value in thinking of them in that way. Undoubtedly, of course, there are other mechanisms behind the institutionalizing of new schemas of political relationship, and they too invite scrutiny.

At a time of intractable economic inequality and sharp political divisions, we need new forms of political solidarity. People grappling with that need have been sensitive to how easily boundaries between "us" and "them" become politically charged. At the same time, they have been confident that creating bonds of intimacy across those boundaries can erode them. I am less confident. But I do not want to retreat to the view that such divisions are inevitable, or that they recede only when groups, usually the less advantaged, are willing to ignore differences of experience, need, and priorities in favor of what is held to be a superordinate identity. To the contrary, I believe that there are many ways in which to imagine the bonds joining us on each side of the boundary as well as across it.

When I was growing up in Switzerland in the 1970s, we eagerly tuned in to a television show called *Jeux sans frontières* (viewers in Great Britain, Germany, and Italy respectively knew it as *It's a Knockout, Spielen ohne Grenzen*, and *Giochi senza frontiere*). The show brought national teams of ordinary people together to compete in funny games; as I recall, there were quite a few human bobbleheads, greased balancing beams, and flying cream pies. Created soon after the establishment of the European Economic Union, the purpose of the show, which ran until the late 1970s, was to foster a newly European collective identity. Evidence of whether it did so is unclear, but I am struck by the power of its sheer silliness. The show invoked national identities and lightheartedly mocked them, depicting nations in relations of competition and conflict, but competition and conflict that was ridiculous. There is something, I believe, to the idea of silly play as the crucible of new solidarities. Or, at the other extreme, consider again the "mere civility" that the American minister Roger Williams endorsed three centuries earlier as a way to deal with differences of religion and race rather than nation. Williams imagined relationships based on talk that was often rancorous. It little resembled an earnest getting-to-know-you and there was no empathizing with the other's plight, but it remained open to the possibility of agreement, and it envisaged a relationship continuing over time. These are just two of the many ways of imagining the ties that bind, evident in the practical talk and action of real people trying to cooperate across lines of difference. We should learn from them.[37]

Notes

PREFACE

1. Caitlin Dickerson and Zolan Kanno-Youngs, "Thousands Are Targeted as ICE Prepares to Raid Undocumented Migrant Families," *New York Times*, 11 July 2019, https://www.nytimes.com/2019/07/11/us/politics/ice-families-deport.html?searchResultPosition=1.

2. Margaret Renkl, "ICE Came to Take Their Neighbor. They Said No," *New York Times*, 5 August 2019, https://www.nytimes.com/2019/08/05/opinion/ice-undocumented-migrants.html?searchResultPosition=1.

3. Frank Newport, "Americans' Long-Standing Interest in Taxing the Rich," *Gallup Polling Matters*, 22 February 2019, https://news.gallup.com/opinion/polling-matters/247052/americans-long-standing-interest-taxing-rich.aspx; Lee Drutman, "Opposing Forces: Issues Dividing Voters Ahead of Election 2020," Voter Study Group, Democracy Fund, August 2019, https://www.voterstudygroup.org/publication/opposing-forces. Thanks to Felicia Wong for drawing my attention to these findings.

CHAPTER ONE

1. Richard Sennett discusses the rise of the "uncooperative self" in *Together: The Rituals, Pleasures and Politics of Cooperation* (New Haven, CT: Yale University Press, 2012). Figures on inequalities in wealth are from Edward N. Wolf, National Bureau of Economic Research Working Paper 24085, "Household Wealth Trends in the United States, 1962 to 2016: Has Middle Class Wealth Recovered?" (National Bureau of Economic Research: 2017); on the top three richest Americans, see Chuck Collins and Josh Hoxie, "Billionaire Bonanza 2018: Inherited Wealth Dynasties in the 21st-Century U.S.," Inequality.Org (an Institute for Policy Studies Project), https://inequality.org/great-divide/billionaire-bonanza-2018-inherited-wealth-dynasties-in-the-21st-century-u-s/; and on ethnic and racial disparities, see Chuck Collins, Dedrick Asante-Muhammed, Josh Hoxie, and Sabrina Terry, "Dreams Deferred: How Enriching the 1% Widens the Racial Wealth Divide," Inequality.Org, 2019, https://inequality.org/wp-content/uploads/2019/01/IPS_RWD-Report_FINAL-1.15.19.pdf. On residential segregation, see 2017 Fair Housing Trends Report, National Fair Housing Alliance.

2. Robert Putnam, "Bowling Alone: The Strange Disappearance of Civic

America," *Journal of Democracy* 6, 1 (1995): 65–78. On what has come to be called "slactivism," see Malcolm Gladwell, "Small Change," *New Yorker*, 4 October 2010, 42–49.

3. On partisan identities as social identities, see Liliana Mason, *Uncivil Agreement: How Politics Became Our Identity* (Chicago: University of Chicago Press, 2018). On our perceptions of partisans on the other side driving our own views, see Anne E. Wilson, Victoria Parker, and Jaslyn English, "The Ties that Blind: How Diverging Definitions and False Polarization Increases Division and Obscures Common Ground," invited talk, Group Processes & Intergroup Relations Pre-conference, annual convention of the Society for Personality and Social Psychology, Atlanta, Georgia, 1–3 March 2018. On partisan identities driving political preferences, see John Sides, Michael Tesler, and Lynn Vavreck, *Identity Crisis: The 2016 Presidential Campaign and the Battle for the Meaning of America* (Princeton, NJ: Princeton University Press, 2018).

4. I will discuss the vast literature on solidarity at several points. For discussions of the virtues and risks of national-level solidarities, see Elizabeth Theiss Morse, *Who Counts as an American? The Boundaries of National Identity* (New York: Cambridge University Press, 2009); Keith Banting and Will Kymlicka, "Introduction: The Political Sources of Solidarity in Diverse Societies," in *The Strains of Commitment: The Political Sources of Solidarity in Diverse Societies*, ed. Keith Banting and Will Kymlicka (New York: Oxford University Press, 2017), 1–58; and David Miller, "Solidarity and Its Sources," in Banting and Kymlicka, *The Strains of Commitment*, 61–79. For a strong case for the power of subnational solidarity in motivating social provision, see Prerna Singh, *How Solidarity Works for Welfare: Subnationalism and Social Development in India* (New York: Cambridge University Press, 2016).

5. Thomas Pettigrew, Linda R. Tropp, Ulrich Wagner, and Oliver Christ draw attention to the value of self-disclosure in "Recent Advances in Intergroup Contact Theory," *International Journal of Intercultural Relations* 35 (2011): 271–280.

6. On intergroup dialogue, see Katherine Cramer Walsh, *Talking about Race: Community Dialogues and the Politics of Difference* (Chicago: University of Chicago Press, 2008). On public deliberation, see chap. 4; on nonprofits' approach to relationship building, see Nina Eliasoph, *Making Volunteers: Civic Life after Welfare's End* (Princeton, NJ: Princeton University Press, 2011); on the sharing economy, see Nicholas A. John, *The Age of Sharing* (New York: John Wiley & Sons, 2017); on advocacy groups, see chap. 5.

7. Hannah Arendt, "On Humanity in Dark Times: Thoughts about Lessing," trans. Clara and Richard Winston, in *Men in Dark Times* (San Diego: Harcourt Brace, 1968), 3–32, at 27.

8. James D. Montgomery, "Toward a Role-Theoretic Conception of Embeddedness," *American Journal of Sociology* 104, 1 (1998): 92–125. The word *relationship* is usually defined simply as the way things are connected, and when it comes to people, as the way people feel about and behave toward one another. The "way" they do, of course, is at once individual and cultural.

9. Ann Swidler, *Talk of Love: How Culture Matters* (Chicago: University of Chicago Press, 2001). See Cara J. Wong, *Boundaries of Obligation in American Politics: Geographic, National, and Racial Communities* (New York: Cambridge University

Press, 2010), on White Americans' imagined closeness with African Americans. Social psychologists discuss people's ideas about different kinds of groups in terms
of group *entitativity*. See Brian Lickel, David L. Hamilton, Grazyna Wieczorkowska,
Amy Lewis, Steven J. Sherman, and A. Neville Uhles, "Varieties of Groups and the
Perception of Group Entitativity," *Journal of Personality and Social Psychology* 78, 2
(2000): 223. On popular assumptions about the relational styles characteristic of
different kinds of groups, see Brian Lickel, David L. Hamilton, and Steven J. Sherman, "Elements of a Lay Theory of Groups: Types of Groups, Relational Styles, and
the Perception of Group Entitativity," *Personality and Social Psychology Review* 5, 2
(2001): 129–140.

10. Sandra R. Levitsky, *Caring for Our Own: Why There Is No Political Demand for
New American Social Welfare Rights* (Oxford: Oxford University Press, 2014); I explore the relational schemas in Levitsky's account in my "The Multiple Meanings
of Familialism," *Law and Social Inquiry* 43, 1 (2018): 230–237.

11. Francesca Polletta, *Freedom Is an Endless Meeting: Democracy in American
Social Movements* (Chicago: University of Chicago Press, 2002).

12. On scholars' vacillating attention to solidarity, see Jeffrey C. Alexander,
"Morality as a Cultural System: On Solidarity Civil and Uncivil," in *The Palgrave
Handbook of Altruism, Morality, and Social Solidarity*, ed. Vincent Jeffries (New York:
Palgrave Macmillan, 2014), 303–310. See also Lawrence Wilde, "The Concept of
Solidarity: Emerging from the Theoretical Shadows?" *British Journal of Politics and
International Relations* 9, 1 (2007): 171–181; and Graham Crow, "Social Solidarities,"
Sociology Compass 4, 1 (2010): 52–60. Christian Smith and Katherine Sorrell, "On
Social Solidarity," in *The Palgrave Handbook of Altruism, Morality, and Social Soli-
darity*, 219–247, attribute interest in solidarity since about 2005 to moral psychologists' discovery of the social bases of morality. Banting and Kymlicka ("Introduction: The Political Sources of Solidarity in Diverse Societies") attribute it to the
perceived weakening of social solidarity in the United States and Europe.

13. With this fairly anodyne definition of solidarity, I have skirted debates about
the topic—for example, about whether solidarity requires action as well as fellow-
feeling and whether it should be considered mainly a feeling or a set of normative
obligations. See Smith and Sorrell, "On Social Solidarity," for some of these debates.
See Alexander Gofman, "Durkheim's Theory of Social Solidarity and Social Rules,"
in *The Palgrave Handbook of Altruism, Morality, and Social Solidarity*, ed. Vincent
Jeffries (New York: Palgrave Macmillan), 45–69, on Durkheim's evolving understanding of solidarity. Sally J. Scholz, *Political Solidarity* (College Station: Penn-
sylvania State University Press, 2008), names categories of solidarity that overlap
with mine. We both refer to social solidarity; however, what I call oppositional
solidarity, she refers to as political solidarity. What she calls civic solidarity centers on citizens' obligations to each other as mediated by the state. I refer instead
to national solidarities and to the solidarities that characterize civil society. Klaus
Peter Rippe, "Diminishing Solidarity," *Ethical Theory and Moral Practice* 1 (1998):
355–373, similarly distinguishes between solidarities that sustain the current state
of things and those that underpin projects for change. Smith and Sorrell discuss
labor movements using the name Solidarity. The essays in Banting and Kymlicka,
The Strains of Social Commitment, focus on the fourth kind of solidarity.

14. The works I have already cited take up the obstacles to solidarity from both normative and empirical perspectives. Talcott Parsons is probably most closely associated with a view of breaches of solidarity reflecting inadequate socialization; see, e.g., his *The Social System* (New York: Free Press, 1968). Michael Hechter, *Principles of Group Solidarity* (Berkeley and Los Angeles: University of California Press, 1987), argues that solidarity increases as members of the group invest more of their own resources in it. Control by the group, in turn, prevents members from acting self-interestedly against the group.

15. Rippe discusses this in his "Diminishing Solidarity." Scholz also takes up the issue in her *Political Solidarity*.

16. This is the Tocquevillian argument, familiar to many from the work of Robert Putnam. See his *Bowling Alone: The Collapse and Revival of American Community* (New York: Simon & Schuster, 2000). For questions like the one I am asking, see Bob Edwards and Michael W. Foley, "Civil Society and Social Capital: A Primer," in *Beyond Tocqueville: Civil Society and the Social Capital Debate in Comparative Perspective*, ed. Bob Edwards, Michael W. Foley, and Mario Diani (Hanover, NH: University Press of New England, 2001), 1–14. Bo Rothstein and Dietlind Stolle, "Social Capital, Impartiality and the Welfare State: An Institutional Approach," *Generating Social Capital: Civil Society and Institutions in Comparative Perspective*, ed. Mark Hooghe and Dietlind Stolle (New York: Palgrave Macmillan, 2003), 191–209, suggest that the causal arrow between solidarity and government may go the other way: accountable governments lead to greater trust and more solidarity.

17. On moral psychologists' new attention to relationships, see Margaret S. Clark, Erica J. Boothby, Elizabeth Clark-Polner, and Harry T. Reis, "Understanding Prosocial Behavior Requires Understanding Relational Context," in *The Oxford Handbook of Prosocial Behavior*, ed. David A. Schroeder and William G. Graziano (New York: Oxford University Press, 2015), 329–345, at 329. On judging failures of omission and commission, see Jonathan Haidt and Jonathan Baron, "Social Roles and the Moral Judgement of Acts and Omissions," *European Journal of Social Psychology* 26, 2 (1996): 201–218; on judging the misbehavior of people who are psychologically close, see Francesca Gino and Adam D. Galinsky, "Vicarious Dishonesty: When Psychological Closeness Creates Distance from One's Moral Compass," *Organizational Behavior and Human Decision Processes* 119, 1 (2012): 15–26.

18. For good discussions of relational approaches, see Mustafa Emirbayer, "Manifesto for a Relational Sociology," *American Journal of Sociology* 103 (1997): 281–317; Ann Mische, "Relational Sociology, Culture, and Agency," in *The Sage Handbook of Social Network Analysis*, ed. John Scott and Peter J. Carrington (Thousand Oaks, CA: Sage, 2011), 80–97; and John Krinsky and Ann Mische, "Formations and Formalisms: Charles Tilly and the Paradox of the Actor," *Annual Review of Sociology* 39 (2013): 1–26. The latter two are especially good in challenging the notion that relational approaches fail to attend to culture. Harrison White and Ann Mische, "Between Conversation and Situation: Public Switching Dynamics Across Network Domains," *Social Research* (1998): 695–724, argue that all ties are constituted discursively. Paul McClean provides an excellent overview of the ways in which social ties create, channel, and are constituted by culture in *Culture in Networks* (Cambridge: John Wiley & Sons, 2016). Paul Lichterman shows how people in

conversation constitute the meaning of ties in *Elusive Togetherness: Church Groups Trying to Bridge America's Divisions* (Princeton, NJ: Princeton University Press, 2005). Viviana Zelizer and her students have explored ties as sources of meaning by studying how people use money to establish and transform those ties. See her *The Purchase of Intimacy* (Princeton, NJ: Princeton University Press, 2005). On relational approaches in economic sociology, see Nina Bandelj, Paul James Morgan, and Elizabeth Sowers, "Hostile Worlds or Connected Lives? Research on the Interplay between Intimacy and Economy," *Sociology Compass* 9 (2015): 115–127. Benedict Anderson, *Imagined Communities: Reflections on the Origin and Spread of Nationalism* (New York: Verso, 1991), uses the term *imagined communities*. Jan A. Fuhse makes a similar case to mine for treating social networks as shaped by cultural expectations about the relationships that make them up in his "Social Relationships between Communication, Network Structure, and Culture," in *Applying Relational Sociology: Relations, Networks, and Society*, ed. François Dépelteau and Christopher Powell (New York: Palgrave Macmillan, 2013), 181–206. See Charles Horton Cooley, *Human Nature and the Social Order* (1922; New York: Routledge, 2017). See also Randall Collins, *Three Sociological Traditions* (New York: Oxford University Press, 1985), on the micro-interactionist tradition, which includes Cooley and George Herbert Mead, as well as Alfred Schutz. On the constitution of the modern self, see Charles Taylor, *Sources of the Self: The Making of the Modern Identity* (Cambridge, MA: Harvard University Press, 1989).

19. On institutional schemas, see Elisabeth S. Clemens and James M. Cook, "Politics and Institutionalism: Explaining Durability and Change," *Annual Review of Sociology* 25 (1999): 441–466; Francesca Polletta and Beth Gharrity Gardner, "Culture and Social Movements," in *Emerging Trends in the Social and Behavioral Sciences*, ed. Robert A. Scott and Stephen M. Kosslyn (New York: Wiley, 2015); and Edwin Amenta and Kelly M. Ramsey, "Institutional Theory," in *The Handbook of Politics*, ed. Kevin T. Leicht and J. Craig Jenkins (New York: Springer, 2010), 15–39. Scholars of mental models of relationships distinguish between a model and a prototype, which is an exemplary model. See Siegwart Lindenberg, "Prosocial Behavior, Solidarity, and Framing Processes," in *Solidarity and Prosocial Behavior: An Integration of Sociological and Psychological Perspectives*, ed. Detlef Fetchenhauer, Andreas Flache, Abraham P. Buunk, and Siegwart Lindenburg (New York: Springer, 2006), 23–44. See also the discussion of schemas in Rogers Brubaker, *Ethnicity without Groups* (Cambridge, MA: Harvard University Press, 2004), 74–78, and more broadly his discussion of ethnicities as ways of seeing.

20. G. P. Ginsburg, "Rules, Scripts and Prototypes in Personal Relationships," in *Handbook of Personal Relationships: Theory, Research and Interventions*, ed. Steve E. Duck, Dale F. Hay, Stevan E. Hobfoll, William Ed Ickes, and Barbara M. Montgomery (New York: John Wiley & Sons, 1988), 23–39, at 30. On relational schemas, see Mark W. Baldwin, "Relational Schemas and the Processing of Information," *Psychological Bulletin* 112 (1992): 461–484. See also E. K. Davis and Michael J. Todd, "Assessing Friendship: Prototypes, Paradigm Cases and Relationship Description," in *Understanding Personal Relationships: An Interdisciplinary Approach*, ed. Steve E. Duck and Daniel Perlman (London: Sage, 1985), 17–38, who refer to a cultural "prototype" for relationships; G. J. McCall, "The Organizational Life Cycle of

198 | NOTES TO CHAPTER ONE

Relationships," in Duck, Hay, Hobfoll, Ickes, and Montgomery, *Handbook of Personal Relationships*, 467–484, who refers to a "cultural blueprint" of a relationship; Peter L. Berger and Hans Kellner, "Marriage and the Construction of Reality: An Exercise in the Microsociology of Knowledge," *Diogenes* 46 (1964): 1–25, who refer to a "collective definition" of a relationship; and Lindenburg, "Prosocial Behavior, Solidarity, and Framing Processes," who refers to "mental models" of relationships.

21. On the function of relationship scripts, see also Myron Wish, Morton Deutsch, and Susan Kaplan, "Perceived Dimensions of Interpersonal Relations," *Journal of Personality and Social Psychology* 33 (1976): 409–420; Baldwin, "Relational Schemas and the Processing of Information"; and Michael Argyle and Monika Henderson, "The Rules of Friendship," *Journal of Social and Personal Relationships* 1 (1984): 211–237. On people characterizing relations similarly, see Wish, Deutsch, and Kaplan, "Perceived Dimensions of Interpersonal Relations"; on confusing those in similar relationships, see Alan P. Fiske, Nick Haslam, and Susan T. Fiske, "Confusing One Person with Another: What Errors Reveal about the Elementary Forms of Social Relations," *Journal of Personality and Social Psychology* 60 (1991): 656–674; on failing to remember script-incongruent behavior, see Sally Planalp, "Relational Schemata: A Test of Alternative Forms of Relational Knowledge as Guides to Communication," *Human Communication Research* 12 (1985): 3–29; and on behaving consistently with the salient relationship, see Mark W. Baldwin and John G. Holmes, "Salient Private Audiences and Awareness of the Self," *Journal of Personality and Social Psychology* 52 (1987): 1087–1098.

22. James M. Jasper, *The Emotions of Protest* (Chicago: University of Chicago Press, 2018), chap. 6, explores the connections between moral commitments and affective ones. Bruce J. Biddle, "Recent Developments in Role Theory," *Annual Review of Sociology* 12 (1986): 37–59, notes role theory's theatrical origins. Role theorists do recognize that roles exist in relationship. In other words, the role of *mother* exists in connection with the roles of *child*, *father*, and so on. But the concept of relationship schemas alerts us more sharply to the interactional demands of role relationships, to the fact that successful role enactments depend on the other party fulfilling his or her role expectations and that she or he can undermine the role claimed by the other by refusing to accede to the terms of the relationship.

23. Alan Page Fiske, *Structures of Social Life: The Four Elementary Forms of Human Relations* (New York: Free Press, 1991). See also Peter A. McGraw, Philip E. Tetlock, and Orie V. Kristel, "The Limits of Fungibility: Relational Schemata and the Value of Things," *Journal of Consumer Research* 30 (2003): 219–229.

24. Paul D. McLean, "A Frame Analysis of Favor Seeking in the Renaissance: Agency, Networks, and Political Culture," *American Journal of Sociology* 104, 1 (1998): 51–91. Fiske discusses the use of schemas in ambiguous situations in *Structures of Social Life*, 693.

25. William Sewell, "A Theory of Structure: Duality, Agency, and Transformation," *American Journal of Sociology* 98, 1 (1992): 1–29; Emily Honig, "Burning Incense, Pledging Sisterhood," *Signs* 10 (Summer 1985): 700–714. On the transposability of schemas, see also Amy Binder, "For Love and Money: Organizations' Creative Responses to Multiple Environmental Logics," *Theory and Society* 36 (2007): 547–571; Patricia H. Thornton, Candace Jones, and Kenneth Kury, "Insti-

tutional Logics and Institutional Change in Organizations: Transformation in Accounting, Architecture, and Publishing," in *Transformation in Cultural Industries*, ed. Candace Jones and Patricia H. Thornton (Boston: Elsevier, 2005), 125–170; and Michael P. Young, *Bearing Witness against Sin: The Evangelical Birth of the American Social Movement* (Chicago: University of Chicago Press, 2006). For a discussion of Luc Boltanski and Laurent Thevenot's somewhat similar concept of institutional "grammars of worth," see Michèle Lamont, "Toward a Comparative Sociology of Valuation and Evaluation," *Annual Review of Sociology* 38 (2012): 201–221.

26. Elisabeth S. Clemens, *The People's Lobby: Organizational Innovation and the Rise of Interest Group Politics in the United States* (Chicago: University of Chicago Press, 1997). George Lakoff, "The Contemporary Theory of Metaphor," in *Metaphor and Thought*, ed. Andrew Ortony, 2nd ed. (New York: Cambridge University Press, 1993): 202–251, has observed that many of the metaphors we use in everyday life are not especially evocative. When we talk about a relationship "going nowhere," a friend being "up," or the soccer season "winding down," we are not offering new ways of seeing relationships, emotions, sports, or seasons. But metaphors can also be "generative," to quote the political scientist Donald A. Schön, "Generative Metaphor: A Perspective on Problem-Setting in Social Policy," in *Metaphor and Thought*, ed. Andrew Ortony (Cambridge: Cambridge University Press, 1979), 137–163. They can promote new perspectives on familiar issues. What if we then had the opportunity to begin to act on those metaphors, and to expect that others would too? Andrew Perrin, *Citizen Speak: The Democratic Imagination in American Life* (Chicago: University of Chicago Press, 2006), identifies something like the capacity to transpose and combine ideas as a wellspring of creativity in democratic life.

27. Zsuzsa Berend, *The Online World of Surrogacy* (New York: Berghahn Books, 2016).

28. Michèle Lamont, *The Dignity of Working Men: Morality and the Boundaries of Race, Class, and Immigration* (New York: Russell Sage Foundation, 2000). In their fascinating account of what went wrong when international donors responded to the scourge of AIDS in Malawi, Ann Swidler and Susan Cotts Watkins, *A Fraught Embrace: The Romance and Reality of AIDS Altruism in Africa* (Princeton, NJ: Princeton University Press, 2017), draw attention to the misunderstandings wrought by the very different relationship schemas on which Malawians and Western donors operated. In particular, Westerners found discomfiting and sometimes outright immoral the expectations of a patron-client relationship that Malawians took for granted.

29. On the history of consensus-based decision making in American social movements, see my *Freedom Is an Endless Meeting*. On the behavioral expectations of friendship, see Marilyn Friedman, "Feminism and Modern Friendship: Dislocating the Community," in *Feminism and Community*, ed. Penny A. Weiss and Marilyn Friedman (Philadelphia: Temple University Press, 1995), 187–207; and Barbara Misztal, *Trust in Modern Societies: The Search for the Bases of Social Order* (Cambridge: Polity Press/Blackwell, 1996). On women's liberationist groups' efforts to implement formal mechanisms for ensuring equality, see Polletta, *Freedom Is an Endless Meeting*, chap. 6.

30. Polletta, *Freedom Is an Endless Meeting*.

31. On friendship's exclusivity, see Rebecca Adams and Rachel Torr, "Factors Underlying the Structure of Older Adult Friendship Networks," *Social Networks* 20 (1998): 51–61; on the threat posed to existing friendship ties by new ones, see Evelien Zeggelink, "Evolving Friendship Networks: An Individual-Oriented Approach Implementing Similarity," *Social Networks* 17 (1995): 83–110. See also Joreen (Jo Freeman), "The Tyranny of Structurelessness," in *Radical Feminism*, ed. Ann Koedt, Ellen Levine, and Anita Rapone (New York: Quadrangle Books, 1973), 285–299.

32. On making friends, see Joan Cassell, *A Group Called Women: Sisterhood and Symbolism in the Feminist Movement* (New York: David McKay, 1977), 146; also interviews with Joan Cassell, 3 October 2000; Ann Sutherland Harris, 29 September 2000; and Chude Pamela Allen, 29 September 1996 and 22 July 2000. Foror is quoted in Alice Echols, *Daring to Be Bad: Radical Feminism in America* (Minneapolis: University of Minnesota Press, 1989), 100. On the collapse of New York Radical Women, see Ros Baxandall, "Catching the Fire," in *The Feminist Memoir Project*, ed. Rachel Blau DuPlessis and Ann Snitow (New York: Three Rivers Press, 1998), 208–224; and Carol Hanisch, "Struggles over Leadership in the Women's Liberation Movement," in *Leadership and Social Movements*, ed. Colin Barker, Alan Johnson, and Michael Lavallette (Manchester: University of Manchester Press, 2001), 77–95.

33. Alan Page Fiske and Philip E. Tetlock, "Taboo Trade-Offs: Reactions to Transactions That Transgress the Spheres of Justice," *Political Psychology* 18 (1997): 255–297; McGraw, Tetlock, and Kristel, "The Limits of Fungibility"; Sally Planalp and J. M. Honeycutt, "Events that Increase Uncertainty in Personal Relationships," *Human Communication Research* 11 (1985): 593–604; and Sally Planalp and Mary Rivers, "Changes in Knowledge of Close Relationships," in *Knowledge Structures in Close Relationships*, ed. Garth Fletcher and Julie Fitness (Mahwah, NJ: Lawrence Erlbaum Press, 1995), 299–324.

34. On the claims made for crowds, as well as criticisms, see Daren C. Brabham, *Crowdsourcing* (Cambridge, MA: MIT Press, 2013). On open-source and peer production, see Daniel Kreiss, Megan Finn, and Fred Turner, "The Limits of Peer Production: Some Reminders from Max Weber for the Network Society," *New Media & Society* 13, 2 (2011): 243–259; and Yochai Benkler, Aaron Shaw, and Benjamin Mako Hill, "Peer Production: A Form of Collective Intelligence," in *Handbook of Collective Intelligence*, ed. Thomas W. Malone and Michael S. Bernstein (Cambridge, MA: MIT Press, 2015), 175–204.

35. William Sewell, "Connecting Capitalism to the French Revolution: The Parisian Promenade and the Origins of Civic Equality in Eighteenth-Century France," *Critical Historical Studies* 1, 1 (2014): 5–46.

36. Anthony Giddens, *The Transformation of Intimacy: Sexuality, Love, and Eroticism in Modern Societies* (Stanford, CA: Stanford University Press, 1992); on confluent love as opening out to one another, see p. 61; the pure relationship is defined on p. 58.

37. He writes, "Equalisation is an intrinsic element in the transformation of intimacy, as is the possibility of communication" (149).

38. Giddens, *The Transformation of Intimacy*, 188 and 196.

39. Nikolas Rose, *Governing the Soul: The Shaping of the Private Self* (New York:

Routledge, 1990), 215–217; Eva Illouz, *Saving the Modern Soul: Therapy, Emotions, and the Culture of Self-Help* (Berkeley and Los Angeles: University of California Press, 2008); Ole Jacob Madsen, *The Therapeutic Turn: How Psychology Altered Western Culture* (New York: Routledge, 2014); and John Durham Peters, *Speaking Into the Air: A History of the Idea of Communication* (Chicago: University of Chicago Press, 1999), 25 ff., Rogers quote at 26.

40. For claims about the triumph of the therapeutic, see, e.g., Didier Fassin and Richard Rechtman, *The Empire of Trauma: An Inquiry into the Condition of Victimhood* (Princeton, NJ: Princeton University Press, 2009); and Frank Furedi, *Therapy Culture: Cultivating Vulnerability in an Uncertain Age* (London: Routledge, 2004). On public deliberation, see Caroline W. Lee, *Do-It-Yourself Democracy: The Rise of the Public Engagement Industry* (New York: Oxford University Press, 2015); on community projects, see Eliasoph, *Making Volunteers*. On the cultural ideas about temporality that shape our actions and experiences, see Iddo Tavory and Nina Eliasoph, "Coordinating Futures: Toward a Theory of Anticipation," *American Journal of Sociology* 118, 4 (2013): 908–942.

41. Eliasoph, *Making Volunteers*, "I'm involved, . . ." 17.

42. On the argument that sharing comes naturally to millennials, see John, *The Age of Sharing*, 86.

43. John, *The Age of Sharing*.

44. Jeffrey C. Alexander, *The Civil Sphere* (New York: Oxford University Press, 2006).

45. Anderson, *Imagined Communities*. David Kahane makes a similar criticism of the literature on nationalism in his "Diversity, Solidarity and Civic Friendship," *Journal of Political Philosophy* 7 (1999): 267–286. See Bart Bonikowski, "Nationalism in Settled Times," *Annual Review of Sociology* 42 (2016): 427–449, for an overview of recent approaches to nationalism. On Aristotle's concept of civic friendship, see Sibyl A. Schwarzenbach, "On Civic Friendship," *Ethics* 107, 1 (1996): 97–128.

CHAPTER TWO

1. Interview with Charles Cobb, Washington, DC, 12 June 1998. On the Freedom Rides, see August Meier and Elliot Rudwick, *CORE: A Study in the Civil Rights Movement* (Champaign, IL: University of Illinois Press, 1975).

2. Interview with Ivanhoe Donaldson, Washington, DC, 12 June 1998. Report on Project in Greenville, Mississippi, from Cobb, 18 May 1963, Southern Regional Council Papers, 1944–1968, microfilm (hereinafter SRC Papers), Reel 179, #739–741. "While at the cafe they met a man by the name of Bobby O'Neal, . . ." West Helena, Arkansas, ND, Student Nonviolent Coordinating Committee Papers, 1959–1972, microfilm (Sanford, NC: Microfilming Corporation of America, 1982; hereinafter SNCC Papers), Reel 5, #329.

3. Interview with Charles Cobb, Washington, DC, 12 June 1998; Complaint from Mrs. Bernice Carter, 18 February 1963, fired by her employer, SRC Papers, Reel 177, #1762. James West Report, "Things That Happened to Me in Jail," n.d. [June 1963], SRC Papers, Reel 179, #1280. For other reports of people threatened with eviction, dismissal, or punishment in school for associating with Freedom Riders, see,

among others, Lee County field report, 15 March 1964, Willie Ricks, SNCC Papers, Reel 7, #496; and Chatfield field report, 28 November 1962, SRC Papers, Reel 178, #449.

4. On SNCC's organizing in Mississippi and southwest Georgia, see Clayborne Carson, *In Struggle: SNCC and the Black Awakening of the 1960s* (Cambridge, MA: Harvard University Press, 1983); Charles E. Cobb, Jr., *This Nonviolent Stuff'll Get You Killed: How Guns Made the Civil Rights Movement Possible* (New York: Basic Books, 2014); James Forman, *The Making of Black Revolutionaries* (Seattle, WA: Open Hand, 1985); and Charles Payne, *I've Got the Light of Freedom: The Organizing Tradition and the Mississippi Freedom Struggle* (Berkeley and Los Angeles: University of California Press, 1995). On later voter registration and turnout in the Mississippi counties in which SNCC worked in the early 1960s, see Kenneth T. Andrews, "The Impacts of Social Movements on the Political Process: The Civil Rights Movement and Black Electoral Politics in Mississippi," *American Sociological Review* 62, 5 (1997): 800–819.

5. Mancur Olson, *The Logic of Collective Action* (Cambridge, MA: Harvard University Press, 1965); see Anthony Oberschall, *Social Conflict and Social Movements* (Englewood Cliffs, NJ: Prentice-Hall, 1973), for the argument that northern White support was crucial to the rise of the civil rights movement.

6. Aldon Morris, *The Origins of the Civil Rights Movement: Black Communities Organizing for Change* (New York: Free Press, 1984); and Doug McAdam, *Political Process and the Development of Black Insurgency, 1930–1970* (Chicago: University of Chicago Press, 1982).

7. On the mobilizing power of prior ties: in the French commune, see Roger Gould, *Insurgent Identities: Class, Community, and Protest in Paris from 1848 to the Commune* (Chicago: University of Chicago Press, 1995). In the Russian Revolution, see Victoria Bonnell, *Roots of Rebellion: Workers' Politics and Organizations in St. Petersburg and Moscow, 1900–1914* (Berkeley and Los Angeles: University of California Press, 1983). On Central American solidarity, see Sharon Nepstad and Christian Smith, "Rethinking Recruitment to High-Risk/Cost Activism: The Case of Nicaragua Exchange," *Mobilization* 4, 1 (1999): 25–40. On environmental activism, see Mario Diani, *Green Networks: A Structural Analysis of the Italian Environmental Movement* (Edinburgh: Edinburgh University Press, 1995). On animal rights activism, see James M. Jasper and Jane D. Poulsen, "Recruiting Strangers and Friends: Moral Shocks and Social Networks in Animal Rights and Anti-Nuclear Protests," *Social Problems* 42, 4 (1995): 493–512. On LGBT and disabled rights activism, see Debra C. Minkoff, "Producing Social Capital: National Social Movements and Civil Society," *American Behavioral Scientist* 40, 5 (1997): 606–619. Elisabeth Jean Wood, *Insurgent Collective Action and Civil War in El Salvador* (New York: Cambridge University Press, 2003), describes the ties of competition that characterized El Salvadoran peasants who worked on elite-controlled haciendas. On the mixed findings on the role of prior ties in movements, see Florence Passy and Gian-Andrea Monsch, "Do Social Networks Really Matter in Contentious Politics?" *Social Movement Studies* 13, 1 (2014): 22–47.

8. On preexisting ties discouraging participation, see James A. Kitts, "Mobilizing in Black Boxes: Social Networks and Participation in Social Movement Orga-

nizations," *Mobilization* 5, 2 (2000): 241–257; and Nepstad and Smith, "Rethinking Recruitment."

9. Payne, *I've Got the Light of Freedom.*

10. Organizers and scholars who write about organizing now often characterize it as "relational." See, for example, Hahrie Han, *How Organizations Develop Activists: Civic Associations and Leadership in the 21st Century* (New York: Oxford University Press, 2014); and Heidi J. Swarts, *Organizing Urban America: Secular and Faith-Based Progressive Movements* (Minneapolis: University of Minnesota Press, 2008). However, the existing literature does not discuss the imaginative dimensions of this relationship-building work. This is what I try to add. Payne, *I've Got the Light of Freedom.*

11. Report to VEP, RE: Mississippi Voter Registration Project, From: Bob Moses, rec'd 5 December 1962, SRC Papers, Reel 177, #1553–1557.

12. Saul Alinsky, *Reveille for Radicals* (Chicago: University of Chicago Press, 1945), 204; see also Sanford D. Horwitt, *Let Them Call Me Rebel: Saul Alinsky—His Life and Legacy* (New York: Vintage, 1989). Georg Simmel, "The Stranger" [1908], in *Georg Simmel*, ed. Donald Levine (Chicago: University of Chicago Press), 143–149. Alessandro Pizzorno, "Some Other Kinds of Otherness: A Critique of 'Rational Choice' Theories," in *Development, Democracy, and the Art of Trespassing: Essays in Honor of Albert O. Hirschman*, ed. Alejandro Foxley, Michael S. McPherson, and Guillermo O'Donnell (Notre Dame, IN: University of Notre Dame Press, 1996), 355–372. Other scholars have discussed the political effects of people's ambiguous social positions. John Padgett and Christopher Ansell, "Robust Action and the Rise of the Medici, 1400–1434," *American Journal of Sociology* 98, 6 (1993): 1259–1319, attribute Cosimo de' Medici's power in seventeenth-century Florence to his interstitial position and the capacities that were as a consequence projected onto him: "The very ambiguity of his placement in self-interest somehow became elevated, in the public mind, into the essence of public interest" (1308). In a related but different line of argument, Ann Mische, *Partisan Publics: Communication and Contention across Brazilian Youth Activist Networks* (Princeton, NJ: Princeton University Press, 2007), shows that interlocutors connect disparate identities through people's capacity to recognize different dimensions of themselves in the interlocutor.

13. For overviews of how social movement scholars have conceptualized collective identity, see Francesca Polletta and James M. Jasper, "Collective Identity and Social Movements," *Annual Review of Sociology* 27 (2001): 283–305; and Cristina Flesher Fominaya, "Collective Identity in Social Movements: Central Concepts and Debates," *Sociology Compass* 4, 6 (2010): 393–404. On identity being as much a product of "'external' identification by others as of 'internal' self-identification," see Richard Jenkins, *Social Identity* (New York: Routledge, 2008), 20; and Pizzorno, "Some Other Kinds of Otherness." Experiments on voting and other forms of participation suggest the power of recognizing social identities. People who were told by experimenters that they were above-average citizens were subsequently more likely to vote (Alice M. Tybout and Richard F. Yalch, "The Effect of Experience: A Matter of Salience?" *Journal of Consumer Research* 6, 4 [1980]: 406–413); and people who were told by an organization of which they were members that "I know you're the kind of person who cares" were more likely to sign an online petition, find out

about an upcoming conference to which they were invited, or reach out to friends as potential recruits (Han, *How Organizations Develop Activists*, 148). Doug McAdam and Ronelle Paulsen, "Specifying the Relationship between Social Ties and Activism," *American Journal of Sociology* 99, 3 (1993): 640–667, describe something like this dynamic in a later episode in the civil rights movement. McAdam and Paulsen studied the northern, mainly White students who applied to travel to Mississippi in 1964 to work as volunteers in registering voters and running freedom schools. The authors were interested in the differences between students who were accepted to the program and those who actually made good on their commitment and traveled to the South. They found that the students who followed through on their commitment did not have more ties to other participants, as the preexisting-ties argument would anticipate. Rather, at the time they applied to the program, these volunteers were involved in groups that defined participation in the movement as central to their identity. They were active in student democratic groups or in religious communities committed to social justice. In Pizzorno's terms, these groups served as identity-constituting circles of recognition, giving their members a sense of being already part of the southern freedom movement.

14. Mustafa Emirbayer, "A Manifesto for a Relational Sociology," *American Journal of Sociology* 103, 2 (1997): 281–317, writes, "Circles of recognition can include 'virtual' circles with cultural ideals and fantasized objects, as well as circles of interpersonal, social relationships" (297).

15. Harrell R. Rodgers, Jr., and Charles S. Bullock III, *Law and Social Change* (New York: McGraw-Hill, 1972), 22–23.

16. On Mississippi registration rates by county, see Payne, *I've Got the Light of Freedom*, 112. On voter registration rates in southwest Georgia, see Stephen G. N. Tuck, *Beyond Atlanta: The Struggle for Racial Equality in Georgia, 1940–1980* (Atlanta: University of Georgia Press, 2003), 163. "It seemed like a good afternoon" is from Chatfield to SNCC, 20–21 December 1962, SRC Papers, Reel 178, #516–517.

17. SNCC's first project, in McComb, Mississippi, in the summer and fall of 1961, was plagued by a series of setbacks: high school students were jailed for trying to desegregate the local Woolworth's, SNCC workers were beaten for accompanying Black residents to the voting registrar, and then, calamitously, the project supporter Herbert Lee was murdered by E. H. Hurst, a White neighbor and state representative, who was later acquitted. In the resulting climate of fear, SNCC workers withdrew. They regrouped in early 1962, joining with Mississippi activists from the Congress of Racial Equality and the NAACP to map out a state registration program. On the development of the Mississippi projects, see Payne, *I've Got the Light of Freedom*. On the southwest Georgia project, see Tuck, *Beyond Atlanta*.

18. On SNCC's relationship with the Voter Education Project, see Tuck, *Beyond Atlanta*, 161, and Payne, *I've Got the Light of Freedom*, 108–109. On field-workers being asked to submit field reports, see Jack Minnis to James Forman, 19 September 1962, SRC Papers, Reel 178, #428; and Jack Minnis to Aaron Henry, 12 January 1963, SRC Papers, Reel 177, #1612–1613.

19. On the role of an older cadre of activists, see Indeed, Memorandum, Miss. Field Trip, 9–11 January 1963, SRC Papers, Reel 177, #1604–1611; the Wiley Branton quote is from Indeed, Memorandum; Report from Charlie Cobb on Voter Regis-

tration Activities in Leland, Miss., 31 January–4 February 1963, SRC Papers, Reel 177, #1668; Report on Voter Registration in Washington County from Curtis Elmer Hayes, 28 January–4 February [1963], SRC Papers, Reel 177, #1670. On southwest Georgia, see Tuck, *Beyond Atlanta*, 169 ff.

20. Bob Moses wrote pessimistically about the involvement of adults in early 1963, "Those adults who have the time, are economically independent of the White man, are willing to join in the struggle, and are not afraid of the tremendous pressure they will face, are a negligible number. . . . It doesn't seem likely that this situation will change very much in the near future," Report to Voter Education Project, Re: Mississippi Voter Registration Project, Bob Moses, 21 January 1963, SNCC Papers, Reel 62, #826–827; on organizing efforts on a single day in 1962, see Payne, *I've Got the Light of Freedom*, 252; Report to VEP, RE: Mississippi Voter Registration Project from Bob Moses, n.d. (rec'd 5 December 1962), SRC Papers, Reel 177, #1553–1557; on southwest Georgia, see Tuck, *Beyond Atlanta*, 165–166; on fears of retaliation, "Voter Canvassing Report," Peter Stone, 1 June 1963, SRC Papers, Reel 179, #1191.

21. "My immediate opposition . . ." is in To: SNCC, From: Willie Blue, Panola County Project, Batesville, 2 October 1963, SNCC Papers, Reel 17, #132–133; "most of the old people . . ." is in Report from Charles R. McLaurin, Washington and Sunflower Counties, Mississippi, 1–16 June 1963, SRC Papers, Reel 179, #846.

22. Stanford University Project South Oral History Collection, 1965 [microform] (Glen Rock, NJ: Microfilming Corp. of America), interviews 162 and 165.

23. On Black clergy's role in Black communities and White ones, see Morris, *Origins*, and Payne, *I've Got the Light of Freedom*. "With us 100% . . ." is in Tate County Field Report, 11 August 1964, SNCC Papers, Reel 6, #1091; "I went to see . . ." is in Report on the Greenville Mississippi Project, from Charlie Cobb, 11 May 1963, SRC Papers, Reel 179, #721–723.

24. 18 March 1963, Report on meeting at Wesley Methodist Church, SRC Papers, Reel 177, #1794.

25. Report from Frank Smith on Voter Registration Project in Holly Springs, Miss., SRC Papers, Reel 177, #1674. Bob Mants and John Perdew told people in Americus, Georgia, that pipes were being put in the Black community as "a result of having as many people registered as we do" (To: Voter Education Project, From Bob Mants, John Perdew, March–April 1964, SRC Papers, Reel 184, #1841). Interviews with Hollis Watkins, Jackson, MS, 22 November 1996; and Ivanhoe Donaldson, Washington, DC, 12 June 1998.

26. Interview with Charles Cobb, Ivanhoe Donaldson, and Dion Diamond, Washington, DC, 12 June 1998.

27. Reginald Robinson to Dear Jim, 30 April 1962, Huntsville, Ala., SNCC Papers, Reel 9, #55.

28. Interview with Charles Cobb, Washington, DC, 12 June 1998.

29. Sherrod to Wiley, 10 March 1963, SRC Papers, Reel 178, #630–631; "a sense of the larger movement" is in Joyce Barrett to SNCC, 10 March to 14 April 1963, SRC Papers, Reel 178, #685–669; "All that happens . . ." is in Charles Sherrod to Wiley Branton, 9 October 1962, SRC Papers, Reel 178, #435; "The importance of this . . ." is in To: Mr. Wiley Branton, From: Charles Sherrod, 9 December 1962, A General

Account of the Present State of the Work in Lee, Terrell, and Sumter Counties, SRC Papers, Reel 178, #467; Prathia [Hall] to Howdy, 4 March 1963, SRC Papers, Reel 177, #1747; Chatfield Field Report, 28 November 1962, SRC Papers, Reel 178, #449. Reverend James quoted in Joanne Grant, *Ella Baker: Freedom Bound* (New York: Wiley, 1998), 147. "Proclaimed that she . . ." is in Chatfield Field Report, 28 November 1962, SRC Papers, Reel 178, #449. Despite Charles Sherrod's conviction that building intercounty unity was essential, few Albany leaders made the trip to counties known for the brutality of their resistance to Black activism. SNCC staffers criticized themselves for having "been very negligent in bringing the few active people from this county in contact with movement people from other places." But an Albany leader confessed, "I know I ought to, but everyone has something they can't do, and going out to Terrell is mine"; quoted in Tuck, *Beyond Atlanta*, 171. The fact that SNCC organizers were unable to make headway in southwest Georgia was undoubtedly due primarily to the depth of African Americans' economic dependence on Whites and the level of racist violence. However, activists' inability to provide the recognition of a wider movement may have also cost them.

30. "This is a report on Ruleville, . . ." SNCC Papers, Reel 7, #29; "So she can be . . ." is in From Milton Hancock to Mr. Robert P. Moses, Voter Education Projects, 24 April 1963, SRC Papers, Reel 179, #1153; "discussed good citizenship" is in Report from Jesse Harris on Voter Registration Activities in Mississippi, 2–14 January 1963, SRC Papers, Reel 177, #1651; "subject was the duties . . ." is in Report on Voter Education, Leflore County, John Hodges, n.d. (12 March 1963), SRC Papers, Reel 177, #1789; "helping the people" is in Report from Mary Lane, March 30, 1963, SRC Papers, Reel 177; "the Negro's responsibility" is in Lee County Voter Registration Project, SNCC Papers, Reel 7, #497–512.

31. "Citizenship Honor Rolls" is in "Report on Forrest County Voter Project," John O'Neal, 8 August 1963, SRC Papers, Reel 179, #1252; "Although we've suffered greatly . . ." is from Mrs. Fannie Lou Hamer, 30 September 1963, Ruleville, SRC Papers, Reel 179, #1338–1344. "More and more Negroes . . ." is in Memorandum [Wiley Branton], Miss. Field Trip, 9–11 January 1963, SRC Papers, Reel 177, #1604–1611.

32. "Would help people . . ." is from the oral history interview with Hollis Watkins, Mississippi Oral History Project, University of Southern Mississippi (hereinafter Miss. Oral History), 23–30 October 1995; Report on meeting at Wesley Methodist Church, 18 March 1963, SRC Papers, Reel 177, #1794; Field Report of Greenwood, Mississippi [n.d.; November 1963], Jane Stembridge, SNCC Papers, Reel 17, #131–132; "were proud to have . . ." is from Faith Holsaert, 19 February 1963, SRC Papers, Reel 178, #639; "My great grandfather . . ." is from Wiley Branton, "Leflore County Chronology Continues," 28 March 1963, SRC Papers, Reel 175, #1860.

33. "Their experiences when . . ." is from interview with Hollis Watkins, Jackson, MS, 22 November 1996; Report on VR in Greenwood, Miss. by Curtis Elmer Hayes, 15 March 1963, SRC Papers, Reel 177, #1803; "The group heard . . ." is from Report on Progress in Ruleville and Other Counties, November 22–29, 1962, SRC Papers, Reel 177, #1615.

34. Payne, *I've Got the Light of Freedom*, 260; "J. C. Morer . . ." is from Joyce Bar-

rett, 11 March 1963, SRC Papers, Reel 178, #635; "Once in a meeting . . ." is from Voice of the Movement, Hattiesburg, Miss. 27 August 1963, SRC Papers, Reel 179, #973–974; Charles Sherrod, An Analysis, Rec'd December 11, 1962, SRC Papers, Reel 179, #496.

35. "He said to be . . ." is from Affidavit of Mrs. Edith Simmons Peters, September 1961, SNCC Papers, Reel 40, #187–190. "Wonderful sermon . . ." is from a memo from Lee County Voter Registration Project, SNCC Papers, Reel 7, #497; "asked the young people . . ." is from Faith Holsaert field report, March 9 1963, SNCC Papers, Reel 6, #1159; "Behind this man . . ." is from Holsaert, 19 February 1963, SRC Papers, Reel 178, #639; "brought eleven-year-old . . ." is from Southwest Georgia Voter Registration Project, Faith Holsaert, Mass meeting in Sumter County, 8 November 1962, SNCC Papers, Reel 6, #1175.

36. "Introduced Jane Johnson . . ." is from the affidavit of Mrs. Cora Campbell, State of Mississippi, County of Leflore, 27 June 1963, SRC Papers, Reel 178, #467. Greenwood Mass Meeting, no author, 11 February 1963, SRC Papers, Reel 177, #1680. "How many . . ." is from To: Branton Wiley, From: Faith S. Holsaert, 11 December 1962, Staff Relationships—Personal Politics, SRC Papers, Reel 178, #485.

37. Interview with Dion Diamond, Washington, DC, 12 June 1998; Dona Richards field report, n.d. [November 1963], SNCC Papers, Reel 17, #136–137.

38. Moore is quoted in Howell Raines, *My Soul Is Rested: The Story of the Civil Rights Movement in the Deep South* (New York: Penguin, 1983), 237; "Bob Moses was a little bitty fella . . ." is in *Voices of Freedom: An Oral History of the Southern Civil Rights Movement from the 1950s through the 1980s*, ed. Henry Hampton (New York: Bantam 1990), 180.

39. Interview with Mike Miller, New York City, 21 August 1998; and Payne, *I've Got the Light of Freedom*, 182.

40. "People from these plantations . . ." is from Payne, *I've Got the Light of Freedom*, 162; "the Negroes from all around the county . . ." is in Leflore County, 23 March 1963, Willie Peacock, SRC Papers, Reel 177, #1819; "people took it to be a personal victory . . ." is from Payne, *I've Got the Light of Freedom*, 162; "many people in Albany . . ." is from Faith Holsaert, 19 February 1963, SNCC Papers, Reel 6, #1160.

41. "Community Organizations," in COFO Mississippi Handbook of Political Programs [1964], SNCC Papers, Reel 41, #76; Ella Baker remarks in Wash. Conf. on Food and Jobs (1963), Zinn Papers, Box 2:10, State Historical Society of Wisconsin.

42. Report from Charlie Cobb on Voter Registration Activities in Leland Miss., from 31 January–4 Feb, 1963, SRC Papers, Reel 177, #1668; Frank Smith field report, Holly Springs, 21 May 1963, SRC Papers, Reel 177, #1524; Report: Holly Springs, 20–22 April 1963, Frank Smith Jr., SRC Papers, Reel 177, #1858; interviews with Wazir Peacock, San Francisco, CA, 29 September 1996; Hollis Watkins, Jackson, MS, 22 November 1996; and Robert Mants, Lowndesboro, AL, 25–29 July 1996.

43. References to "strong" people appear in Outline of Mississippi project areas, n.d. [probably spring 1964], SNCC Papers, Reel 64, #1193–1197; Report to: Cleve Sellers, From Ivanhoe Donaldson, Re: Mississippi, 16 August 1965, SNCC Papers, Reel 40, #1066–1067; Nancy and Gene Turvitz to Dear Friends, 10–14 July 1965, SNCC Papers, Reel 61, #1071–1072; NA to Dear Bill, 14 April 1966, Reel 42, #377.

44. Fannie Lou Hamer is described in Report on Activity in Ruleville and Sunflower County from August 19th to December 28th (1962), Charles McLaurin, SRC Papers, Reel 177, #1528–1531; "I think the kind of people . . ." in To: Staff Coordinator, SNCC, From: Charles Cobb, Re: Greenville Mississippi, Nov. 8 [1963], SNCC Papers, reel 17, #125–128; Moses in transcript of SNCC staff meeting, 9–11 June 1964, SNCC Papers, reel 3, #975–992.

45. "People asking questions . . ." is from Memo: Miss Voter Education Project, Report from Sunflower County, Dec. 3–8, McLaurin, Jones, and Harris, Rec'd Dec. 21 1962, SRC Papers, Reel 177, #1585. "Some of the people have asked . . ." is from Report on progress in Voter Registration in Ruleville, 10-11-62, SRC Papers, Reel 177, #1616. On organizers having to work hard, see Report on Project in Greenville, Mississippi, from Cobb, 18 May 1963, SRC Papers, Reel 179, #739–741.

46. Report on VR activities in Greenwood, Miss., from Ida Holland, 11–22 February 1963, SRC Papers, Reel 177, #1701. Carson, *In Struggle*, discusses SNCC workers' views of the SCLC.

47. Field report by Ralph Allen, n.d. [1964], SNCC Papers, Reel 37, #863–868.

48. I discuss this further in *Freedom Is an Endless Meeting*, chap. 4; see also Payne, *I've Got the Light of Freedom*, and Carson, *In Struggle*.

49. I discuss this further in *Freedom Is an Endless Meeting*.

50. On movements' ability to appropriate a preexisting collective identity, see William A. Gamson, "Commitment and Agency in Social Movements," *Sociological Forum* 6, 1 (1991): 27–50; on the fact that this is sometimes difficult, see David A. Snow and Doug McAdam, "Identity Work Processes in the Context of Social Movements: Clarifying the Identity/Movement Nexus," *Self, Identity, and Social Movements*, ed. Sheldon Stryker, Timothy Joseph Owens, and Robert W. White (Minneapolis: University of Minnesota Press, 2000): 41–67. On identity work in repressive contexts, see Rachel L. Einwohner, "Identity Work and Collective Action in a Repressive Context: Jewish Resistance on the 'Aryan Side' of the Warsaw Ghetto," *Social Problems* 53, 1 (2006): 38–56.

51. See Marilynn Brewer and Wendi Gardner, "Who Is This 'We'? Levels of Collective Identity and Self Representations," *Journal of Personality and Social Psychology* 71, 1 (1996): 83–93.

52. Lynne J. Millward, "Contextualizing Social Identity in Considerations of What It Means to Be a Nurse," *European Journal of Social Psychology* 25 (1995): 303–324. On the constructed character of identities, see Harrison White and Ann Mische, "Between Conversation and Situation: Public Switching Dynamics across Network Domains," *Social Research* (1998): 695–724.

53. Marshall Berman, *All That Is Solid Melts into Air* (New York: Simon & Schuster, 1982), 284. Research on efforts to promote voting likewise suggests the relevance both of personal ties and of imagined social identities. People are more likely to vote when the get-out-the-vote message is delivered by someone who lives in their neighborhood (personal tie), and they are more likely to vote when they are told that they are the kind of person who votes (social identity). See Todd Rogers, Craig R. Fox, and Alan S. Gerber, "Rethinking Why People Vote: Voting as Dynamic Social Expression," in *The Behavioral Foundations of Public Policy*, ed. Eldar Shafir (Princeton, NJ: Princeton University Press, 2013), 91–107.

54. See, e.g., Han, *How Organizations Develop Activists*. I will discuss this kind of community organizing again in chaps. 4, 5, and 6.

55. The excerpt appeared in the radio broadcast *This American Life*, "The Incredible Rarity of Changing Your Mind," April 24, 2015, https://www.thisamericanlife.org/555/the-incredible-rarity-of-changing-your-mind. The program reported on the research of a political scientist, Michael LaCour, that was later found to be fraudulent. However, the canvassing efforts LaCour claimed to have studied were around marriage equality; the recording I cite came instead from canvassing around reproductive rights.

CHAPTER THREE

1. Karl Marx and Friedrich Engels, "Manifesto of the Communist Party," in Robert C. Tucker, *The Marx-Engels Reader* (New York: Norton, 1978), 475; see also Karl Polanyi, *The Great Transformation* (Boston: Beacon, 2001), and more ambivalently, Georg Simmel, *The Philosophy of Money* (New York: Routledge, 2004); see also the discussion in Marion Fourcade and Kieran Healy, "Moral Views of Market Society," *Annual Review of Sociology* 33 (2007): 285–311.

2. All names in the following are pseudonyms.

3. Émile Durkheim, *The Division of Labor in Society*, trans. George Simpson (Glencoe, IL: Free Press, 1966).

4. The research consisted of interviews with twenty-six agents, negotiators, and agency owners between fall 2011 and summer 2014 and field observations at two debt-settlement firms in the fall and winter of 2011. Zaibu Tufail was employed as a telemarketer and agent at a debt-settlement agency from November 2009 to April 2011. After the firm closed, she retained contact with several agents. Those agents provided contact information for other agents, negotiators, and firm owners for interviews. I developed a questionnaire and Tufail conducted interviews in person. Interviews, which were tape-recorded, ran from forty-five minutes to three and a half hours, the median being one and three-quarters hours. Questions addressed the agent's standard procedure for trying to sign clients and the kinds of resistance he or she encountered; the sources of variation in clients' views of debt; the skills that were required of the jobs of agent and negotiator, and, in interviews with both agents and negotiators, the kinds of emotional experiences that came with the job. I went over Tufail's notes after each interview to identify patterns and to add questions for subsequent interviews.

Initial interviews drew my attention to a surprising pattern. Men and women were both hired as agents. But women were much more likely to quit, interviewees said, or to shift over to the job of negotiator when it was offered. Indeed, all but one of the women negotiators interviewed or observed began as agents. The job of a negotiator was not better paid than that of an agent, and it was acknowledged to be a more stressful one. I wondered, therefore, why men tended to stay on as agents and women tended to accept jobs as negotiators. This was especially puzzling because the work of agents seemed to involve the kinds of emotional labor that women's jobs typically involve, namely, solicitousness and concern toward clients who were worried about their financial troubles, along with a comforting optimism that signing up with the firm was the solution to those troubles.

I therefore developed a second questionnaire, and Tufail conducted a second round of interviews in 2013–2014 to probe men's and women's experiences of being an agent. Interviews were conducted either by phone or in person with eight of the original interviewees, along with two agency owners, two agents, and four negotiators who had not been interviewed the first time. Tufail asked interviewees to discuss who tended to hold the jobs of agent and negotiator and why that was the case. She also asked interviewees to compare the jobs in terms of their remuneration, stress, and satisfaction. Interviewees in both rounds had between one and thirteen years of experience in the debt-settlement industry, with a median of four years. Collectively, they had worked at more than two dozen firms. Ten interviewees were women; the rest were men. Thirteen of the interviewees were White, five were Latino, four were African American, and three were Asian or Asian American. Interviewees ranged in age from twenty to forty-five, with a median age of thirty years. Their educational attainment ranged from a high school diploma to a postgraduate degree, but 62 percent did not have a college degree. Again, we use pseudonyms for all interviewees.

Tufail also made contact with the heads of two debt-settlement firms located in the Los Angeles area. I refer to the firms here by the pseudonyms Second Chance Settlement and Red Heron Financial Services. According to interviewees, both firms were typical in terms of their clientele, the kinds of debts they dealt with, and their revenue. Second Chance Settlement operated from 2008 to shortly after our observation period ended in 2011, during which it employed between eighteen and twenty-three agents. Red Heron was established in 2008 and operated as a debt-settlement firm until 2011. After that, it expanded its range of services to include settlements in personal injury and workers' compensation claims. During the period of our observation, eleven agents worked there. Tufail observed agents and negotiators at work in both firms for a total of twenty-nine hours. With the permission of the client or collector, agents and negotiators allowed Tufail to listen to their phone conversations (however, since we did not obtain formal consent from clients or collectors, we do not quote them). After the calls, Tufail was able to ask the agent or negotiator questions about how he or she had handled the client or collector. In addition, she paid special attention to the ways in which men and women agents interacted with clients. Tufail was also able to ask seven women agents about their experiences.

5. On equity theory, see Elaine Walster, William G. Walster, and Ellen Berscheid, *Equity: Theory and Research* (Boston: Allyn & Bacon, 1978). On challenges to the notion of a single principle of fairness, see the essays in *Justice and Social Interaction*, ed. Gerold Mikula (New York: Springer-Verlag, 1980).

6. William Austin and Elaine Hatfield, "Equity Theory, Power, and Social Justice," and Thomas Schwinger, "Just Allocations of Goods: Decisions among Three Principles," both in *Justice and Social Interaction*, ed. Gerold Mikula (New York: Springer-Verlag), 25–61 and 95–125. See also Mikula's introductory essay in that volume, 13–23.

7. Alan P. Fiske, "The Four Elementary Forms of Sociality: Framework for a Unified Theory of Social Relations," *Psychological Review* 99 (1992): 689–723. See also Alan Page Fiske, *Structures of Social Life: The Four Elementary Forms of Human Relations* (New York: Free Press, 1991).

8. Alan Page Fiske and Phillip E. Tetlock, "Taboo Trade-Offs: Reactions to Trans-

actions That Transgress the Spheres of Justice," *Political Psychology* 18, 2 (1997): 255–297; see also A. Peter McGraw, Philip E. Tetlock, and Orie V. Kristel, "The Limits of Fungibility: Relational Schemata and the Value of Things," *Journal of Consumer Research* 30, 2 (2003): 219–229.

9. Fiske, "The Four Elementary Forms," 704.

10. Laura M. Tach and Sara Sternberg Greene, "Robbing Peter to Pay Paul: Economic and Cultural Explanations for How Lower-Income Families Manage Debt," *Social Problems* 61, 1 (2014): 1–21.

11. Vivianna Zelizer, "How I Became a Relational Economic Sociologist and What Does That Mean?" *Politics & Society* 40, 2 (2012): 153.

12. On the debt-settlement industry, see Peter S. Goodman, "Peddling Relief, Firms Put Debtors in a Deeper Hole," *New York Times*, 19 June 2010, A1. On federal legislation, see Federal Trade Commission, "Public Forum on Debt Relief Amendments to the Telemarketing Sales Rule" (Washington, DC, November 2009), http://ftc.gov/bcp/rulemaking/tsr/tsr-debtrelief/transcript.pdf; Senate Committee on Commerce, Science, and Transportation, "Field Hearing: Protecting Consumers from Deceptive Debt Settlement Schemes" (Washington, DC: Government Printing Office, 2010); Edward Wyatt, "New Restrictions Placed on Debt Settlement Companies," *New York Times*, 30 July 2010, B2; Stephanie Wilshusen, "Meeting the Demand for Debt Relief," Payment Cards Center Discussion Paper No. 11, 4 (Federal Reserve Bank of Philadelphia, 2011). On agency practices after the legislation, see Leslie Parrish and Ellen Harnick, *The State of Lending in America and Its Impact on U.S. Households: Debt Settlement* (Durham, NC: Center for Responsible Lending, June 2014), www.responsiblelending.org.

13. On credit card debt carried by debt-settlement customers, see Goodman, "Peddling Relief," and Parrish and Harnick, "The State of Lending." See Wilshusen, "Meeting the Demand," on debt-settlement clients' inability to make debt-management payments.

14. Richard A. Briesch, "Economic Factors and the Debt Management Industry," 2009 paper prepared for Americans for Consumer Credit Choice.

15. On debt as disempowering, see Bruce G. Carruthers and Wendy Nelson Espeland, "Money, Meaning, and Morality," *American Behavioral Scientist* 41, 10 (1998): 1384–1408; Gustav Peebles, "The Anthropology of Credit and Debt," *Annual Review of Anthropology* 39 (2010): 225–40; Deborah Thorne, "Women's Work, Women's Worry? Debt Management in Financially Distressed Families," in *Broke: How Debt Bankrupts the Middle Class*, ed. Katherine Porter (Stanford, CA: Stanford University Press, 2012), 136–153; Deborah Thorne and Leon Anderson, "Managing the Stigma of Personal Bankruptcy," *Sociological Focus* 39, 2 (2006): 77–97; and Rachel Dwyer, "Credit, Debt, and Inequality," *Annual Review of Sociology* 44 (2018): 237–261.

16. Tach and Greene, "Robbing Peter to Pay Paul," 13.

17. Parrish and Harnick, "The State of Lending in America."

18. Charles Everett Hughes, "'Work and Self," in *The Sociological Eye: Selected Papers* (New Brunswick, NJ: Transaction Press, 1984), 338–347; and Blake E. Ashforth and Glen E. Kreiner, "'How Can You Do It?': Dirty Work and the Challenge of Constructing a Positive Identity," *Academy of Management Review* 24, 3 (1999): 413–434, at 418.

19. Arlie Russell Hochschild, *The Managed Heart: The Commercialization of Feeling in Everyday Life* (Berkeley and Los Angeles: University of California Press, 1983). While "surface-acting" emotions leads to burnout, "deep-acting" emotions apparently does not. See Amy S. Wharton, "The Sociology of Emotional Labor," *Annual Review of Sociology* 35 (2009): 147–165; Dieter Zapf and Melanie Holz, "On the Positive and Negative Effects of Emotion Work in Organizations," *European Journal of Work and Organizational Psychology* 15, 1 (2006): 1–28; Céleste M. Brotheridge and Alicia A. Grandey, "Emotional Labor and Burnout: Comparing Two Perspectives of 'People Work,'" *Journal of Vocational Behavior* 60, 9 (2002): 17–39; and Peter Totterdell and David Holman, "Emotion Regulation in Customer Service Roles: Testing a Model of Emotional Labor," *Journal of Occupational Health Psychology* 8, 1 (2003): 55–73.

20. On why women were able to hold a job, that of negotiator, that is typically associated with men, see Zaibu Tufail and Francesca Polletta, "The Gendering of Emotional Flexibility: Why Angry Women are Praised and Devalued in Debt Settlement Firms," *Gender and Society* 29, 4 (2015): 484–508.

21. One might argue that, with women's domination of K–12 education, the role of the educator is a stereotypically feminine one. However, since the clients of debt-settlement agents were adults, the imagined relationship was closer to one between a university instructor and a student, and university instructors are stereotyped as men. The fact that clients were working class may have made them even more respectful of instructors' authority. On university instructors seen as properly men, see Michael A. Messner, "White Guy Habitus in the Classroom: Challenging the Reproduction of Privilege," *Men and Masculinities* 2 (2000): 457–469; and Lana R. Rakow, "Gender and Race in the Classroom: Teaching Way Out of Line," *Feminist Teacher* 6, 1 (1991): 10–13. On poor and working-class adults' view of educators, see Annette Lareau, *Unequal Childhoods: Class, Race, and Family Life* (Berkeley and Los Angeles: University of California Press, 2003).

22. Federal Reserve Bank of New York, Center for Microeconomic Data, *Household Debt and Credit* (New York: Federal Reserve Bank, 2017). On Americans' indebtedness, and especially the forces that are responsible for inequalities in indebtedness and its consequences, see Dwyer, "Credit, Debt, and Inequality." C. Everett Hughes suspected that all jobs involved some dirty work: "It is hard to imagine an occupation in which one does not appear, in certain repeated contingencies, to be practically compelled to play a role of which he thinks he ought to be a little ashamed morally," "Work and Self," 343.

23. Tach and Greene, "Robbing Peter to Pay Paul."

24. On the association of women's jobs with valued social roles of womanhood and mothering, see Hazel-Anne M. Johnson and Paul E. Spector, "Service with a Smile: Do Emotional Intelligence, Gender, and Autonomy Moderate the Emotional Labor Process?" *Journal of Occupational Health Psychology* 12, 4 (2007): 319–333; and Heather Ferguson Bulan, Rebecca J. Erickson, and Amy S. Wharton, "Doing for Others on the Job: The Affective Requirements of Service Work, Gender, and Emotional Well-Being," *Social Problems* 44, 2 (1997): 235–256.

25. Inspired by Carol Gilligan, *In a Different Voice: Psychological Theory and Women's Development* (Cambridge, MA: Harvard University Press, 1982), theorizing

on a feminist ethic of care has divided between those who see untapped political potential in women's caregiving practices and those who see caregiving practices as unfairly stratified and unrewarded. For a good discussion of these two strands, see Elisabeth Conradi, "Theorising Care: Attentive Interaction or Distributive Justice?" *International Journal of Care and Caring* (2019), https://doi.org/10.1332/239788219X15633663863542.

CHAPTER FOUR

1. Pete Hamill, "Thrilling Show of People Power," *New York Daily News*, 22 July 2002, 8.

2. For overviews of public deliberation, see John Gastil and Peter Levine, *The Deliberative Democracy Handbook: Strategies for Effective Civic Engagement in the Twenty-First Century* (San Francisco: Jossey-Bass, 2005); and Tina Nabatchi, John Gastil, Matt Leighninger, G. Michael Weiksner, and Matt Leighninger, eds., *Democracy in Motion: Evaluating the Practice and Impact of Deliberative Civic Engagement* (Oxford and New York: Oxford University Press, 2012). On participatory budgeting, see Gianpaolo Baiocchi and Ernesto Ganuza, *Popular Democracy: The Paradox of Participation* (Palo Alto, CA: Stanford University Press, 2016). On Canada's constitutional agenda, see Graham Smith, *Democratic Innovations: Designing Institutions for Citizen Participation* (New York: Cambridge University Press, 2009). On Finland's constitution, see Manuel Castells, *Networks of Outrage and Hope: Social Movements in the Internet Age* (New York: John Wiley & Sons, 2013).

3. Michael Sorkin, "Power Plays at Ground Zero: Backroom Schemes, Laptop Democracy, and a Howl of Protest," *Architectural Record* 109, 9 (2002): 67–68.

4. Among the many critiques of contemporary forms of participation, see the essays in Caroline Lee, Michael McQuarrie, and Edward Walker, eds., *Democratizing Inequalities* (New York: New York University Press, 2014).

5. See, e.g., Kathrin Braun and Susanne Schultz, "'. . . A Certain Amount of Engineering Involved': Constructing the Public in Participatory Governance Arrangements," *Public Understanding of Science* 19, 4 (2010): 403–419; and David Smilde, Introduction, in *Venezuela's Bolivarian Democracy: Participation, Politics, and Culture under Chávez*, ed. David Smilde and Daniel Hellinger (Durham, NC: Duke University Press, 2011), 1–27.

6. For good introductions to deliberative democratic theory and design, see Smith, *Democratic Innovations*; and Dennis F. Thompson, "Deliberative Democratic Theory and Empirical Political Science," *Annual Review of Political Science* 11 (2008):497–520.

7. Jürgen Habermas, *The Structural Transformation of the Public Sphere: An Inquiry into a Category of Bourgeois Society*, trans. Thomas Burger (Cambridge, MA: MIT Press, 1991); and Habermas, *The Theory of Communicative Action*, trans. Thomas McCarthy (New York: Beacon Press, 1985).

8. On deliberation in Europe, see Beate Kohler-Koch and Barbara Finke, "The Institutional Shaping of EU–Society Relations: A Contribution to Democracy via Participation?" *Journal of Civil Society* 3, 3 (2007): 205–221; on deliberation about science and technology, see Rob Hagendijk and Alan Irwin, "Public Delibera-

tion and Governance: Engaging with Science and Technology in Contemporary Europe," *Minerva* 44, 2 (2006): 167–184; on participatory budgeting in Brazil, see Gianpaolo Baiocchi, *Militants and Citizens: The Politics of Participatory Democracy in Porto Alegre* (Stanford, CA: Stanford University Press, 2005); on participatory initiatives in India, see Paromita Sanyal and Vijayendra Rao, *Oral Democracy* (New Delhi: Cambridge University Press, 2019).

9. On the development of public deliberation and dialogue in the United States, see Matt Leighninger, *The Next Form of Democracy: How Expert Rule Is Giving Way to Shared Governance* (Nashville, TN: Vanderbilt University Press, 2006); Katherine Cramer Walsh, *Talking about Race: Community Dialogues and the Politics of Difference* (Chicago: University of Chicago Press, 2008); Caroline W. Lee, *Do-It-Yourself Democracy: The Rise of the Public Engagement Industry* (New York: Oxford University Press, 2015); and Carmen Sirianni and Lewis Friedland, *Civic Innovation in America: Community Empowerment, Public Policy, and the Movement for Civic Renewal* (Berkeley and Los Angeles: University of California Press, 2001). James S. Fishkin, *Voice of the People: Public Opinion and Democracy* (New Haven, CT: Yale University Press, 1995). On urban visioning projects, see Amy Helling, "Collaborative Visioning: Proceed with Caution! Results from Evaluating Atlanta's Vision 2020 Project," *Journal of the American Planning Association* 64, 3 (1998): 335–349; and Joshua Pacewicz, *Partisans and Partners: The Politics of the Post-Keynesian Society* (Chicago: University of Chicago Press, 2016).

10. On the merging of dialogue and deliberation see, from a practitioner's perspective, Martha L. McCoy and Patrick L. Scully, "Deliberative Dialogue to Expand Civic Engagement: What Kind of Talk Does Democracy Need?" *National Civic Review* 92 (2002): 117–135. See also Walsh, *Talking about Race*; Lee, *Do-It-Yourself Democracy*; and Francesca Polletta and Pang Ching Bobby Chen, "Gender and Public Talk: Accounting for Women's Variable Participation in the Public Sphere," *Sociological Theory* 31, 4 (2013): 291–317. I conducted the 2009 survey together with Caroline W. Lee. See Lee, *Do-It-Yourself Democracy*, and my and Chen's "Gender and Public Talk."

11. For feminist criticisms of deliberation, see Lynn Sanders, "Against Deliberation," *Political Theory* 25 (1997): 347–376; and Iris Marion Young, "Communication and the Other: Beyond Deliberative Democracy," in *Democracy and Difference: Contesting the Boundaries of the Political*, ed. Seyla Benhabib (Princeton, NJ: Princeton University Press, 1996), 121–135. For an overview of findings on group dynamics, see Tali Mendelberg, "The Deliberative Citizen: Theory and Evidence," in *Political Decision-Making, Deliberation and Participation*, ed. Michael X. Dell Carpini, Leonie Huddie, and Robert Y. Shapiro, Research in Micropolitics 6 (Bingley, UK: Emerald Group, 2002), 151–193. John R. Hibbing and Elizabeth Theiss-Morse, *Stealth Democracy: Americans' Beliefs about How Government Should Work* (New York: Cambridge University Press, 2002), argue that deliberation may lead to skepticism about politics. Marie Boor Tonn, "Taking Conversation, Dialogue, and Therapy Public," *Rhetoric and Public Affairs* 8 (2005): 405–430, argues that it may lead to a therapeuticizing of politics.

12. See Walsh, *Talking about Race*, on the integration of dialogue tools into deliberation. Daniel Yankelovich, Steven Rosell, Heidi Gantwerk, and Will Fried-

man write in "The Next Big Step in Deliberative Democracy," *Kettering Review* (Fall 2006): 54–66, "How can public engagement be crafted into a useful political strategy? How can we bring elected leaders into this process at an earlier stage to better connect public dialogue with political decision making?" (65).

13. Alessandro Maranta, Michael Guggenheim, Priska Gisler, and Christian Pohl, "The Reality of Experts and the Imagined Lay Person," *Acta Sociologica* 46, 2 (2003): 150–165. On publics in deliberative exercises, see Julie Barnett, Kate Burningham, Gordon Walker, and Noel Cass, "Imagined Publics and Engagement around Renewable Energy Technologies in the UK," *Public Understanding of Science* 21, 1 (2012): 36–50; and Alan Irwin, "The Politics of Talk: Coming to Terms with the 'New Scientific Governance,'" *Social Studies of Science* 36, 2 (2006): 299–320; and the works cited below.

14. Javier Lezaun and Linda Soneryd, "Consulting Citizens: Technologies of Elicitation and the Mobility of Publics," *Public Understanding of Science* 16 (2007): 279–297, at 280; Braun and Schultz, ". . . A Certain Amount of Engineering Involved"; P. Lehoux, G. Daudelin, and J. Abelson, "The Unbearable Lightness of Citizens within Public Deliberation Processes," *Social Science & Medicine* 74, 12 (2012): 1843–1850; and Mark Learmonth, Graham P. Martin, and Philip Warwick, "Ordinary and Effective: The Catch-22 in Managing the Public Voice in Health Care?" *Health Expectations* 12, 1 (2009): 106–115.

15. I interviewed the organizers of Listening to the City and participated in the daylong event, along with briefings before and afterward. My research team interviewed fifty participants immediately after the forum, and reinterviewed twenty-four of them a year later. I joined the steering committee of Imagine New York in December 2001 and was trained and worked as a facilitator, helped to plan the workshops and to synthesize ideas generated in them for the draft visions, and interviewed organizers. My research team and I observed twelve workshops and the summit, and interviewed thirty-two workshop participants by phone (see Francesca Polletta and Lesley Wood, "Public Deliberations after 9/11," in *Wounded City: The Social Impact of 9/11 on New York City*, ed. Nancy Foner [New York: Russell Sage Foundation, 2005], 321–346, for a fuller discussion). In our interviews with participants in Imagine and Listening to the City, we asked several questions designed to get at the conversational and political models on which participants operated. For example, we asked, "Have you ever done anything like Listening to the City (or Imagine) before?" and "when you decided to come to Listening to the City, what did you imagine that you would do in it?" We also paid close attention to the analogies that people cited in answer to other questions.

16. Maria Powell, Mathilde Colin, Daniel Lee Kleinman, Jason Delborne, and Ashley Anderson, "Imagining Ordinary Citizens? Conceptualized and Actual Participants for Deliberations on Emerging Technologies," *Science as Culture* 20, 1 (2011): 37–70, at 65. For similar calls, see Lehoux, Daudelin, and Abelson, "Unbearable Lightness"; Javier Lezaun and Linda Soneryd, "Consulting Citizens: Technologies of Elicitation and the Mobility of Publics," *Public Understanding of Science*, 16, 3 (2007): 279–297; and Alison Mohr, Sujatha Raman, and Beverley Gibbs, "Which Politics? When? Exploring the Policy Potential of Involving Different Publics in Dialogue around Science and Technology," *Sciencewise-ERC, Didcot* (2013), http://

www.sciencewise-erc.org.uk/cms/which-publics-when. Carolyn M. Hendriks, "When the Forum Meets Interest Politics: Strategic Uses of Public Deliberation," *Politics & Society* 34, 4 (2006): 571–602; and Barnett, Burningham, Walker, and Cass, "Imagined Publics and Engagement," call for the recognition of laypeople's competencies. Ulrike Felt and Maximilian Fochler examine participants' understandings of the purposes and possibilities of their own participation in "Machineries for Making Publics: Inscribing and De-scribing Publics in Public Engagement," *Minerva* 48, 3 (2010): 219–238.

17. Yankelovich, Rosell, Gantwerk, and Friedman, "The Next Big Step," 56; Center for Advances in Public Engagement, *Public Engagement: A Primer from Public Agenda* (New York: Public Agenda, 2008), 1; Carolyn J. Lukensmeyer, Joe Goldman, and Steve Brigham, "A Town Meeting for the Twenty-First Century," in *The Deliberative Democracy Handbook*, ed. John Gastil and Peter Levine (San Francisco: Jossey-Bass, 2005), 154–163; alienated citizens in Doug Henton and John Melville, "Collaborative Governance: A Guide for Grantmakers" (Menlo Park, CA: William and Flora Hewlett Foundation, 2005); "Free for all" quoted in Citizen Choicework (2008) on the National Coalition for Dialogue and Deliberation (NCDD) website, http://ncdd.org/rc/item/2359; Yankelovich, Rosell, Gantwerk, and Friedman, "The Next Big Step"; and Carolyn J. Lukensmeyer, "Key Challenges Facing the Field of Deliberative Democracy," *Journal of Public Deliberation* 10, 1 (2014): article 24.

18. "Ordinary citizens" and "usual suspects" appear in, inter alia, Everyday Democracy, "How to Recruit Dialogue Participants," https://www.everyday-democracy.org/tips/how-recruit-dialogue-participants; Center for Advances in Public Engagement, "Public Engagement: A Primer from Public Agenda"; Greg Keidan, "Talking about Guns and Violence: Strategies for Facilitating Constructive Dialogues," for the University of Arizona's National Institute for Civil Discourse, downloaded from the NCDD website, http://ncdd.org/rc/item/8181; NCDD, "Citizen Choicework." "To reach out to voices that are not heard" was how Imagine New York was described in a coalition meeting; author's notes, 26 April 2002. Fishkin, *Voice of the People*, describes deliberative polls. "A broad cross-section" and "diverse" participants are in *Everyday Democracy*, "How to Recruit Dialogue Participants"; "diverse representation" is in Sandy Heierbacher, "Dialogue & Deliberation Methods," NCDD, http://ncdd.org/rc/item/4856/; "all voices at the table" is in Lukensmeyer, Goldman, and Brigham, "A Town Meeting for the Twenty-First Century," 157. "One of the biggest challenges" is in Everyday Democracy, "How to Recruit Dialogue Participants."

19. Yankelovich, Rosell, Gantwerk, and Friedman, "The Next Big Step," 60, characterize participants as "unorganized." On recruiting from community institutions, see Leighninger, *The Next Form of Democracy*, and Alison Kadlec and Will Friedman, "Deliberative Democracy and the Problem of Power," *Journal of Public Deliberation* 3, 1 (2007): article 8. McCoy and Scully, "Deliberative Dialogue," argue that deliberation organizers should use the tools of community organizing as well as those of dialogue.

20. "Ground rule" in Keidan, "Talking about Guns and Violence"; "exploration of personal opinions" in Sarah L. Campbell, *A Guide for Training Study Circle Facilitators*, 2nd ed. (Pomfret, VT: Study Circles Resource Center, 2006), 50; Public Conversations Project, on NCDD website, http://ncdd.org/rc/item/1591; the facilita-

tor is described in Jane Mansbridge, Janette Hartz-Karp, Matthew Amengual, and John Gastil, "Norms of Deliberation: An Inductive Study," *Journal of Public Deliberation* 2, 1 (2006): article 7, at 34.

21. "Narrowly defined negotiation" is in McCoy and Scully, "Deliberative Dialogue," 125; "bargaining among pre-established preferences" is in Mark Button and David Ryfe, "What Can We Learn from the Practice of Deliberative Democracy?" in *The Deliberative Democracy Handbook: Strategies for Effective Civic Engagement in the Twenty-First Century*, ed. John Gastil and Peter Levine (San Francisco: Jossey-Bass, 2005), 20–34; "bargaining" and "voting, negotiating a consensus, bargaining," are in David Matthews, *Naming and Framing Difficult Issues to Make Sound Decisions: A Cousins Research Group Report on Democratic Practices* (Dayton, OH: Kettering Foundation, 2016); other writers who contrast deliberation with bargaining include Hendriks, "When the Forum Meets Interest Politics," 571; Jon Elster, "Introduction," in *Deliberative Democracy*, ed. Jon Elster (New York: Cambridge University Press), 1–18, at 7; and James Bohman, *Public Deliberation: Plurality, Complexity, and Democracy* (Cambridge, MA: MIT Press, 1996).

22. On using multiple communicative forms, see McCoy and Scully, "Deliberative Dialogue"; Mansbridge, Hartz-Karp, Amengual, and Gastil, "Norms of Deliberation"; and James Fishkin and Cynthia Farrar, "Deliberative Polling: From Experiment to Community Resource," in *The Deliberative Democracy Handbook*, 68–78. On emphasizing common ground more than consensus, see Mansbridge, Hartz-Karp, Amengual, and Gastil, "Norms of Deliberation." Walsh, *Talking about Race*, chap. 3, points out that although dialogue programs tend to emphasize more than deliberation's proponents the need to recognize differences rather than moving too quickly to consensus, they also hold out unity as the goal.

23. Walsh, *Talking about Race*, identifies outcomes of the study circle dialogues sponsored by Everyday Democracy. Sandy Heirbacher, "Running a D and D Program—The Basics," NCDD, 2010, http://ncdd.org/rc/running-a-dd-program/; NCDD, "21st Century Town Meeting," NCDD, 2008, http://ncdd.org/rc/item/2768/; and McCoy and Scully, "Deliberative Dialogue," 127.

24. To preserve the confidentiality of interviewees and ease of reading, I have not named interviewees.

25. Susan Herbst, "History, Philosophy, and Public Opinion Research," *Journal of Communication* 43, 4 (1993): 140–145.

26. Pamela Johnston Conover, Donald D. Searing, and Ivor M. Crewe, "The Deliberative Potential of Political Discussion," *British Journal of Political Science* 32, 1 (2002): 21–62. Thompson, "Deliberative Democratic Theory," 508, makes a point similar to mine.

27. Mark B. Brown, "Survey Article: Citizen Panels and the Concept of Representation," *Journal of Political Philosophy* 14, 2 (2014): 203–225.

28. Matthews, *Naming and Framing*; and Mansbridge, Hartz-Karp, Amengual, and Gastil, "Norms of Deliberation," 23.

29. National Issues Forums, "Moderating Deliberative Forums—An Introduction," Powerpoint (National Issues Forums, 2016); on AmericaSpeaks' inclusion of "stakeholders," see Lukensmeyer, Goldman, and Brigham, "A Town Meeting for the Twenty-First Century."

30. Polletta notes from Imagine NY Summit, 1 June 2002, New York City.

31. AmericaSpeaks, "The AmericaSpeaks Model: Taking Democracy to Scale" (2002), www.americaspeaks.org/history.html, p. 1.

32. Phone interview with Holly Leicht, Municipal Art Society, 17 October 2002; and David Kallick, email to author, 14 November 2011.

33. For a fuller discussion of the case, see Francesca Polletta, "Social Movements in an Age of Participation," *Mobilization* 21, 4 (2016): 485–497.

34. On deliberation professionals' neutrality, see Lee, *Do-It-Yourself Democracy*. Criticisms of AmericaSpeaks's forums on the budget deficit include Dean Baker, "America Speaks Back: Derailing the Drive to Cut Social Security and Medicare," *Huffington Post*, 21 June 2010; and Richard Eskow, "America 'Speaks' on Saturday, but There's an Anti–Social Security Script," *Huffington Post*, 23 June 2010. In defense of the forums, see Archon Fung, "Public Deliberation: The Left Should Learn to Trust Americans," *Huffington Post*, 28 June 2010.

35. Alison Kadlec and Will Friedman, "Deliberative Democracy and the Problem of Power," *Journal of Public Deliberation* 3, 1 (2007): article 8.

36. Lee, *Do-It-Yourself Democracy*.

37. Sirianni and Friedland, *Civic Innovation in America*, 239, 242, 243.

38. Pacewicz, *Partisans*.

39. Pacewicz, *Partisans*, 296.

40. Interview, Alex Garvin, New York City, 3 July 2003. For a fuller discussion of the relations between the civic coalitions and policymakers, see Francesca Polletta, "Deliberation and Contention," in *Democratizing Inequalities*, ed. Caroline Lee, Michael McQuarrie, and Edward Walker (New York: New York University Press, 2014), 222–243.

41. Walsh, *Talking about Race*, 249.

42. Jane Mansbridge, "Recursive Representation," in *Creating Political Presence: The New Politics of Democratic Representation*, ed. Dario Castiglione and Johannes Pollak (Chicago: University of Chicago Press, 2019), 298–337. Recursive representation, as Mansbridge defines it, does not bind representatives to the recommendations that citizens arrive at through a deliberative process. Rather, the accountability comes from the fact that representatives must give accounts of their decision-making process, and they must do so repeatedly. For representatives, ongoing conversations with constituents as well with administrators, who in turn are in conversation with people affected by decisions, are an opportunity to learn about their constituents' concerns, priorities, and experiences. On one effort to create this kind of communication between constituents and their representatives (albeit lacking the iterative character of Mansbridge's model), see Michael A. Neblo, Kevin M. Esterling, and David M. J. Lazer, *Politics with the People: Building a Directly Representative Democracy* (New York: Cambridge University Press, 2018).

43. Kathryn S. Quick and Martha S. Feldman, "Distinguishing Participation and Inclusion," *Journal of Planning Education and Research* 31, 3 (2011): 272–290.

44. Quick and Feldman, "Distinguishing Participation," 279.

45. David Plotke, "Representation Is Democracy," *Constellations* 4, 1 (1997): 19–34, at 19.

46. On changing views of the crowd, see Christian Borch, *The Politics of Crowds: An Alternative History of Sociology* (New York: Cambridge University Press, 2012);

James Surowiecki, *The Wisdom of Crowds: Why the Many Are Smarter than the Few and How Collective Wisdom Shapes Business, Economies, Societies, and Nations* (New York: Doubleday, 2004); Howard Rheingold, *Smart Mobs: The Next Social Revolution* (Cambridge: Basic Books, 2002); Clay Shirky, *Here Comes Everybody: The Power of Organizing without Organizations* (New York: Penguin, 2008). Yochai Benkler, Aaron Shaw, and Benjamin Mako Hill, "Peer Production: A Form of Collective Intelligence," in *Handbook of Collective Intelligence*, ed. Thomas W. Malone and Michael S. Bernstein (Cambridge, MA: MIT Press, 2015), 175–204, rehearse some of the claims made for peer production as well as criticisms of it.

47. Daren C. Brabham, *Crowdsourcing* (Cambridge, MA: MIT Press, 2013); Daniel Kreiss, Megan Finn, and Fred Turner, "The Limits of Peer Production: Some Reminders from Max Weber for the Network Society," *New Media & Society* 13, 2 (2011): 243–259; and José Van Dijck and David Nieborg, "Wikinomics and Its Discontents: A Critical Analysis of Web 2.0 Business Manifestos," *New Media & Society* 11, 5 (2009): 855–874. See Fred Turner, *From Counterculture to Cyberculture: Stewart Brand, the Whole Earth Network, and the Rise of Digital Utopianism* (Chicago: University of Chicago Press, 2006), on how tensions between collectivism and libertarianism were central to personal computing from the very beginning.

CHAPTER FIVE

1. Peter Singer, *The Life You Can Save: How to Do Your Part to End World Poverty* (New York: Random House, 2010).

2. On the challenge facing humanitarian groups, see Luc Boltanski, *Distant Suffering: Morality, Media and Politics*, trans. Graham D. Burchell (Cambridge: Cambridge University Press, 1991); Lilie Chouliaraki, *The Ironic Spectator: Solidarity in the Age of Post-Humanitarianism* (Cambridge: Polity Press, 2013); and Shani Orgad and Bruna Irene Seu, "'Intimacy at a Distance' in Humanitarian Communication," *Media, Culture & Society* 36, 7 (2014): 916–934.

3. Ronald Reagan is quoted in Paul Bloom, "The Baby in the Well: The Case against Empathy," *New Yorker*, 20 May 2013, https://www.newyorker.com/magazine/2013/05/20/the-baby-in-the-well. On the famine in Darfur, see Ray Bush, "Hunger in Sudan: The Case of Darfur," *African Affairs* 8, 346 (1988): 5–23.

4. Orgad and Seu, "'Intimacy at a Distance.'"

5. For examples, see Meyer Foundation, *Stories Worth Telling: A Guide to Strategic and Sustainable Nonprofit Storytelling* (Washington, DC: Georgetown University and Meyer Foundation, 2014), http://meyerfoundation.org/sites/default/files/files/SWT-whitepaper-FINAL.pdf; Working Narratives, *Storytelling and Social Change*, 2nd ed. (2016), http://workingnarratives.org/project/story-guide/; and Hattaway Communications, *Digital Storytelling for Social Impact* (New York: Rockefeller Foundation, 2014) https://assets.rockefellerfoundation.org/app/uploads/20140506171356/Digital-Storytelling-for-Social-Impact.pdf.

6. Klaus Peter Rippe, "Diminishing Solidarity," *Ethical Theory and Moral Practice* 1 (1998): 355–373.

7. Eva Illouz, *Saving the Modern Soul: Therapy, Emotions, and the Culture of Self-Help* (Berkeley and Los Angeles: University of California Press, 2008). See also

Steven Seidman, "State and Class Politics in the Making of a Culture of Intimacy," in *Intimacies: A New World of Relational Life*, ed. Alan Frank, Patricia T. Clough, and Steven Seidman (Oxford and New York: Routledge, 2013), 27–43; and Linda Nicholson, "Let Me Tell You Who I Am: Intimacy, Privacy and Self-Disclosure," in Frank, Clough, and Seidman, *Intimacies*, 44–60. On the role of communication in management, see Daniel Wren, *The Evolution of Management Thought*, 3rd ed. (New York: Wiley, 1987), 253.

8. John Durham Peters, *Speaking into the Air: A History of the Idea of Communication* (Chicago: University of Chicago Press, 2012), Rogers and Sullivan quoted at 26.

9. Illouz, *Saving the Modern Soul*, 29, and quoting *Redbook*, 34; Anthony Giddens, *The Transformation of Intimacy: Sexuality, Love, and Eroticism in Modern Societies* (Stanford, CA: Stanford University Press, 1992), 190.

10. On the professionals charged with improving such talk, see Deborah Cameron, *Good to Talk? Living and Working in a Communication Culture* (Thousand Oaks, CA: Sage, 2000). Cameron writes: "Now that talk is thought of more as the glue holding personal relationships together, people turn for guidance to the professionals who are thought to have specialist knowledge about human behavior, emotions and relationships: psychologists, therapists and counsellors" (30).

11. Peggy Hoy, Oliver Raaz, and Stefan Wehmeier, "From Facts to Stories or From Stories to Facts? Analyzing Public Relations History in Public Relations Textbooks," *Public Relations Review* 33, 2 (2007): 191–200. In 2012 the Public Relations Society of America reported that after a yearlong member-engagement process and a public vote, the Society finalized a "modern definition of PR": "Public relations is a strategic communication process that builds mutually beneficial relationships between organizations and their publics" (https://www.prsa.org/all-about-pr/). Cameron, *Good to Talk?* describes debates within communication training about whether such training should be "values-based" rather than neutral—that is, emphasize communication aimed at moral benefit such as conflict resolution and enhanced self-esteem (31).

12. Caroline W. Lee, *Do-It-Yourself Democracy: The Rise of the Public Engagement Industry* (New York: Oxford University Press, 2015).

13. Nikolas Rose, *Powers of Freedom: Reframing Political Thought* (Cambridge: Cambridge University Press, 1999), describes social problems being made "amenable to technique" (79), which involves defining an "intelligible field with specifiable limits and particular characteristics . . . defining boundaries, rendering that within them visible, assembling information about that which is included and devising techniques to mobilize the forces and entities thus revealed" (33). Tania Murray Li, "Rendering Society Technical: Government through Community and the Ethnographic Turn at the World Bank in Indonesia," *Adventures in Aidland: The Anthropology of Professionals in International Development*, ed. David Mosse (New York: Berghahn Books, 2011): 57–79, refers to experts "rendering technical" political problems.

14. My students Tania DoCarmo and Kelly Ward and I recruited interviewees in several ways. After I proposed a study of advocates who use storytelling to the Health Media Initiative of the Open Society Foundations, the Initiative invited its grantees to participate. Those who were interested contacted me. Nine of our interviewees came to the study via this route. In addition, my students and I contacted

people in advocacy whom we knew and asked for leads to people who used story-telling in their work. At the end of each interview, we asked for leads for other people it would be worth talking to. Finally, we searched online for organizations focused on storytelling in advocacy and contacted them. We conducted semi-structured interviews via Skype, which ran from forty-five minutes to two hours. After completing our interviews, we compiled a list of stories that interviewees identified as especially successful, either in our initial interview or in response to a follow-up email I sent asking for examples of stories that "got wide attention or seemed to have an impact on policymakers or funders." A third student, Jessica Callahan, analyzed forty-five of the stories that were intended for an Internet audi-ence and therefore available online, coding for emotional expression, dramatic conflict, and the performance of victimhood and agency. Finally, I read numerous consultant-produced handbooks, articles, blog entries, and reports on how to tell stories effectively. I participated in two one-day workshops on narrative strategies; my students and I participated in a shorter workshop on storytelling; and my stu-dents participated in online webinars on storytelling. All of these were offered by narrative consultants like the ones we interviewed.

15. On the effectiveness of personal storytelling in winning marriage equality, see Matt Foreman, "Hearts and Minds: How the Marriage Equality Movement Won Over the American Public," *Nonprofit Quarterly*, 27 June 2016, https://nonprofitquarterly .org/hearts-minds-marriage-equality-movement-won-american-public/; and Marc Solomon, *Winning Marriage: The Inside Story of How Same-Sex Couples Took On the Politicians and Pundits—And Won* (Lebanon, NH: Foredge, 2014); and in the Dream-ers movement, see Walter Nicholls, *The DREAMers: How the Undocumented Youth Movement Transformed the Immigrant Rights Debate* (Stanford, CA: Stanford Univer-sity Press, 2013); on the lessons taken from those movements, see David Callahan, "A Closer Look at Atlantic's End Game—And Where It's Putting the Biggest Money," *Inside Philanthropy*, 20 August 2014, https://www.insidephilanthropy.com/home /2014/8/20/a-closer-look-at-atlantics-end-gameand-where-its-putting-the.html; The Culture Group, *Culture Matters: Understanding Cultural Strategy and Mea-suring Cultural Impact*, https://theculturegroupcollaborative.wordpress.com/20 13/08/30/reports-culture-matters/; Steph Herold, "Four Ways to Create Culture Change around Abortion," *Rewire News*, 22 May 2014, https://rewire.news/article /2014/05/22/four-ways-create-culture-change-around-abortion/; and Ann McQueen, *Compton Foundation: Art as a Strategy for Change*, Americans for the Arts (2013), http://animatingdemocracy.org/resource/compton-foundation-art-strategy -change. On storytelling by messaging consultants, see Hattaway Communica-tions, *Digital Storytelling for Social Impact*; Brennen Jensen, "Strength in Storytell-ing," *Chronicle of Philanthropy* 27, 2 (6 November 2014): 20; Simon Hodges, "What's So Special about Storytelling for Social Change?" 21 January 2014, https://www .opendemocracy.net/transformation/simon-hodges/what's-so-special-about -storytelling-for-social-change; and Jonah Sachs, *Winning the Story Wars: Why Those Who Tell—and Live—the Best Stories Will Rule the Future* (Cambridge, MA: Harvard Business Press, 2012). On public interest communications, see Jasper Fessmann, "The Emerging Field of Public Interest Communications," in *Strategic Communica-tions for Non-Profit Organizations: Challenges and Alternative Approaches* (Wilming-

ton, DE: Vernon Press, 2016), 13–33; and Edward Downes, "'Doing Good' Scholarship: Considerations for Building Positive Social Change Through the Emerging Field of Public Interest Communications," *Journal of Public Interest Communications* 1, 1 (2017), 31–44; the Goodman Center, http://www.thegoodmancenter.com. On public health communication, see Emily Moyer–Gusé, "Toward a Theory of Entertainment Persuasion: Explaining the Persuasive Effects of Entertainment–Education Messages," *Communication Theory* 18, 3 (2008): 407–425. On storytelling by foundations, see Darlene M. Siska, "Story Time," *Chronicle of Philanthropy* 17, 22 (1 September 2005): 35–37; Michael Scutari, "Another Day, Another Storytelling Initiative (This Time from Sundance)," *Inside Philanthropy*, 1 November 2016, https://www.insidephilanthropy.com/home/2016/11/1/another-day-another-new-storytelling-initiative-this-time-from-sundance. Foundations funding storytelling for advocacy include the Atlantic Philanthropies (now closed, shortly after launching, with the Ford Foundation, the Narrative Initiative), the Compton Foundation, the Nathan Cummings Foundation, the Ford Foundation, the Bill and Melinda Gates Foundation, the William and Flora Hewlett Foundation, the Robert Wood Johnson Foundation, the Meyer Foundation, the Open Society Foundations, the David and Lucille Packard Foundation, the Rockefeller Foundation, and the Skoll Foundation. For a critique of contemporary advocacy storytelling that is different from mine, see Sujatha Fernandes, *Curated Stories: The Uses and Misuses of Storytelling* (New York: Oxford University Press, 2017).

16. See, e.g., "Storybanking: A Bank That Always Builds Interest," The Nonprofit Marketing Blog, 26 March 2009, Network for Good, https://www.networkforgood.com/nonprofitblog/storybanking-bank-always-builds-interest/; on supply-side and demand-side issues, see Rockefeller Foundation, *Storytelling for Social Impact*.

17. Examples of criticisms of victim storytelling include Didier Fassin and Richard Rechtman, *The Empire of Trauma: An Inquiry into the Condition of Victimhood* (Princeton, NJ: Princeton University Press, 2009), Frank Furedi, *Therapy Culture: Cultivating Vulnerability in an Uncertain Age* (London: Routledge, 2004); and Thomas Laqueur, "We Are All Victims Now," *London Review of Books*, 8 July 2010, 19. For criticism of the notion that victims gain closure from transitional justice initiatives, see Nicola Henry, "Witness to Rape: The Limits and Potential of International War Crimes Trials for Victims of Wartime Sexual Violence," *International Journal of Transitional Justice* 3, 1 (2009): 114–134. On the potentially damaging psychological effects of storytelling in transitional justice initiatives, see Henry, "Witness to Rape"; Laurel E. Fletcher and Harvey M. Weinstein, "Violence and Social Repair: Rethinking the Contribution of Justice to Reconciliation," *Human Rights Quarterly* 24, 3 (2002): 573–639; Jonathan Doak, "The Therapeutic Dimension of Transitional Justice: Emotional Repair and Victim Satisfaction in International Trials and Truth Commissions," *International Criminal Law Review* 11, 2 (2011): 263–298; and Diana T. Meyers, *Victims' Stories and the Advancement of Human Rights* (New York: Oxford University Press, 2016); in trials for sexual assault, see Kate Crowe, "Sexual Assault and Testimony: Articulation of/as Violence," *Law, Culture and the Humanities* 15, 2 (2019): 401–420; after disasters, see Jerome Groopman, "The Grief Industry," *New Yorker*, 1 January 2004, 30–38.

18. Meyer Foundation, *Stories Worth Telling*, 14.

19. Taylor Griffith, "How I Found Authenticity in My Writing, Without Becoming a Secret Agent," *Huffington Post*, 5 March 2014, http://www.huffingtonpost.com /taylor-griffith/how-i-found-authenticity-_b_4906398.html.

20. How-to guides for storytelling in advocacy include The Narrative Initiative, *Toward New Gravity: Charting a Course for the Narrative Initiative* (New York: The Narrative Initiative, 2017), https://www.narrativeinitiative.org; Simone Joyaux, "Storytelling: For Fundraising . . . and Life, Too," *Nonprofit Quarterly*, 21 March 2014, https://nonprofitquarterly.org/storytelling-for-fundraising-and-life-too/; Hattaway Communications, *Digital Stories for Social Impact*; Meyer Foundation, *Stories Worth Telling*; and Working Narratives, *Storytelling and Social Change*.

21. See also Sam Gregory, "Cameras Everywhere: Ubiquitous Video Documentation of Human Rights, New Forms of Video Advocacy, and Considerations of Safety, Security, Dignity and Consent," *Journal of Human Rights Practice* 2, 2 (2010): 191–207; Renee Bracey Sherman and the Sea Change Program, "Saying Abortion Aloud: Research and Recommendations for Sharing Your Abortion Story Publicly," http:// seachangeprogram.org/our-work/untold-storiesproject/storytelling-research/; and Aspen Baker, *Pro-Voice: How to Keep Listening When the World Wants a Fight* (Oakland, CA: Berrett-Koehler, 2015).

22. On narratives' power to alter brain patterns, see, for example, Working Narratives, *Storytelling and Social Change*; Bioneers, "Social Change Campaign Strategy," 8 November 2017, https://bioneers.org/social-change-campaign -strategy-the-importance-of-storytelling-ze0z1711/; on human brains as "wired" to remember stories, see Community Land Trust Network, "Storytelling for Advocacy" (2015), http://cltnetwork.org/wp-content/uploads/2015/05/Storytelling-for -Advocacy-2015.pdf; on storytelling as "basic to what it is to be human," see Narrative Initiative, *Toward New Gravity*; on people as "narrative animals," see Bioneers, "Social Change Campaign Strategy." The Barbara Hardy quote appears in Narrative Initiative, *Toward New Gravity*, unpaginated.

23. Blurb on Working Narratives, *Storytelling and Social Change*. In addition to our interviews, several handbooks and briefs for narrative refer to story sharing. Among them are Narrative Initiative, *Toward New Gravity*; Hattaway Communications, *Digital Storytelling*; Community Trust Land Network, "Storytelling for Advocacy." Nicholas A. John, *The Age of Sharing* (New York: Polity Press, 2016); and Alan Page Fiske, *Structures of Social Life: The Four Elementary Forms of Human Relations* (New York: Free Press, 1991).

24. Ruth McCambridge, "Pity Charity: When 'Storytelling' Is Abuse," *Nonprofit Quarterly*, 22 November 2013, https://nonprofitquarterly.org/2013/11/22/pity-char itywhen-storytelling-is-abuse/.

25. Chouliaraki, *The Ironic Spectator*.

26. "American Refugees: The Beast Inside," YouTube video, 19 May 2014, https:// www.youtube.com/watch?v=nwg8nZFhBEE; The Center for Reproductive Rights, "Jemima Kirke Shares Her Story about Ending a Pregnancy," YouTube video, 14 April 2015, https://www.youtube.com/watch?v=m1DhscWRT9w.

27. Meyer Foundation, *Stories Worth Telling*, 14; Jerome Deroy, "Sense-Based Storytelling," 16 August 2018, *Narrativ* blog, https://narativ.com/2018/08/16/sense -based-storytelling/.

28. Kate Marple, "5 Ways for Nonprofits to Tell an Ethical Story," *Nonprofit Quarterly*, 22 October 2014, https://nonprofitquarterly.org/5-ways-organizations -can-empower-storytellers/; Meyer Foundation, *Stories Worth Telling*; Bridgespan Group, "Why Nonprofits Need to be Great Storytellers: An Interview with Andy Goodman," n.d., accessed 15 May 2019, https://www.bridgespan.org/insights/li brary/leadership-development/why-nonprofits-need-to-be-storytellers.

29. Marple, "Five Ways for Nonprofits to Tell an Ethical Story"; see also Hodges, "What's So Special about Storytelling for Social Change?"

30. In her ethnography of a sanctuary group for undocumented immigrants, Grace Yukich, "Constructing the Model Immigrant: Movement Strategy and Immigrant Deservingness in the New Sanctuary Movement," *Social Problems* 60, 3 (2013): 302–320, found that activists chose as "sanctuary representatives"—people they saw as exemplifying the injustices of the system and whom they would help to secure permanent residency—intact families rather than single people or people whose family members remained in their home country, people without a criminal record or one in the distant past, Asian and Latino people rather than Black ones, and people who were hardworking, energetic, sad, and frustrated, but not angry. Yet there seemed to be very little discussion of the possible consequences of these choices for those who did not fit the picture activists wanted to forward. Ruth Braunstein, "Storytelling in Liberal Religious Advocacy," *Journal for the Scientific Study of Religion*, 51, 1 (2012):110–127, describes religious advocacy groups struggling with this issue.

31. Shuo Zhou and Jeff Niederdeppe, "The Promises and Pitfalls of Personalization in Narratives to Promote Social Change," *Communication Monographs* 84, 3 (2017): 319–342.

32. On the benefits of self-disclosure in intergroup contact initiatives, see Thomas Pettigrew, Linda R. Tropp, Ulrich Wagner, and Oliver Christ, "Recent Advances in Intergroup Contact Theory," *International Journal of Intercultural Relations* 35 (2011): 271–280. On the different desires of dominant and subordinate group members, see Tamar Saguy, John F. Dovidio, and Felicia Pratto, "Beyond Contact: Intergroup Contact in the Context of Power Relations," *Personality and Social Psychology Bulletin* 34, 3 (2008): 432–445.

33. Emile G. Bruneau and Rebecca Saxe, "The Power of Being Heard: The Benefits of 'Perspective-Giving' in the Context of Intergroup Conflict," *Journal of Experimental Social Psychology* 48, 4 (2012): 855–866. On the other hand, initiatives in which members of dominant groups were exposed to the stories of members of subordinate groups backfired when dominant group members experienced the stories as blaming them; see Elizabeth Levy Paluck, "Is It Better Not to Talk? Group Polarization, Extended Contact, and Perspective Taking in Eastern Democratic Republic of Congo," *Personality and Social Psychology Bulletin* 36, 9 (2010): 1170–1185.

34. On policymakers' expectation of a clear "ask," see American Association of Family Physicians, *AAFP Annual Chapter Leader Forum*, Legislative Communications (n.d.), https://www.aafp.org/dam/AAFP/documents/events/alf_ncsc/alf_hand outs/effective-legislative-testimony-handout.pdf.

35. On nonprofits' efforts to comply with foundations' request for evidence of their impacts, see Nina Eliasoph, *Making Volunteers: Civic Life after Welfare's End* (Princeton, NJ: Princeton University Press, 2011).

36. In this vein, undocumented student Dreamers carefully crafted stories for the public while also reserving time to share their more personal stories with fellow Dreamers, as observed in Thomas Swerts, "Gaining a Voice: Storytelling and Undocumented Youth Activism in Chicago," *Mobilization* 20 (2015): 345–360. Danielle S. Allen, *Talking to Strangers: Anxieties of Citizenship since* Brown v. Board of Education (Chicago: University of Chicago Press, 2004), discusses the everyday sacrifices made by activists, and Peters, *Speaking into the Air*, describes the act of communicating in a way that people will understand as a sacrifice. I draw on these two ideas in suggesting that personal storytelling in advocacy may often involve a necessary sacrifice.

37. Ruth Braunstein, *Prophets and Patriots: Faith in Democracy Across the Political Divide* (Berkeley and Los Angeles: University of California Press, 2017), 165. See Marshall Ganz, "Public Narrative, Collective Action, and Power," *Accountability through Public Opinion: From Inertia to Public Action*, ed. Sina Odugbemi and Taeku Lee (Washington, DC: World Bank, 2011), 273–289, on stories' use in organizing.

38. Lee, *Do-It-Yourself-Democracy*.

CHAPTER SIX

1. See, e.g., the criticisms in Kevin Durrheim and John Dixon, "Intergroup Contact and the Struggle for Social Justice," in *The Oxford Handbook of Social Psychology and Social Justice*, ed. Phillip L. Hammack, Jr. (New York: Oxford University Press, 2018), 367–377.

2. Alexis de Tocqueville, *Democracy in America*, vols. 1 [1835] and 2 [1840], trans. Henry Reeve (New York: Bantam, 2000); and Robert D. Putnam, *Bowling Alone: The Collapse and Revival of American Community* (New York: Simon and Schuster, 2000).

3. On Putnam's emphasis on the socializing functions of voluntary institutions, along with a broader critique of social capital perspectives, see Bob Edwards and Michael W. Foley, "Civil Society and Social Capital: A Primer," in *Beyond Tocqueville: Civil Society and the Social Capital Debate in Comparative Perspective*, ed. Bob Edwards, Michael W. Foley, and Mario Diani (Hanover, NH: University Press of New England, 2001), 1–14. Bo Rothstein and Dietlind Stolle, "Social Capital, Impartiality and the Welfare State: An Institutional Approach," in *Generating Social Capital: Civil Society and Institutions in Comparative Perspective*, ed. Mark Hooghe and Dietlind Stolle (New York: Palgrave Macmillan, 2003), 191–209, argue that rather than interpersonal trust leading to trust in government, the relationship may be the reverse. They provide evidence suggesting that perceptions of government as fair lead to trust in others.

4. Émile Durkheim, *Elementary Forms of Religious Life*, trans. Karen E. Fields (New York: Free Press, 1995); on rituals helping to construct new solidarities, see David I. Kertzer, *Ritual, Politics, and Power* (New Haven, CT: Yale University Press, 1989). Patricia Ewick and Marc Steinberg, "The Dilemmas of Social Movement Identity and the Case of the Voice of the Faithful," *Mobilization* 19, 2 (2014): 209–227, show that a Catholic activist group formed during the clergy sexual abuse crisis used rituals to form a new schema for Catholics' relationship to the Church.

5. Nadja Mosimann and Jonas Pontusson, "Solidaristic Unionism and Support

for Redistribution in Contemporary Europe," *World Politics* 69, 3 (2017): 448–492. Peter A. Hall, "The Political Sources of Social Solidarity," *The Strains of Commitment: The Political Sources of Solidarity in Diverse Societies*, ed. Keith Banting and Will Kymlicka (New York: Oxford University Press, 2017), 201–232, summarizes other explanations for differences in national support for redistribution.

6. Mosimann and Pontusson, "Solidaristic Unionism."

7. Gary Adler, "An Opening in the Congregational Closet? Boundary-Bridging Culture and Membership Privileges for Gays and Lesbians in Christian Religious Congregations," *Social Problems* 59, 2 (2012): 177–206.

8. Ruth Braunstein, Brad R. Fulton, and Richard L. Wood, "The Role of Bridging Cultural Practices in Racially and Socioeconomically Diverse Civic Organizations," *American Sociological Review* 79, 4 (2014): 705–725.

9. Paul Lichterman, *Elusive Togetherness: Church Groups Trying to Bridge America's Divisions* (Princeton, NJ: Princeton University Press, 2005), 62.

10. The "do, don't talk" approach in action is described in Lichterman, *Elusive Togetherness*, 69; dialogue groups' talk, 46–47; "Christ-like care," chap. 5.

11. Lichterman, *Elusive Togetherness*, 45.

12. Among the many studies of Occupy and the May 15 movement, see Marina Sitrin and Dario Assellini, *They Can't Represent Us! Reinventing Democracy from Greece to Occupy* (London: Verso Books, 2014); Jeffrey S. Juris, "Reflections on, #Occupy Everywhere: Social Media, Public Space, and Emerging Logics of Aggregation," *American Ethnologist* 39, 2 (2012): 259–279; Manuel Castells, *Networks of Outrage and Hope: Social Movements in the Internet Age* (Hoboken, NJ: John Wiley & Sons, 2013); Kate Khatib, Margaret Killjoy, and Mike McGuire, eds., *We Are Many: Reflections on Movement Strategy from Occupation to Liberation* (Oakland, CA: AK Press, 2012); and Maple Razsa and Andrej Kurnik, "The Occupy Movement in Žižek's Hometown: Direct Democracy and a Politics of Becoming," *American Ethnologist* 39, 2 (2012), 238–258, all of which offer valuable insights into the groups' interactional styles. On democratic relationships in the global justice movement, see Nicole Doerr, *Political Translation: How Movement Democracies Survive* (New York: Cambridge University Press, 2018); Donatella Della Porta and Dieter Rucht, eds., *Meeting Democracy: Power and Deliberation in Global Justice Movements* (New York: Cambridge University Press, 2013); Jeffrey S. Juris, *Networking Futures: The Movements against Corporate Globalization* (Durham, NC: Duke University Press, 2008); and Marianne Maeckelbergh, *Will of the Many: How the Alterglobalisation Movement Is Changing the Face of Democracy* (New York: Palgrave Macmillan, 2009). On contemporary anarchist activism, see Dana M. Williams, "Contemporary Anarchist and Anarchistic Movements," *Sociology Compass* 12, 6 (2018): e12582.

13. For common criticisms of consensus-based decision making, see Francesca Polletta, "Consensual Decision Making," in *The Wiley-Blackwell Encyclopedia of Social and Political Movements* (Hoboken, NJ: Blackwell, 2013), 249–251.

14. On the concept of prefiguration, see Wini Breines, *Community and Organization in the New Left, 1962–1968: The Great Refusal* (New Brunswick, NJ: Rutgers University Press, 1989), and Francesca Polletta and Katt Hoban, "Why Consensus: Prefiguration in Three Activist Eras," *Journal of Social and Political Psychology* 4, 1 (2016): 286–301.

15. Joreen, "The Tyranny of Structurelessness," in *Radical Feminism*, ed. Ann Koedt, Ellen Levine, and Anita Rapone (New York: Quadrangle Books, 1973), 285–299. I elaborate on the argument I make here in *Freedom Is an Endless Meeting: Democracy in American Social Movements* (Chicago: University of Chicago Press, 2002), chap. 6.

16. On the evolution of consensus decision making after the 1960s, see Sitrin and Azzellini, *They Can't Represent Us!*; Polletta and Hoban, "Why Consensus;" Juris, *Networking Futures*; Barbara Epstein, *Political Protest and Cultural Revolution: Nonviolent Direct Action in the 1970s and 1980s* (Berkeley and Los Angeles: University of California Press, 1991); Andrew Cornell, *Oppose and Propose! Lessons from Movement for a New Society* (Oakland, CA: AK Press, 2011); and Polletta, *Freedom Is an Endless Meeting*.

17. On the role of informal norms in organizational decision making, see Leigh Thompson and Reid Hastie, "Social Perceptions in Negotiation," *Organizational Behavior and Human Decision Processes* 47 (1990): 98–123; Marshall Scott Poole, David R. Siebold, and Robert D. McPhee, "The Structuration of Group Decisions," in *Communication and Group Decision-Making*, 2nd Ed., ed. Randy Y. Hirokawa and Marshall Scott Poole (Beverly Hills: Sage, 1996), 114–146; and Sim B. Sitkin and Nancy L. Roth, "Explaining the Limited Effectiveness of Legalistic Remedies for Trust/Distrust," *Organization Science* 4 (1993): 367–392.

18. Christoph Haug and Dieter Rucht, "Structurelessness: An Evil or an Asset? A Case Study," in *Meeting Democracy*, 179–213; Darcy K. Leach, "Culture and the Structure of Tyrannylessness," *Sociological Quarterly* 54 (2013): 159–228, at 188; Darcy K. Leach, "When Freedom Is Not an Endless Meeting: A New Look at Efficiency in Consensus-Based Decision Making," *Sociological Quarterly* 57, 1 (2016): 36–70, at 57.

19. Polletta and Hoban, "Why Consensus," 296. On activists' views of decision making as a site for challenging inequalities, see Lisa Fithian and David Mitchell, "Anti-Oppression," in *Beautiful Trouble: A Toolbox for Revolution*, ed. Andrew Boyd and David Oswald Mitchell (New York: OR Books, 2012), 212–215; and H. Walia, "Consensus Is a Means, Not an End," in *Beautiful Trouble*, 116–117.

20. Juris, *Networking Futures*. Maeckelbergh, *Will of the Many*, discusses horizontalists' efforts to turn conflict into a source of political innovation.

21. On *encuentros*, see Marianne Maeckelbergh, "Horizontal Democracy Now: From Alterglobalization to Occupation," *Interface* 4, 1 (2012): 207–234; on affinity groups, see Juris, *Networking Futures*; on working groups, see Donatella della Porta, "Making the Polis: Social Forums and Democracy in the Global Justice Movement," *Mobilization* 10, 1 (2005): 73–94.

22. On Occupy's reversal of the roles of general assemblies and working groups, see Maeckelbergh, "Horizontal Democracy Now"; on decisions being made behind the scenes by a small group, see Jackie Smith and Bob Glidden, "Occupy Pittsburgh and the Challenges of Participatory Democracy," *Social Movement Studies* 11, 3–4 (2012): 288–294; and Jonathan Matthew Smucker, "Occupy: A Name Fixed to a Flashpoint," *Sociological Quarterly* 54, 2 (2013): 219–225; activists quoted in Polletta and Hoban, "Why Consensus," 295; on the 15M movement, see Maekelbergh, "Horizontal Democracy Now," and Simon Tormey, John Keane, Ramon A. Feenstra,

and Andreu Casero-Ripollés, *Refiguring Democracy: The Spanish Political Laboratory* (New York: Routledge, 2017), chap. 1.

23. Leach, "When Freedom Is Not an Endless Meeting."

24. On contemporary activists' dislike of representation, see Simon Tormey, *The End of Representative Democracy* (Malden, MA: Polity Press, 2015). David Plotke, "Representation Is Democracy," *Constellations* 4, 1 (1997): 19–34.

25. Richard L. Wood and Brad R. Fulton, *A Shared Future: Faith-Based Organizing for Racial Equity and Ethical Democracy* (Chicago: University of Chicago Press, 2015), note the wider scope of today's community organizing; David Walls, *Community Organizing* (Malden, MA: Polity Press, 2015), discusses organizers' antipathy to horizontalist activism.

26. Walls, *Community Organizing*, 97–91, describes such a meeting in detail.

27. Heidi Swarts, "Drawing New Symbolic Boundaries Over Old Social Boundaries: Forging Social Movement Unity in Congregation-Based Community Organizing," *Sociological Perspectives* 54, 3 (2011): 453–477, at 469.

28. Hahrie Han, *How Organizations Develop Activists: Civic Associations and Leadership in the 21st Century* (New York: Oxford University Press, 2014), 109. Swarts, "Drawing New Symbolic Boundaries," 465.

29. Swarts, "Drawing New Symbolic Boundaries," 466. "Target means, . . ." Ruth Braunstein, *Prophets and Patriots: Faith in Democracy Across the Political Divide* (Berkeley and Los Angeles: University of California Press, 2017), 159; "we're not here to bludgeon, . . ." 160; "as potential partners, . . ." 161.

30. " 'Oh, I mean, flattery and nice things, . . .'" Swarts, "Drawing New Symbolic Boundaries," 467; the PICO coalition's standard question, "Who do you love?" is in Heidi Swarts, *Organizing Urban America: Secular and Faith-Based Progressive Movements* (Minneapolis: University of Minnesota Press, 2008), 22; the New York organizer is quoted in Walls, *Community Organizing*, 52.

31. Braunstein, *Prophets and Patriots*.

32. William H. Sewell, Jr., "Connecting Capitalism to the French Revolution: The Parisian Promenade and the Origins of Civic Equality in Eighteenth-Century France," *Critical Historical Studies* 1, 1 (2014): 5–46.

33. Sewell, "Connecting Capitalism," 35.

34. Benjamin L. Shepard, M. Bogad, and Stephen Duncombe, "Performing vs. the Insurmountable: Theatrics, Activism, and Social Movements," *Liminalities: A Journal of Performance Studies* 4, 3 (2008): 1–30; on Critical Mass bike rides, see Dana M. Williams, "Happiness and Freedom in Direct Action: Critical Mass Bike Rides as Ecstatic Ritual, Play, and Temporary Autonomous Zones," *Leisure Studies* 37, 5 (2018): 589–602.

35. On the danger that the bracketing of inequality in a limited space contributes to inequality outside the space, see Carl Cassegård, "Contestation and Bracketing: The Relation between Public Space and the Public Sphere," *Environment and Planning D: Society and Space* 32, 4 (2014): 689–703. Jodi Dean, *Crowd and Party* (London: Verso, 2016), argues that the Left's emphasis on momentary experiences of democratic potential is counterproductive: "They mistake an opening, an opportunity, for an end. They imagine the goal of politics as the proliferation of multiplicities, potentialities, differences. The unleashing of the playful, carnivalesque,

and spontaneous is taken to indicate political success, as if duration were but a multiplication of movements rather than itself a qualitative change" (125).

36. Katherine C. Kellogg, "Operating Room: Relational Spaces and Microinstitutional Change in Surgery," *American Journal of Sociology* 115, 3 (2009): 657–711. In 1984 Libby Zion was an eighteen-year-old admitted to a New York hospital for a fever; her death that night may have been caused by an interaction between the antidepressants she was taking and drugs administered at the hospital, as well as by hospital residents' initial failure to evaluate her response. Zion's father, the columnist Sidney Zion, publicized the fact that the residents on the case routinely worked thirty-six hours straight, and the ensuing controversy led the official body governing medical education to limit the hours of doctors in training. See Barron Lerner, "A Life-Changing Case for Doctors in Training," *New York Times*, 3 March 2009, D5.

37. Kellogg, "Operating Room," 693.

38. Nicole Doerr, "The Disciplining of Dissent and the Role of Empathetic Listeners in Deliberative Publics: A Ritual Perspective," *Globalizations* 8, 4 (2011): 519–534.

39. See Betsy Leondar-Wright, *Missing Class: Strengthening Social Movement Groups by Seeing Class Cultures* (Ithaca, NY: Cornell University Press, 2014), on how styles of talk are associated with class backgrounds—and are read that way by people in cross-class movements. See also Francesca Polletta, "How Participatory Democracy Became White: Culture and Organizational Choice," *Mobilization* 10, 2 (2005): 271–288.

40. Kathleen M. Blee, *Democracy in the Making: How Activist Groups Form* (New York: Oxford University Press, 2012), 112.

41. On domestic partnerships, see Mary Bernstein, "The Movement towards Marriage Equality in Advanced Industrialized Countries," in *Handbook on Gender and Social Policy*, ed. Sheila Shaver (Northampton, MA: Edward Elgar, 2018), 307–323; on minority group ally-ship, see Patrick R. Grzanka, Jake Adler, and Jennifer Blazer, "Making Up Allies: The Identity Choreography of Straight LGBT Activism," *Sexuality Research and Social Policy* 12, 3 (2015): 165–181; on cooperatives and collectives, see Joyce Rothschild, "Creating Participatory Democratic Decision-Making in Local Organizations," in *Handbook of Community Movements and Local Organizations in the 21st Century*, ed. Ram A. Cnaan and Carl Milofsky (New York: Springer, 2018), 127–140; on consensus management, see Art Kleiner, *The Age of Heretics: A History of the Radical Thinkers Who Reinvented Corporate Management* (San Francisco: Jossey-Bass, 2008).

CHAPTER SEVEN

1. Nell Lake, "Language Wars" *Harvard Magazine*, March–April 2002, https://harvardmagazine.com/2002/03/languagewars. For a review of work on national solidarities, see Bart Bonikowski, "Nationalism in Settled Times," *Annual Review of Sociology* 42 (2016): 427–449. On the virtues and dangers of strong national identity, see Elizabeth Theiss Morse, *Who Counts as an American? The Boundaries of National Identity* (New York: Cambridge University Press, 2009); on cosmopolitan-

ism, see Craig Calhoun, "Cosmopolitanism and Nationalism," *Nations and Nationalism* 14, 3 (2008): 427–448.

2. Hans Kohn, *The Idea of Nationalism: A Study in Its Origins and Background* (New York: Macmillan, 1944). On the ethnic/civic distinction, see Rogers Brubaker, *Ethnicity without Groups* (Cambridge, MA: Harvard University Press, 2004); Rogers M. Smith, *Civic Ideals: Conflicting Visions of Citizenship in U.S. History* (New Haven, CT: Yale University Press, 1997).

3. Deborah Jill Schildkraut, *Press One for English: Language Policy, Public Opinion, and American Identity* (Princeton, NJ: Princeton University Press, 2005); Deborah J. Schildkraut, "Defining American Identity in the Twenty-First Century: How Much 'There' Is There?" *Journal of Politics* 69, 3 (2007): 597–615; and Bart Bonikowski and Paul DiMaggio, "Varieties of American Popular Nationalism," *American Sociological Review* 81, 5 (2016): 949–980.

4. Brubaker, *Ethnicity without Groups*; Schildkraut, *Press One for English*; and Deborah Condor, "Temporality and Collectivity: Diversity, History and the Rhetorical Construction of National Entitativity," *British Journal of Social Psychology* 45 (2006): 657–682. See also Gérard Bouchard's elegant discussion of the myths that underpin national identities in his *Social Myths and Collective Imaginaries*, trans. Howard Scott (Toronto: University of Toronto Press, 2017).

5. See Bonikowski, "Nationalism in Settled Times," for an overview of these research findings.

6. Qiong Li and Marilyn Brewer, "What Does It Mean to Be an American? Patriotism, Nationalism, and American Identity after 9/11," *Political Psychology* 25, 5 (2004): 727–739.

7. Alan Page Fiske, *Structures of Social Life: The Four Elementary Forms of Human Relations* (New York: Free Press, 1991); Kathleen E. Powers, "Nationalism, Social Identity Content, and Foreign Policy Attitudes," paper prepared for presentation at the 2018 International Studies Association Annual Meeting, San Francisco, CA, 4–7 April.

8. Iseult Honohan, "Friends, Strangers or Countrymen? The Ties between Citizens as Colleagues," *Political Studies* 49, 1 (2001): 51–69. Of course, solidarity as the bonds between co-workers, as Honohan understands it, is different than solidarity as the bonds between workers, the ideal that has long animated workers' movements. Opposition to management, and sometimes, to the owners of the means of production, is central to the latter, but not the former. Hazel Rose Markus, "American = Independent?" *Perspectives on Psychological Science* 12, 5 (2017): 855–866, discusses Americans' ambivalence about being interdependent.

9. Diana C. Mutz and Jeffrey J. Mondak, "The Workplace as a Context for Cross-Cutting Political Discourse," *Journal of Politics* 68, 1 (2006): 140–155.

10. Eleanor Miles and Richard J. Crisp, "A Meta-Analytic Test of the Imagined Contact Hypothesis," *Group Processes & Intergroup Relations* 17, 1 (2014): 3–26, report on a meta-analysis showing the effects of imagined contact across groups on attitudes, behavioral intentions, and behavior. Richard Dagger, "Rights, Boundaries, and the Bonds of Community: A Qualified Defense of Moral Parochialism," *American Political Science Review* 79, 2 (1985): 436–447, argues that we have special obligations to our compatriots neither because we consented to those obligations

in a contractual way nor because we share some primordial kinship with them, but rather because we jointly participate in a cooperative enterprise. When we use public roads and facilities, enter into contracts secured by law, send our children to public schools, and so on, we take advantage of opportunities provided by this cooperative enterprise, and accordingly, we have a duty to reciprocate.

11. Danusha Laméris, "Small Kindnesses," in *Healing the Divide: Poems of Kindness and Connection*, ed. James Crews (Brattleboro, VT: Green Writers Press, 2019), 56.

12. Honohan herself does not maintain that colleagueship is the best metaphor for citizenship, and in her "Metaphors of Solidarity," in *Political Language and Metaphor: Interpreting and Changing the World*, ed. Terrell Carver and Jernej Pikalo (New York: Routledge, 2008), 85–98, she offers additional, somewhat fanciful metaphors such as those of a stream, flow, network, orchestra, and web. Rogers M. Smith, *Stories of Peoplehood: The Politics and Morals of Political Membership* (New York: Cambridge University Press, 2003).

13. Paige Raibmon, "Provincializing Europe in Canadian History; Or, How to Talk about Relations between Indigenous Peoples and Europeans," Active History Blog, 24 October 2018.

14. Raibmon, "Provincializing Europe."

15. Teresa M. Bejan, *Mere Civility: Disagreement and the Limits of Toleration* (Cambridge, MA: Harvard University Press, 2017).

16. Bonikowski, "Nationalism in Settled Times," discusses some of the ways in which national identities are communicated. Peter A. Hall, "The Political Sources of Social Solidarity," in *The Strains of Commitment: The Political Sources of Solidarity in Diverse Societies*, ed. Keith Banting and Will Kymlicka (New York: Oxford University Press, 2017), 201–232, argues that policies may produce solidarity as much as the reverse.

17. Hall, "The Political Sources of Social Solidarity"; Hansson quote at 218.

18. Irene Bloemraad, "Solidarity and Conflict," in *The Strains of Commitment: The Political Sources of Solidarity in Diverse Societies*, ed. Keith Banting and Will Kymlicka (New York: Oxford University Press, 2017), 327–363. Schildkraut attributes the currency of an incorporationist vision of American identity to movements on behalf of racial minorities in "Defining American Identity."

19. The literature on institutional scripts is vast. See, for classics, Walter K. Powell and Paul J. DiMaggio, eds., *The New Institutionalism in Organizational Analysis* (Chicago: University of Chicago Press, 1991), on how scripts influence organizations; and John W. Meyer, John Boli, George M. Thomas, and Francisco O. Ramirez, "World Society and the Nation-State," *American Journal of Sociology* 103, 1 (1997): 144–181, on how institutional scripts influence nations. For people's creativity in resisting and transforming institutional scripts, see Patricia H. Thornton, William Ocasio, and Michael Lounsbury, *The Institutional Logics Perspective: A New Approach to Culture, Structure, and Process* (New York: Oxford University Press, 2012); Amy Binder, "For Love and Money: Organizations' Creative Responses to Multiple Environmental Logics," *Sociological Theory* 36 (2007): 547–571; W. E. Douglas Creed, Maureen A. Scully, and John R. Austin, "Clothes Make the Person? The Tailoring of Legitimating Accounts and the Social Construction of Identity," *Organiza-*

232 | NOTES TO CHAPTER SEVEN

tion Science 13 (2002): 475–496; and Tim Hallett and Marc J. Ventresca, "Inhabited Institutions: Social Interactions and Organizational Forms in Gouldner's *Patterns of Industrial Bureaucracy*," *Sociological Theory* 35 (2006): 213–236.

20. For example, Hallett and Ventresca, "Inhabited Institutions," quote from Gary Fine's study of why restaurant workers tend to stay with one establishment, distinguishing in brackets the effects of structure from those of unstructured interactions: "While the conditions of the job [read: structure] contribute to satisfaction, friendships . . . [read: unstructured interactions] . . . tether workers to the organization." In their interpretation, job salary and hours are structural; friendships are not. My point is that the relationship schema of friendship is also a structure, and it also constrains workers. Interestingly, Fine himself writes elsewhere: "Sociologists must use the investigation of interpersonal situations as a strategy through which broader social forces, properties, and processes can be understood as constituted in practice. Sociologists are skilled in emphasizing the power of structure in top-down models, but they are less concerned with the ways actors shape structure from the bottom up." Gary Alan Fine and Corey D. Fields, "Culture and Microsociology: The Anthill and the Veldt," *Annals of the American Academy of Political and Social Science* 619 (2008): 130–148. Viviana Zelizer argues similarly to Hallett and Ventresca that to capture the constraints on the relational work people do with money, scholars should distinguish "between top-down forms of monetary earmarking, such as those instituted by the state or other powerful agencies and bottom-up differentiations created by people's everyday relations." Viviana A. Zelizer, "How I Became a Relational Economic Sociologist and What Does That Mean?" *Politics & Society* 40 (2012): 145–174, at 163. Some scholars in an inhabited institutions approach have defined agency as people's capacity to modify and transpose institutional schemas (e.g., Creed, Scully, and Austin, "Clothes Make the Person?" 475). This misses the extent to which people agentically reproduce institutional schemas.

21. G. P. Ginsburg, "Rules, Scripts and Prototypes in Personal Relationships," in *Handbook of Personal Relationships: Theory, Research and Interventions*, ed. Steve E. Duck, Dale F. Hay, Stevan E. Hobfoll, William Ed Ickes, and Barbara M. Montgomery (New York: John Wiley, 1988), 23–39 and see my discussion in chap. 1. For a fascinating historical analysis of friendship, see Allan Silver, "Friendship and Trust as Moral Ideals: An Historical Approach," *Archives européenes de sociologie* 30 (1989): 274–297.

22. Benedict Anderson, *Imagined Communities: Reflections on the Origin and Spread of Nationalism* (New York: Verso, 1991). Marilyn B. Brewer, "The Importance of Being *We*: Human Nature and Intergroup Relations," *American Psychologist* 62, 8 (2007): 728–738, cites social psychological evidence that in-group members may not necessarily be hostile toward out-group members.

23. Fred Turner, *From Counterculture to Cyberculture: Stewart Brand, the Whole Earth Network, and the Rise of Digital Utopianism* (Chicago: University of Chicago Press, 2006); and Rebecca Bordt, *The Structure of Women's Nonprofit Organizations* (Bloomington: Indiana University Press, 1997).

24. See Ferdinand de Saussure, *Course in General Linguistics* (1916), excerpted in Jeffrey C. Alexander and Steve Seidman, eds., *Culture and Society: Contemporary*

Debates (New York: Cambridge University Press, 1990), 55–63; and Jeffrey C. Alexander and Philip Smith, "The Discourse of American Civil Society: A New Proposal for Cultural Studies," *Theory and Society* 22, 2 (1993): 151–207, on the power of culture structures of analogy and opposition. In Francesca Polletta, "How Participatory Democracy Became White: Culture and Organizational Choice," *Mobilization* 10, 2 (2005): 271–288, and Francesca Polletta and Pang Ching Bobby Chen, "Gender and Public Talk: Accounting for Women's Variable Participation in the Public Sphere," *Sociological Theory* 31, 4 (2013): 291–317, I show that the perceived utility of two forms of decision making—consensus and deliberation—was shaped by their symbolic association with social groups: middle-class Whites in the first case, and women in the second.

25. Anthony Giddens, *The Transformation of Intimacy: Sexuality, Love, and Eroticism in Modern Societies* (Stanford, CA: Stanford University Press, 1992), 196.

26. Katherine Cramer Walsh, *Talking about Race: Community Dialogues and the Politics of Difference* (Chicago: University of Chicago Press, 2007); and Nina Eliasoph, *Making Volunteers: Civic Life after Welfare's End* (Princeton, NJ: Princeton University Press, 2011). For an example of a recent civility initiative, see Better Angels, https://www.better-angels.org.

27. For a critique of scholars' unwillingness to admit emotions into the public sphere, see Elaine Swan, "'You Make Me Feel like a Woman': Therapeutic Cultures and the Contagion of Femininity," *Gender, Work & Organization* 15, 1 (2008): 88–107.

28. The danger that self-disclosing talk be taken as a sign that equality has already been achieved exists in intimate relationships in the private sphere as much as in relationships in the public sphere. There, too, intimate, reciprocal, and egalitarian communication between partners may coexist with real inequalities in the relationship and indeed may compensate for such inequalities. See Lynn Jamiesen, "Intimacy Transformed? A Critical Look at the 'Pure Relationship,'" *Sociology* 33, 3 (1999): 477–494. In an Australian study of heterosexual couples who shared labor, Jacqueline Goodnow and Jennifer Bowes found that some couples engaged in considerable talk to arrive at an arrangement perceived as fair, and others did not. Some couples' arrangement was based on partners' personal tastes in tasks, and others were not. Most adopted principles—fairness, having a "pleasant time"—that they sought to enact in their division of labor. Jacqueline J. Goodnow and Jennifer M. Bowes, *Men, Women and Household Work* (Melbourne: Oxford University Press, 1994). On intergroup contact, see Tamar Saguy, John F. Dovidio, and Felicia Pratto, "Beyond Contact: Intergroup Contact in the Context of Power Relations," *Personality and Social Psychology Bulletin* 34, 3 (2008): 432–445; Emile G. Bruneau and Rebecca Saxe, "The Power of Being Heard: The Benefits of 'Perspective-Giving' in the Context of Intergroup Conflict," *Journal of Experimental Social Psychology* 48, 4 (2012): 855–866; and the discussion in chap. 5.

29. Nicholas A. John, *The Age of Sharing* (New York: Polity, 2016).

30. On time-, disk-, and file-sharing, see John, *The Age of Sharing*, 49; "Facebook helps you connect," and "where friends share their lives," 61; "Share what's important to you," 64; Zuckerberg quoted at 65.

31. John, *The Age of Sharing*, 86. Interestingly, as attention has focused on people's use of social media to display a personal life that is enviably adventurous,

socially connected, and successful, the term *sharing* may be increasingly inflected with a recognition of its status-seeking purposes along with the desire to connect emotionally.

32. Jane Mansbridge, *Beyond Adversary Democracy* (New York: Basic Books, 1980), makes the important point that people tend to be comfortable with discrepancies in influence as long as they agree with the decisions that result. Walsh, *Talking about Race*.

33. Eliasoph, *Making Volunteers*.

34. Jane Mansbridge, "Recursive Representation," in *Creating Political Presence: The New Politics of Democratic Representation*, ed. Dario Castiglione and Johannes Pollak (Chicago: University of Chicago Press, 2019), 298–337.

35. Jodi Dean, *Crowds and Party* (London: Verso, 2016), engages in the kind of experimentation I have in mind, albeit conceptually. She argues that modern capitalism's "dominant ideology of singularity, newness, and now" (21) has been adopted by contemporary leftist politics, foreclosing possibilities for real impact. On the other hand, drawing on theorists such as Elias Canetti, she argues that in crowds, people have an experience not only of collectivity but of collective power. The challenge is to connect that evanescent experience to political forms capable of focusing and sustaining that power—in her view, the Communist party.

36. Hannah Arendt, "On Humanity in Dark Times: Thoughts about Lessing," trans. Clara and Richard Winston, in *Men in Dark Times* (San Diego: Harcourt Brace, 1968), 3–32, at 27. On civic friendship, see Sibyl A. Schwarzenbach, "On Civic Friendship," *Ethics* 107, 1 (1996): 97–128. While Martha Nussbaum, "Human Functioning and Social Justice: In Defense of Aristotelian Essentialism," *Political Theory* 20 (1992): 2012–2046, emphasizes Aristotle's acknowledgment of and attention to difference, David Kahane, "Diversity, Solidarity and Civic Friendship," *Journal of Political Philosophy* 7, 3 (1999): 267–286, maintains that Aristotle viewed difference as a threat to friendship.

37. Jérôme Bourdon, "Unhappy Engineers of the European Soul: The EBU and the Woes of Pan-European Television," *International Communication Gazette* 69, 3 (2007): 263–280, recounts the origins of *Jeux sans frontières* and notes the lack of evidence on its impact on a European identity. Cornel Sandvoss, "On the Couch with Europe: The Eurovision Song Contest, the European Broadcast Union and Belonging in Europe," *Popular Communication* 6, 3 (2008): 253–289, offers an alternative interpretation of how cultural productions like *Jeux sans frontières*, and specifically the Eurovision Song Contest, work in relation to collective identities. Sandvoss, in "Jeux sans frontières? Europeanisation and the Erosion of National Categories in European Club Football Competition," *Politique européenne* 1, 36 (2012): 76–101, shows how European sports leagues have fostered both local and supranational identities. Bejan, *Mere Civility*.

Index

debt-settlement firms (*continued*)
ships and, 29, 60, 84, 178, 180–81;
industry characteristics, 65; male
agents in, 75, 76–77, 78–80, 83;
market-pricing relationship schema
and, 64; negotiator's job in, 60, 66;
obligations of clients of, 8, 9, 73;
poor record of, 75; ranking of debts
in, 66–70; self-interest of clients
and, 10–11, 59, 60, 61, 84–85; studied
with interviews and field observations, 61, 209n4; women agents in,
9, 18, 29, 61, 75, 77–81, 84, 85–86,
212n21
deep-acting emotions, 83, 212n19
deliberation. *See* public deliberation
Deliberative Polls, 95
democracy: contemporary ideals of
intimacy and, 22; egalitarian intimacy as model for, 183; network
metaphor for, 153; participatory, in
movements, 6–7, 18–20; polarization
as threat to, 2; public deliberation
and, 87, 88, 90, 91, 123; relationship
schemas and, 112–13; social movements with new schemas for, 151
democratic deliberation. *See* public
deliberation
democratic representation, 114–15, 155
democratic solidarity: certain kind of
talk and, 23, 186; egalitarian intimacy and, 120; ethic of care and, 29;
negotiating equality and, 186; voluntary organizations and, 143–44. *See
also* solidarity
dialogue and deliberation specialists,
91, 110, 120, 122–23, 141, 184
Diamond, Dion, 44, 49
difference: consensus-based decision
making and, 155; dialogue organizers discouraging discussion of,
110; egalitarian intimacy and, 141;
as obstacle to solidarity, 11, 12; real
people trying to cooperate across,
191; recognized in civil society
groups, 30; rituals and, 146, 148, 163;

solidarity built across, 141, 143–45,
161, 179–80. *See also* diversity
DiMaggio, Paul, 168
direct action, 155, 190
dirty work, 76, 212n22
diversity: of public deliberation participants, 95, 98–99, 100, 114; solidarity
and, 179–80. *See also* difference
Doar, John, 44
DoCarmo, Tania, 124, 132, 220n14
Dolly, Mama, 46
domestic partnerships, 165
Donaldson, Ivanhoe, 33, 44
Douglas, Mary, 59
Dreamers, undocumented student,
124, 225n36
Durkheim, Émile, 10
Durkheimian solidarity: defined, 10;
forged in civil society, 144; rituals
and, 145–46; self-interest and, 10–11,
61, 177–78

economic inequality, 1, 191
egalitarian decision making, 152, 154,
186. *See also* consensus-based decision making
egalitarian intimacy: advocates wanting to create relationships of, 119;
building solidarity with alternatives to, 6, 151, 162–63; communicative style used for, 3, 6, 24–25, 141,
142, 183–89; as go-to model for civic
actors, 183; inadequate for solidarity
among church volunteer groups,
149; limitations for building civic
solidarity, 6, 26–27, 120, 149, 184–85,
187–89; in public deliberation, 24,
91, 113, 141, 183, 188; as relationship
schema, 21; self-disclosure and, 3, 6,
22, 183; in storytelling for advocacy,
119, 127, 128, 129–30, 132, 139, 140,
141, 142, 183; as time-limited relationship in civic initiatives, 24, 188.
See also intimacy
egalitarianism: eighteenth-century
commerce and, 160; of friendship,

Parisian promenade, eighteenth-century, 160, 163

Parsons, Talcott, 196n14

participatory democracy in movements, 6–7, 18–20

participatory learning, 140

partisanship, viii, 2, 144, 191

partnership, relationship schema of, 115, 116, 141

partnership with government: in civic renewal movement, 108–9; community organizers using confrontation instead of, 157–59; deliberation organizers aiming for, 98, 108, 109, 113, 114, 141, 180, 182

Payne, Charles, 37, 48, 50–51

Peacock, Wazir, 50, 52

peer-to-peer networks, 21

Peters, John Durham, 22, 143

Pettigrew, Thomas, 3

philosophes, 160, 161, 190

PICO (Pacific Institute for Community Organization), 157, 158

Pizzorno, Alessandro, 38–39, 204n13

play, 159, 160–61, 165, 190, 191, 228n35

Plotke, David, 114–15, 155

policy makers: community organizing and, 156, 157, 188; conceptualization of public by, 92–93, 95–96; metaphors of belonging used by, 190–91; public deliberation and, 113, 114, 141, 161, 180, 182; telling stories to, 138, 139

political accountability: confrontation by community organizers and, 159, 190; imagined relationships and, 6; public deliberation and, 11–12, 88; recursive representation and, 111–12, 218n42

political institutions, trust in, 2, 29, 144

political partisanship, 2, 144, 191

political polarization, 2, 88, 224n33

political solidarity: ethics of care and, 86; need for new forms of, 191. *See also* solidarity

Pontusson, Jonas, 146

power: in activist groups, 152–53, 154; to choose relationship schema, 61; community organizers and challenging of, 145, 155, 156, 158; in debt settlement situation, 180–81; to define relationship, 18; equality and, 4; intergroup contact initiatives and, 138; in participatory democratic groups, 19; practitioners of public deliberation and, 107–8, 141–42, 180; refusal of claimed relationship by the powerful, 180; rituals that recognize asymmetries of, 164; self-disclosure not changing inequalities in, 185; storytelling in community organizing and, 140. *See also* empowerment by storytelling; empowerment projects

Powers, Kathleen E., 170

prefiguration, 156, 161, 226n14

progressive stack, 152

psychotherapeutically informed communication techniques, 3, 22–23, 91, 120–22, 183–84

psychotherapeutic approaches: criticisms of, 23–24, 92, 122, 126; in debt settlement, 78–79, 84; in deliberation, 91, 123; diffusion of, 22–23, 84, 91, 120–22, 126, 189; in transitional-justice initiatives, 126

Public Agenda, 94–95

Public Conversations Project, 96

public deliberation: agendas of diverse initiatives in, 90–91; authenticity and, 95, 120, 123, 141; compromise in, 99–101, 102, 110, 113–14; conceptualization of public by organizers and policy makers, 92–94, 95–96; criticisms of, 88, 89, 91–93, 141–42; decision makers and, 92, 97, 104, 106, 109, 141; diversity of participants in, 95, 98–99, 100, 114; egalitarian intimacy in, 24, 91, 113, 141, 183, 188; without enduring civic relationships, 188–89; imagined rela-

tive, 15; of partnership, 115, 116, 141; play and, 159, 161–62, 165; power of some people to choose, 61; in public deliberation, 113–15, 141; rituals and, 145–46; structural ties distinguished from, 13, 176; with a telos, 140, 156, 162, 163, 189; transposed to new settings, 17–18, 179, 199n26; in voluntary civic organizations, 144–45. *See also* creating new relationship schemas; egalitarian intimacy; Fiske, Alan Page; metaphors

representation: democratic, 114–15, 155; recursive, 111–12, 189, 218n42

reproductive surrogates, 18

Rheingold, Howard, 115

Richards, Dona, 49

Rippe, Klaus Peter, 120

rituals: of Chinese women mill workers in 1940s, 17; of church volunteer groups, 148; of civil society groups, 30; of community organizers, 147–48, 156, 157, 159, 163–64; of consensus-based decision making, 155; creating new modes of interaction through, 162, 165, 190; solidarity-building functions of, 163–64, 165; in sustaining new relationship schemas, 145–46

Robinson, Jackie, 47

Robinson, Reggie, 45

Rogers, Carl, 22–23, 121

roles, vs. relationships, 15, 198n22

Rose, Nikolas, 22

Rosenvallon, Pierre, 87

Rucht, Dieter, 152

schemas, 14. *See also* relationship schemas

Schildkraut, Deborah, 168

SCLC (Southern Christian Leadership Conference), 43, 53

scripts, 15. *See also* relationship schemas

Searing, Donald, 101

self-disclosure: communication characterized by, 23; egalitarian intimacy by way of, 3, 6, 22, 183; Giddens's confluent love and, 22; intergroup contact and, 3; not providing equality, 24–25, 26, 143, 185, 186, 233n28; as sharing, 185; solidarity not based on, 190

self-interest: capitalism and, 59; community organizers appealing to, 57; of debt-settlement clients, 10–11, 59, 60, 61, 84–85; Durkheimian solidarity and, 10–11, 61, 177–78; free-riding and, 178; moral norms and, 61, 84; as obstacle to solidarity, 10, 29; redistributive policies and, 146; relationship schemas used to pursue, 17

Seu, Bruna, 118

Sewell, William, 17, 21, 159–61

sexual orientation, 145, 147, 162

sharing: social media and, 26, 186, 233n31; storytelling for advocacy and, 129–30, 137–38, 185; two meanings of, 25–26, 129–30, 185–86

sharing economy, 3, 25–26, 185–86

Shepherd, Benjamin, 161

Sherrod, Charles, 45–46, 48–49, 206n29

Shirky, Clay, 115

Simmel, Georg, 38

Sirianni, Carmen, 108

Smart Mobs (Rheingold), 115

Smith, Frank, 44, 51

Smith, Jean, 49

Smith, Rogers, 168, 172

social capital, 28

social media, 26, 138, 186, 233n31

social movements: creating new relationship schemas in, 27, 151, 153–54, 155; factors affecting participation in, 54–58; groups that emphasize doing rather than talking, 164; outsiders in, 35, 37–39, 51, 52–54, 56; radical equality in, 150–55; under repression, 35–37, 161; resources for mobilization of, 35–36; solidarity in,